From the moment the club was first dreamed up in 2005 through their treble triumph in 2017, Toronto FC has consistently been at the vanguard of pushing Major League Soccer forward. The results haven't always pretty, but TFC has almost always been ahead of the curve in terms of support, willingness to spend, and, at least since 2015, results. In *Come On You Reds*, Kloke chronicles the club's birth, those long years of mismanagement and misguided ambition, and its rise and ultimate triumph in a way that will entertain and inform the most ardent TFC supporters, casual Toronto sports fans, and fans of other MLS clubs alike. This isn't just a story about a team — this is a book about how, if it's done right, an MLS club can become a continental power and a true part of the fabric of their city.

— Sam Stejskal, MLSsoccer.com

COME ON YOU REDS

COME ON YOU REDS

the story of Toronto FC

Joshua Kloke

Foreword by Michael Bradley

DUNDURN
TORONTO

Cover image: © Carmen Giraudy
Printer: Webcom

Library and Archives Canada Cataloguing in Publication

Kloke, Joshua, 1983-, author
        Come on you Reds : the story of Toronto FC / Joshua Kloke ; foreword by Michael Bradley.

Includes bibliographical references and index.
Issued in print and electronic formats.
ISBN 978-1-4597-4237-6 (softcover).--ISBN 978-1-4597-4238-3 (PDF).--
ISBN 978-1-4597-4239-0 (EPUB)

        1. Toronto FC (Soccer team)--History. 2. Soccer teams--Ontario--
Toronto--History. I. Bradley, Michael, 1987-, writer of foreword II. Title.

GV943.6.T6K56 2018   796.334'6309713541   C2018-903621-4
                                                        C2018-903622-

21 2 3 4 5   22 21 20 19 18

We acknowledge the support of the **Canada Council for the Arts**, which last year invested $153 million to bring the arts to Canadians throughout the country, and the **Ontario Arts Council** for our publishing program. We also acknowledge the financial support of the **Government of Ontario**, through the **Ontario Book Publishing Tax Credit** and the **Ontario Media Development Corporation**, and the **Government of Canada**.

Nous remercions le **Conseil des arts du Canada** de son soutien. L'an dernier, le Conseil a investi 153 millions de dollars pour mettre de l'art dans la vie des Canadiennes et des Canadiens de tout le pays.

VISIT US AT

dundurn.com | @dundurnpress | dundurnpress | dundurnpress

Dundurn
3 Church Street, Suite 500
Toronto, Ontario, Canada
M5E 1M2

For Jess, who knows what it means to be a fan

Contents

Foreword

I SAID THIS RIGHT AFTER the 2017 MLS Cup, on the field: for 364 days a group of guys had to live with the ghosts of losing a final at home on penalties — and all of the pain, disbelief, suffering, frustration, heartbreak, tears, and everything that goes along with it. There was not one day that I did not think about losing that final and trying to get back to the next one. We lived that together. You feel like your chance at redemption is never going to come. So you just work every single day. You keep chipping away, with this idea: in the end, if you give enough, you'll get another chance. We did all of that.

There's a pride in doing that, of living that, with your teammates, with your coaches, with everybody at the club, with the city, with the fans, because you look at the south end and you see the same faces every game. In any other city, you lose a final at home and all anybody would've wanted to say is "You idiots. You blew it. All you had to do was win a game at home and we were going to get to lift the trophy, and you blew it." And that's the nice version. There's places, and I've played at one, where there would be fans waiting outside the training ground or outside your house and there'd be some issues. With *our* fans and *our* city, it was the complete opposite. People were heartbroken, but people weren't angry. Nobody pointed fingers, nobody blamed anybody. There was heartbreak, but then there was pride. People felt like they had been a part of something different and unique and something that made them *feel*.

I can remember in the days after that first final, when we started to get out a little more, the reaction from fans and people we'd see in the city: I was almost embarrassed because they were congratulating me as if we'd won. It was so genuine. I thought to myself, *You know we lost, right?* But there was this pride in what they'd seen and been a part of that was just so overriding to anything else in that moment.

In 2017, to be able to win at home and to give every person in the city a chance to celebrate with no asterisk, to celebrate to the absolute fullest, that part was amazing. In so many ways they had made us feel like we'd won the year before, but we hadn't. The part for us that was so special was our relationship with the fans. For us to be able to say "You believed in us, you stuck with us, you didn't turn on us. And here you go. This is for all of us."

So what does TFC mean to me? It's all of this. Every single one of these experiences. At this point I've had more of the biggest moments in my career at BMO Field than in any other stadium in the world. That's pretty incredible. You win, and in the days after the game, so much sticks with you. From the day I got here, people at the club, from Corey Wray to Mike Masaro to Jaime McMillan to Jimmy Brennan, would say the same thing: "Wait until you see the city when we win." Every step along the way, reality has blown away expectations.

I don't presume to speak for everybody on the team, but in a lot of ways I think we were exactly what each of us was looking for at that moment. Up to 2014, there had been some long, hard, frustrating years; and, more than anything, a revolving-door sequence of players and coaches. The club had no identity on the field. The club's identity was in the stands, with the people and the fans who continued to come and support the team even in the darkest moments. They did it because they loved the club, the colours, the city. Obviously you can do that, and it shows real love and loyalty and devotion, but at a certain point there has to be something out there to give you some kind of hope or something to believe in. I was at a point in my career where I had been to a lot of different clubs and lived in a lot of places, but I wanted something different: I wanted to go to a place where I could play a huge part in what went on and could try to make things special and different. I wanted to make a place home.

In that moment, TFC, the city, and the fans were exactly what I was looking for. In a small way, I think I was part of what they were looking for: a player who was going to come here and say *This is my team, this is my club, and I'm not going anywhere. It might take a little while but I'm going to give you everything I have to try and get us to where we all want to be.* With that journey, and all the experiences along the way, Toronto's home for me.

At the end of the day, I'm a sports fan. I like to read about sports, I like to watch sports, and I always have. I've always had a huge amount of admiration for guys like Derek Jeter, Kobe Bryant, Paolo Maldini, and Francesco Totti — guys who get to play their entire career in one city, in some cases their hometown. There's something about that. It's so amazing. What they mean to that club and that city. For a million reasons, that was never going to be possible for me. For an American soccer player, if you want to challenge yourself, it requires moving yourself up the ladder and changing teams.

When I came to Toronto, I wanted, with time, to be able to feel just one-billionth of what those guys feel in terms of having a connection with a club and a city that's special and unique. More than any other place my family and I have lived, Toronto is our home. When the season ends, it's not like we go anywhere. The connection I have with the club, the city, but more than that, with the people and the fans — that part means a lot to me. Especially given the road that we've all taken together to get here, it makes it mean all that much more.

Michael Bradley
January 2018

Prologue

I'LL NEVER FORGET THAT FLAG.

I wasn't even 10 years old the first time I walked into Soccer City, an indoor soccer facility that doubled as a roller-hockey pad, on Sunray Street in Whitby, Ontario. It was before the 1994 FIFA World Cup in the United States and, being raised in the hockey-centric city of Oshawa, and having played soccer only in the summers, my knowledge of the soccer infrastructure in the Greater Toronto Arena was limited. But I was training indoors in the winter for the first time, in the hopes of eventually convincing my childhood friends, all of them born with skates on their feet, that soccer was a noble, viable option to be played year-round. I cheered for the Toronto Maple Leafs, because I was a child of a Leafs fan in the suburbs, and that's just what you do. But I always felt an inherent disconnect with the team because, as a child, I knew I would never be able to become a Maple Leaf myself. I couldn't skate for shit; so, being the grandson of German immigrants, I fell for soccer.

So when I first saw the dark blue and white, classic-looking logo on a flag hanging inside the lobby of this strange, new soccer facility, I assumed it was Toronto's soccer team's. Finally, my preteen self had something to aspire to become a part of and to align myself with; a badge I could wear as well.

"Is that Toronto's soccer team?" I asked my father as we walked through the lobby.

"*Errr*, I don't know," he replied, clearly frustrated.

He could rattle off information about Tiger Williams, Dave Keon, and Darryl Sittler with ease, but in not being able to identify what logo was on the flag, or, upon further grilling, what Toronto's soccer team's logo might even look like, we had an even bigger problem: If I was in love with the game of soccer and lived in or near Toronto in the early '90s, what was I a part of?

And was there even a team in Toronto to cheer for? The answer, like so much of the history of the sport in the city, is not easy to find.

This book is not my story, of course, but my experience is not uncommon in Toronto at the time. When the World Cup rolled around months later, I sat on the floor of my grandparents' living room, watching German players I knew from the trading cards I'd asked distant cousins to send me from half a world away: Klinsmann, Matthäus, Sammer — men who I knew were great because they were on TV. But these were also men who would never sign my cards at a local Canadian Tire event.

As much as I wanted to prove otherwise to my friends, soccer was beloved, but soccer was still a strange, foreign thing here.

That flag, as it turned out, belonged to a diehard Glasgow Rangers fan. My confusion only intensified when I learned that Scotland, the country that the proprietor of Soccer City came from, wasn't even going to be playing in the World Cup. Just how enormously popular was this sport, I wondered, and why, in a city that boasted the Leafs, the Blue Jays, the Argonauts, and very soon after, the Raptors, on TV regularly, was I having such a hard time figuring out who someone like me could belong to?

My plight was only exacerbated by those playing at a semi-professional level.

Pat Onstad was born in Vancouver. But at the age of 22, the goalkeeper had arrived in Toronto to begin playing with the Toronto Blizzard of the then nascent Canadian Soccer League. Onstad, still deep in his university studies, had already made stops with the Vancouver 86ers and Winnipeg Fury. These clubs were part of a league trying to capitalize on the men's national team's surprising qualification for the 1986 World Cup. When Onstad landed in Canada's largest city, he expected similarly extensive support.

Instead, his time at the Blizzard reinforced the belief that many Torontonians were still struggling to understand the sport, and, because of its lack of popularity, the prospect of soccer taking hold in Toronto as it had in nearly every other world-class city still seemed like more of a dream than a possibility.

The CSL and its ownership groups suffered, according to Onstad, for being without a push from ownership groups and from a lack of foresight and vision as to what soccer could become in Toronto and Canada. The entire league was just struggling to catch up to a flash-in-the-pan success of a few years previous and showed little understanding of the nuances of the game.

"I think people looked at it, and to a certain extent, probably rightfully so, as a second-tier league and not a league that was striving to be seen on the international [stage] as a developing league," said Onstad.

The CSL was, at the time, strictly for the Canadian player, and as such, could offer only limited compensation. "It was a good summer job for me," admits Onstad. His first contract in the league was for just $4,500 (CAD) for the season. "It wasn't like I was putting money away," he said.

He remembers being a child in Vancouver, watching the Whitecaps in the old North American Soccer League and seeing some of the world's best-ever come for victory laps in the NASL, from Pelé to Franz Beckenbauer to Johan Cruyff. That's where Onstad caught the soccer bug. The CSL, in his mind, "didn't even come close to that level."

The Toronto Blizzard were forced to move from Varsity Stadium in downtown Toronto to Centennial Stadium in nearby Etobicoke during that season. In the bowels of the 2,000-plus-seat stadium, Blizzard coach Tony Taylor used a few spare locker rooms to set up a laundry room and a few haphazard physiotherapy tables. Perhaps laughable by the standards of other leagues, but not in the CSL. "Most clubs didn't have that, so we were a prestigious club," remembers Onstad.

After another stop in Winnipeg, Onstad returned to Toronto in 1994 for a stint with the Toronto Rockets of the American Professional Soccer League (APSL). Onstad realized the only reason the Rockets were a step up was because the league featured teams from the United States and the overall quality of the league benefited.

Even with the World Cup happening just south of Toronto, Onstad saw no discernable change in the interest level among fans. "At that stage, it was still in its infancy," he said.

The Canadian men's national team had come within a game of qualifying for that World Cup a year earlier when they jumped to a 1–0 lead against Mexico in the 17th minute of a CONCACAF qualifying game at Varsity Stadium. Had they kept that lead, Canada would have gone to their second-ever World Cup. But Mexico stormed back to claim a 2–1 win and an automatic berth in the World Cup. Canada would lose to Australia on penalties in a two-leg interconfederation playoff series.

What Onstad did feel was how far behind clubs like the Blizzard and the Rockets were in terms of fan support compared to the city's clubs of the past, including Toronto Italia and Toronto Croatia. These were teams that had very much been extensions of the community they were born out of and spoke to a collection of fans who had simply brought their inherent passion for the game with them from Europe. As unifying as these teams were for their respective communities, they ultimately proved exclusive for soccer fans across Toronto as a collective.

After venturing both east and west with stops at the Montreal Impact and the Edmonton Drillers, Onstad completed a rare Toronto soccer trifecta, playing for the inaugural season of the Toronto Lynx in what was then called the A-League. Even at just 29, Onstad had learned that for all the good intentions in the Canadian soccer landscape, there was a lack of long-term vision for sustainability. Many Canadian soccer clubs were being treated more like a get-rich-quick scam: maybe the growing game would catch on with this club or that club, even if very few people in Toronto had any idea how to connect these clubs with the wider population.

Onstad's various tours of duty throughout haphazard leagues and teams with little to no support found him at the end of his rope. "At that stage, from my perspective, I was chasing a paycheque," said Onstad. "Here's another franchise that just isn't going to make it. In Toronto, it felt like nothing was going to [grab] hold."

In 2003, after a few more stops, in Scotland and the United States, Onstad eventually landed in Major League Soccer, which was still finding its feet but had a promising outlook in its eighth season. He'd win an MLS Cup and MLS Goalkeeper of the Year in his first season, before winning two more MLS Cups and another Goalkeeper of the Year award later.

After his retirement, he landed with Toronto FC as chief scout and could barely comprehend how the club was managing to put close to 20,000 fans in their stadium game after game when, not 20 years earlier, Onstad's own clubs had struggled to fill a stadium a fraction of that size.

Quickly, Onstad realized that all the soccer fans of Toronto had wanted was a team to call their own. "You could feel the passion of the fans there," said Onstad. "They were really frustrated and angry and had all this pent-up energy. They were just waiting to release it. They just needed something successful. And you could tell that if this thing could snowball, they'd get some success."

He can't help looking at how far back those three old Toronto-based teams were from what Toronto FC and Major League Soccer have become. "Light years," said Onstad, laughing.

1

Message Boards, Manna Dropping from Heaven, and an Armani Suit

A CLAIM COULD BE MADE that Toronto FC's birthplace was either in the Maple Leaf Sports and Entertainment offices of 50 Bay Street in downtown Toronto or in the Major League Soccer offices across the border in New York City.

But, as it turns out, TFC as a club was first dreamt up in a space much more difficult to pin down and then eventually conceived in a setting where so many fans still watch games to this day.

Midway through the first decade of the 2000s, soccer had not yet broken into the mainstream consciousness of Canadians. Lionel Messi and Cristiano Ronaldo, the two iconic global brands who would usher the sport into the homes of Canadians via a generation of young, impressionable teenagers clamouring for the next star, were just beginning their careers at Barcelona and Manchester United, respectively. David Beckham was himself a star recognized around the world after incredibly impressive spells at Manchester United and Real Madrid, but in North America he could have just as easily been identified as the husband of Spice Girl Victoria Beckham or the player Keira Knightley wanted to imitate in 2002's *Bend It Like Beckham*. Before Beckham's historic move to the Los Angeles Galaxy in 2007, soccer magazines from England could usually be found only at the back of the magazine rack, past the hockey, basketball and, well, motocross glossies.

Soccer, for better or worse, was still a fringe sport in North America's biggest cities, such as Toronto. Many in that city could only look with confused curiosity at the thousands of people who congregated along two of the larger streets, Danforth Avenue and Dundas Street, to watch two unlikely teams, Greece and Portugal, face off in the final of Euro 2004.

That a Greece team without a single superstar defeated a heavily favoured Portuguese side was one thing. But how could this dull 1–0 win, on the other side of the world, motivate jubilant supporters of Greece to close down 10 blocks of the major thoroughfare in Toronto? It only confirmed what many unfamiliar with the sport suspected: soccer is strange.

But beyond the ouzo-soaked fans on Danforth revelling in patriotic fervour were many other people who also revelled in that strangeness. And there was a degree of patriotism involved there, as well; albeit without much return up to that point.

And without a street to call their own, they congregated where so many fanatics met and congregated in that decade: on message boards on the internet.

For all the future influence that the club could have on the growth of the game on Canadian soccer pitches across the country, Toronto FC would not exist without internet message boards.

Every day early in the 2000s, hundreds of fans would log in to a message board called Big Soccer to discuss their obsession: not a giant club on the other side of the planet, like Arsenal or Liverpool (though many of these fans had their allegiances), but instead, the players that represented them in red Canadian jerseys.

The Voyageurs were a country-wide group of Canadian soccer supporters that was founded in 1996 and, spread out across a large country, enabled like-minded people online to discuss Canadian soccer. It's worth noting that the national men's side, after achieving their best-ever FIFA ranking at 40th in 1996, would plummet to being ranked 101st in the world two years later.

But as the century turned, interest on these message boards did not dissipate. Fans still gathered and critically examined the state of the local game. And, given that local soccer still garnered very few, if any, headlines in national newspapers, and both local and national men's teams games weren't always featured prominently on national television broadcasts, internet message boards were the place where those who didn't feel their needs were being satisfied by mainstream media would meet.

Sean Keay was a member of those early message boards. He remembers them as a forum for people to gather, share thoughts on Canada's teams, and perhaps even bridge that divide between online and "real life" friendships.

"Even though it was a much different time and they were just these simple message boards, I wouldn't be in the situation I'm in now without that community," said Keay, who is now a manager of digital strategy at Maple Leaf Sports and Entertainment (MLSE). "The first time I met the Voyageurs, I was sixteen and my brother said 'I met these people on the internet and we're going to go watch Canada play in World Cup qualifying.' And I was like, 'No, that's the thing your parents tell you *not* to do.' But that's exactly where the community came from and grew from."

It was a community that Paul Beirne had to listen to.

Beirne is, in many ways, the founding father of Toronto FC. He had been overseeing ticket sales and service for the Leafs and Raptors with MLSE. With Richard Peddie at the pinnacle of power as president and CEO of MLSE, the owners of the company, the Ontario Teachers' Pension Plan, had given Peddie and MLSE a mandate for enterprise value growth.

"It was an era when you saw MLSE trying new things," said Beirne. It was during this time that MLSE launched Leafs TV; welcomed the Leafs farm club, the Marlboros, back from St. John's to Toronto; and continued commercial development outside of Maple Leaf Square.

Beirne had begun to feel bored with his role and saw his peers at MLSE being given opportunities. So when he heard that Peddie and MLSE were going to acquire an MLS expansion franchise, he put his hand up. He was quickly entrusted with figuring out whether an MLS team could work in Toronto.

"Everyone, without exception, thought I was crazy to buy into soccer in Toronto," said Beirne.

Seeking validation, he began to conduct research about the viability of an MLS franchise in Toronto in the message boards. At first he lurked, but eventually he came to a realization, combining what he saw online with data from presentations at MLSE meetings: past attempts to get a professional soccer franchise off the ground in Toronto had failed, but not for lack of ticket-buying support.

The fans were there, online, and the manner in which they dissected games and players showed an enthusiasm that was promising. Here was a community of forgotten fans, that had been marginalized by the other professional franchises in Toronto.

"It was clear there was a market people weren't recognizing for soccer," said Beirne.

So Beirne began trying to connect with those fans and to gauge their interest in an MLS club and, also, what they thought that club should look like. When Beirne had volunteered to lead the charge in understanding what fans of an MLS club in Toronto would want, he also had to be honest with himself: he himself was not a soccer fan, having gone to just one World Cup game in 1994. He was driving blind and needed soccer's fervent underground community to help take the wheel.

Beirne's goal was to keep the club as authentic as possible.

"We shouldn't try and propose a brand," he remembers thinking.

On October 29, 2005, Beirne registered in the Big Soccer online forum with the username mlsintoronto.

And on January 28, 2006, Beirne piped up as himself, creating a thread called "Market Research," and leading off with one of his first posts:

> Full Disclosure: I'm employed by Maple Leaf Sports and I'm part of a team working on the MLS ramp up. Judging by the lurking I've been doing in this board lately it appears that soccer in Toronto has a huge potential, but a long way to go. I'm interested in your opinions — please dump them all here. Please resist the urge to slag us over basket-ball or hockey issues (but go ahead and shower us with accolades if you must). For what it's worth, for a name, I'm in favour of simple modest soccer. Nothing flashy: Toronto Football Club.

The feedback ranged from outright support to blatant suspicion.

"Must be the journalist in me," replied Duane Rollins, a part-time journalist under the username SweetOwnGoal. "My Bull$hit meter is waaaaaaaaaaaayyyyyyyyyyyyyyyyyy up. All the money MLSE has and it's doing 'market research' on a discussion board. Interesting."

"Back then, there were so many stops and starts, so I didn't want to be teased anymore," said Rollins. "We were always told this would happen or that would happen, but the rug would be pulled out."

Rollins's suspicion stemmed from Beirne's employer, Maple Leaf Sports and Entertainment, and the giant corporate undertones it presented. "The culture back then was very niche, very fan-driven," Rollins said. "And this outsider comes in and says he's going to fix things for you, and you're like, 'Wait.'"

Soccer geeks, as Rollins put it, are not unlike Trekkies. "It was such a small little community," he said of Toronto's hard-core soccer supporters at the time.

But Beirne wanted to break down the barriers and prove himself to those fans. And he did so in a manner that soccer fans universally appreciate: he offered to buy them a beer.

A meeting was organized at the Duke of York pub in Toronto's Annex neighbourhood for Beirne to get formally acquainted with some of the Voyageurs and to hear their ideas for an MLS club. Two tables-worth of supporters showed up and surrounded Beirne. At one table were a group of enthusiastic supporters, eager to pick Beirne's brain about what an MLS club could look like, and to contribute what they believed would be important in a new professional soccer franchise.

"We were all very intrigued," said David Bailey, who sat at the table with a chatty and down-to-earth Beirne.

The supporters were impressed that MLSE was reaching out to the grassroots, and they were optimistic. Beirne allowed them to peek behind the curtain at what MLSE had been planning for the club. In a time when MLSE was known for their monolith, the Toronto Maple Leafs, and the Leafs were able to influence millions of people, Beirne's engagement was encouraging to the soccer fans gathered.

"MLSE is reaching out," said Bailey, "to the little people."

What struck Bailey was Beirne's and MLSE's vision for forming a team: namely, to present an authentic product that true soccer fans would appreciate. "They didn't want this to be going after the soccer moms," said Bailey.

Meanwhile, at the other table sat Rollins and some of the other Voyageurs who were much quieter and much, much more skeptical. They welcomed Beirne with snide comments from under their breath.

But eventually, as Beirne's plan for an authentic club emerged, they changed their tone. "Paul is a natural salesman, but he came off as sincere in his desire to make this work. He understood that it was a bit of a closed society and that he needed to slowly work his way in by being patient and not force a relationship," said Rollins.

Rollins and others drew hope from the fact that, compared to other sports executives, Beirne was quite young and had an understanding of soccer and how many young people were quickly becoming interested in the sport.

And Beirne himself was learning. His notion of supporters moved beyond that of traditional youth soccer after that meeting and he took a "quantum leap forward" in terms of his understanding of what supporters' clubs could be. "It became a mutually supportive ecosystem," he said.

By the end of the meeting, surrounded by empty pint glasses, the Voyageurs walked away even more optimistic. "Paul is the most important figure in MLS history," said Rollins, "that no one knows."

There was a brief time, however, when Beirne could have lost that credibility. In the lead-up to announcing TFC to the public, MLSE had registered a number of possible names for the club as trademarks. The Northmen and Toronto Reds were among them. Some were real considerations and some were decoys, as Beirne assumed that, given that the trademark registrations were in the public record, these names would eventually leak out.

And while Beirne had originally mentioned "Toronto FC" as a possible name, MLSE had another horse in the race that was gaining momentum: Inter Toronto.

The idea behind that name made sense: Toronto was a cosmopolitan city and Beirne needed the city's Italian, Portuguese, and Colombian communities, along with many others, to come together and support the club. MLSE were convinced that having Inter Toronto was the perfect way to encapsulate the international feel of the city. "The idea was that you can have a supporting interest here on Saturday afternoon and you're wearing red," said Beirne, "but you can be at the pub in the morning supporting your club and be wearing blue."

It was the connotations of that colour, blue, that still rubbed some the wrong way. Even the most casual of supporter was aware of Inter Milan, the Italian club that would go on to win the Serie A title five seasons in a row from 2005 to 2010, and were, at the time, one of the most well-known clubs in the world. Upon the leak, Beirne received an overwhelming wave of negative feedback.

"Oh, it's just like Real Salt Lake," Beirne remembers being told. "It's a fake name."

The club was risking alienating any possible fans who weren't Italian and didn't want to be associated with an Italian club (and even fans of other Italian clubs who might not want to be closely associated with the new team if it suggested support for Inter.)

And while TFC could have ridden the wave of Inter Milan's popularity during their first seasons, especially with their 2010 UEFA Champions League title, a vocal section of the incipient club's supporters, especially Beirne, talked themselves out of the name.

It was another early part of the learning process, and it reinforced the modus operandi that would dictate their approach: don't sell supporters and their understanding of the game short, and don't try to be something you're not.

"[The name] Toronto FC didn't offend anybody," said Beirne, relying on a classically, inoffensively Canadian approach. "It better executed what we wanted to achieve."

It might have appeared at times during Toronto FC's rather miserable early existence as if the club would never achieve any success on the pitch. It's almost easy to forget that, had it not been for a series of small steps, the club would not even exist as it's currently known today.

Toronto's former mayor, David Miller, who spent part of his childhood in England and acquired a love for soccer there, brought that passion back to Canada when he moved here in 1967.

He remembers, sometimes fondly, the many failed soccer franchises that came and went in Toronto between 1967 and when he was elected mayor in 2003.

Miller can't recall exactly where he was when he first heard the news of a new soccer stadium in Toronto, but he remembers being surprised. Shocked, even.

The then mayor of Toronto, and lifelong supporter of English second-division side Ipswich Town FC, heard the news through channels: the federal government was going to call a news conference on May 21, 2004, near the University of Toronto, to make a pivotal announcement: a partnership was being formed with the city's "community, athletic and sports leaders" to rebuild Varsity Stadium. The stadium had been demolished in 2002 after skyrocketing costs became higher than any revenue generated. Temporary seating was put up around the field after, simply to provide somewhere for fans to watch university football games.

And Toronto soccer fans, like Miller, took note, because this new stadium would be "a major component in the bid of the Canadian Soccer Association (CSA) for Canada to host the 2007 FIFA Men's Under-20 [World Cup]."

The feds also promised that this new stadium would act as the permanent home and "focal point for Canadian soccer." For good measure, they even tacked on the idea that the 25,000-seat venue would serve as home to the Argonauts as well, because, well, why not?

At the time, federal Human Resources and Skills Development Minister Joe Volpe promised that the new stadium would "provide a critical boost" in the CSA bid to host the 2007 FIFA Men's U-20 World Cup. Volpe added that he believed the World Cup would bring "as much as fifteen million dollars in benefits coming directly to Toronto."

And throughout all of this, Miller sat stunned. A new stadium was being proposed in the city he effectively ran, and he didn't receive so much as a phone call. "It indicated the dysfunctionality of [the] Canadian political system," said Miller. Nobody from the federal government had ever consulted with Miller about the ideal place for the stadium in Toronto.

Miller felt only a bit slighted; but, because the municipal government, councillors, civil servants, and the Office of the Mayor, who "actually understand the city because that's their job," weren't consulted, Miller also knew that the plan was destined to fail.

He, like so many others in Toronto, believed that something needed to be done at the Varsity Stadium site, but was also well aware of the challenges that a 25,000-seat stadium in that location would present.

First, given the extremely limited parking in and around the University of Toronto, patrons of the stadium would be forced to rely on the TTC to get to and from the stadium. And while a reliance on public transit as opposed to travelling by car intrigued Miller, he also knew there would be capacity issues on the TTC, especially given that some games could be played during rush hour. And anyone who has relied on Toronto's subway system day-in and day-out might be inclined to agree.

Another issue lay in the fact that the University of Toronto is a federation. "And unless you did your homework properly, you faced the risk that not all colleges would agree properly," said Miller.

So, as much as he liked the historical ties of the stadium — given that athletic events had been hosted there since the late 19th century — he knew the plan simply would not work.

The University of Toronto eventually voted down the proposal, citing concerns of cost and disturbance to students.

In the fall of 2004, the same cast of characters took the dog-and-pony show north of the city to York University's Keele Campus. Volpe was again on hand to announce that York University, the provincial government, as well as the owners of the Argonauts would all be kicking in money for the new stadium; but that plan also failed when the finances didn't add up.

For Miller, there was always only one choice when it came to building a new soccer-specific stadium in Toronto: Exhibition Place, on the shore of Lake Ontario.

City-building had always been a priority for Miller and he believed a new stadium in a developing neighbourhood would do just that:

> One of the benefits to public investment in a stadium of this kind is a spinoff to local communities in terms of customers to local bars and restaurants. The logical place for this to happen was Liberty Village. And on the other side of the tracks, the King and Dufferin area was undergoing a job revitalization at the time.

The neighbourhood was just begging for an attraction of this sort. Long known as a hub for young professionals with disposable income, Liberty Village appeared to be the perfect destination for a new team in the city to lay down roots.

And, as Miller was quick to remind anyone who would listen, Exhibition Place was well-served by both the TTC and GO Transit, and it had plenty of parking space. "For people who aren't living in the boundaries of the 416," said Miller, "it's easier to get to than Varsity."

Miller had always believed that if the City of Toronto owned the land that the stadium was built on, and if there were to be significant public investment, the city itself should be publicly involved. So, he sat back and waited.

And in August 2005, his phone rang.

The Canadian Soccer Association was panicking. They didn't have a flagship stadium in the country's biggest market and were now worried that they would lose the rights to host the U-20 World Cup. "We're in danger," Miller recalls being told.

And while Miller was slightly put off by how long it took for the parties to involve the city and its soccer-loving mayor, he got to work. His first call was to then Maple Leafs Sports and Entertainment president and CEO, Richard Peddie. Peddie was already in talks with MLS regarding expansion to Toronto, so the two had a mutual interest. The key issue for the two men was to make up for the $10 million hole in the budget that had been created now that the Argonauts had pulled out (the team had opted to renew their lease at the Rogers Centre, rather than commit to the planned new stadium).

But even more importantly, Miller stood firm on his belief that Exhibition Place was the right location for a stadium, even if he would need to get the motion to that effect through city council. And he wanted MLSE to back his plan. "I need you to publicly say that Exhibition Place is the right place for us," Miller told Peddie.

Miller wanted the corporation's public support, but stood firm that the city needed to own the stadium and that it needed to be built on city land. This was Miller's attempt to push back against a federal government that had been trying to drive the whole procedure and to get credit for it.

And while some would argue that Miller was driving a hard bargain, he also knew that he had leverage because the entire stadium deal was, in his words, "teetering on the edge. When I got these calls, people were *really* desperate."

Miller proposed to invest $10 million of the city's money into the new venue. But some were worried that the stadium would become a white elephant and that the city would never recoup the investment.

Still, the mayor got to work convincing council of the stadium's viability, that Exhibition Place was the logical place to hold events in the city, and that the infrastructure surrounding it made perfect sense.

And in late October 2005, Miller got what he wanted, when Toronto city council voted 25 to 13 in favour. "We look forward to working with the three levels of government as we prepare for construction of the stadium in early 2006 and while we finalize our franchise agreement with Major League Soccer," said Richard Peddie at the time.

Finally, all three levels of government had worked together. Through Infrastructure Canada, the federal government contributed $27 million and the Ontario government ponied up $8 million. The City of Toronto contributed $9.8 million and retained ownership of the stadium. Miller's real stroke of genius was retaining that ownership while also protecting himself and the city. Through an agreement between the city, Exhibition Place, the CSA, and MLSE, MLSE would be responsible for the management of the stadium and also would pay $18 million ($8 million for construction and $10 million for stadium naming rights) and would provide a $2 million guarantee against operational losses.

Essentially, the city would receive half of the profits from the stadium but accept none of the losses. "It was brilliantly negotiated by city staff," said Miller. "Everyone saved face."

And for Miller, the announcement brought a sense of personal satisfaction as well. Soccer, to him, had always appealed to his political sensibilities simply because it's not an expensive sport to play and thus does not become marked by class differences, like golf or hockey:

> Everybody can play it. And when you're the mayor of Toronto, you're very cognizant of the fact that the demographics of the city represent everybody in the world. So, the importance of bringing the U-20 World Cup and Toronto FC wasn't just because 'David Miller's a soccer fan,' it's actually an incredibly important thing to have a sport that everybody in Toronto can feel a part of and we can coalesce on. It's a really beautiful and important thing.

And whenever Miller walks through the turnstiles of BMO Field as a long-time season-ticket holder, he remembers that feeling of satisfaction at delivering for the city he still calls home. "We were called upon to rescue it," said Miller, "and truly, had we not stepped in, it would not have happened."

Richard Peddie still had work to do on his end. As much as the CSA, an organization bound by tradition, needed BMO Field to be the flagship stadium for the 2007 U-20 World Cup, they also wanted to ensure that Peddie and MLSE played by their rules and, given that the club would play on their turf, would get approval from them before purchase.

The ownership groups of the Vancouver Whitecaps and Montreal Impact, also hoping to make the jump up the pyramid to MLS, reached out in the hopes that MLSE would not jump the queue. Perhaps the three clubs could enter MLS closer together?

"Fuck off, I'm buying this thing," Peddie remembers thinking.

It was Peddie's determination that redeemed him with MLS commissioner Don Garber and MLS itself. "It was a little bit of manna dropping from heaven," Garber said of Peddie's involvement.

Garber was in awe of Peddie, the head of a powerful North American sports and entertainment company that had been following the league. Garber remembers not only how quickly the deal to purchase the club came together, but the gusto with which Peddie acted.

One of the final negotiations took place in Peddie's conference room at the MLSE offices. Halfway through the negotiations, Peddie received a call from the NHL offices: the league was about to announce the cancellation of the 2004–5 season because of a lockout and Peddie had to head downstairs to conduct a press conference.

Forty-five minutes later, Peddie returned, not rattled in the slightest. "Okay," he said, "where did we leave off?"

So when Peddie walked into the CSA offices to eventually request their approval, he ultimately wanted to make the decision for them. Dressed in an Armani suit, he was his "aggressive best" in his presentation. "My opening slide was, 'I don't know anything about football,'" he said, mimicking a dropping microphone.

The CSA was naturally aghast, but MLSE's financial investment in the club and the stadium was hard to overlook. Peddie eventually appealed to the organization's more emotional side by promising that this club would help grow the sport in the country and eventually make the national team more competitive. Not surprisingly, the CSA relented.

As Peddie strutted out of the CSA offices, even he likely could not have predicted how well the city's soccer community would buy into what MLSE was selling.

When season tickets first went on sale, MLSE announced that Leafs and Raptors season-seat holders could purchase tickets at a discount. Once season ticket sales hit 5,000, Peddie instructed Beirne to stop the discounts. Peddie says the ticket sales took off the way a "bullet train in Japan" picks up speed. "We need to think big," Peddie remembers thinking. "We had momentum going for us."

On May 11, 2006, MLSE officially chose Toronto FC as the name of the 13th MLS club. And MLS commissioner Don Garber understood how important the city's diverse population would be not only to the club's success, but also to the growth of the league. "The launch of TFC and its representation of an authentic soccer culture in a very important global city is, without a doubt, one of the most important factors in helping Major League Soccer to be what we are today," said Garber. "I say that because it comes out of a time period when, in the early part of the decade, 2001–3, we had gone through a major reorganization. It was very traumatic."

Garber recalls how, before TFC entered MLS, the league was in dire straits, with teams being operated by the league because of a lack of private-ownership investment. He and MLS understood they needed to find a path forward that would require a real, energized, and deep re-launch, which included Philip Anschutz taking ownership of five teams, the league folding teams in Miami and Tampa Bay due to lack of revenue, and the launch of Soccer United Marketing, which created the economic engine that would keep the league alive. All signs pointed to the league attempting to reinvent itself.

"Coming out of that period in 2003, we knew we needed to expand," said Garber. "If we didn't, we wouldn't have been able to move forward. And I say that because if that was MLS 1.0-plus, and if we were not able to get new investors to believe in this new path forward, we would've had to fold."

The league added Real Salt Lake and Chivas USA in 2005, which was in Garber's estimation the first sign of new investors believing that MLS could at least move forward for a few years with the new model.

Yet it was the addition of a Toronto-based club backed by one of the most successful sports and entertainment brands in North America that truly extinguished any doubts Garber had of the future of the league. A precedent had been set with the success of the Leafs and the Raptors, and Garber couldn't contain his excitement.

"It wasn't until the next team," Garber said of TFC, "which took us many years to get finalized in Toronto in 2007, that we actually believed, 'Hey guys, I think we got this.' And that was because a big market, with a big time global sports and entertainment company in MLSE that was validating our league by saying, 'We want in. And we want in with a downtown stadium, with an authentic brand.'"

On a stage at the Ricoh Coliseum, steps away from where Toronto FC would eventually play, the team's first kit was revealed. To no one's surprise, red was chosen as the primary colour in an attempt to honour the club's Canadian heritage. They were the first Canadian expansion club.

"Toronto provides the perfect backdrop for the world's number-one sport, given our city's diversity and affinity for soccer," said Tom Anselmi, executive vice-president and COO of MLSE. "We're committed to making Toronto FC and Major League Soccer a success."

The club's first slogan was also revealed: "All For One."

Rollins understands that while "All For One" is a marketing slogan, he believes that when it was announced, it "meant something." "They were able to strip down the resistance," said Rollins of the club's ability to unite a diverse fan base with very diverse allegiances to other clubs. "It wasn't 'I'm a Juventus fan,' 'I'm a Bayern fan.'"

For the first time, the club's logo was also revealed. The time of the outlandish and oft-provocative logos of the '90s was long gone, and above the heart on the red kit was a large grey *T* with the words *Toronto FC* in red and white, worked into a simple, classic crest.

Beirne would eventually reveal that MLS's design team had refined an early take on the logo; then downtown design agency AmoebaCorp further evolved it. The ties to the city were only strengthened further when designer Ryan Smolkin, who would eventually open local mainstay Smoke's Poutinerie and become the easily identifiable face on the logo of that busy fast-food joint, was the one assigned to the TFC logo.

The logo, in Beirne's words, was meant to be "classic, inoffensive." Beirne was proud of how the club eschewed the sort of overtly Canadian imagery that would have been a two-foot putt. "There's no beaver in it," he said. "It's trying to be the real thing."

The songs fans hear at Toronto FC games might seem expertly choreographed. At specific moments throughout the 90 minutes, a full performance, often sung by the entire south end, will break out in a rousing manner and can quickly sweep up the entire stadium.

It's not unlike what a newcomer to a match with fervent supporters in Europe would hear. Those clubs, of course, have the luxury of a much longer history than TFC and time to not only develop those songs, but have them become deeply ingrained in the game-day experience.

Months before kickoff of TFC's first game, there was still division within the various TFC supporters' groups over which songs would be used, and when.

Red Patch Boys and U-Sector both believed themselves to be the dominant supporters' group, each with good reason to think so. Red Patch Boys had the numbers and the unyielding passion of a start-up, while U-Sector had the history, having led their own chants at Toronto Lynx games in the A-League years earlier.

Debates continued on various online message boards over which songs should be used at TFC games. "Everybody wanted to support," said Jack DePoe, an early founder of the Red Patch Boys. "Opinions on how to do so were as varied as the cultural backgrounds of Toronto."

DePoe pointed out to his fellow Red Patch Boys members that there were different styles of support in different countries of the world. For TFC, the singing and chanting that had been popularized in England was what struck a chord for them.

It was just before Christmas 2006 that things came to a head. Various supporters realized they were just months away from TFC kicking off and that the factions within the supporters' groups could derail the excitement that, as a collective, they all shared. So, invites were extended to various supporters' groups to meet for a "Song Night" at the Rhino Restaurant and Bar in Toronto's Parkdale neighbourhood, just a short walk from BMO Field. The plan was simple, according to Keay: "Everyone stop bitching and complaining about your politics and let's go to the Rhino and let's just hang out, sing some songs, and let's try to get along."

Keay realized there was a lot of work to be done if the groups were to create something special. And so, with copious amounts of beer to ease the mood, one fan would start out with a line from a song and would continue until everyone else understood the song and would then belt it out. Throughout the evening, a strong sense of bravado became evident. "It was very *West Side Story*," said Keay.

As the beer continued to flow, more songs came out of the groups and a sense of camaraderie built from the excitement of what was happening: the rise of a club to be shared among thousands of supporters from different walks of life. Regardless of previous allegiances, it was at the Rhino that TFC first became a club that more than just one group took ownership of. And this paved the way for what TFC would ultimately become: a club that speaks to people of different backgrounds and one that values diversity and inclusivity.

"It was," said Keay, "a come-to-Jesus type moment."

After the original meeting with possible supporters at the Duke of York and then the reveal of a classic-looking club, the idea of what soccer could eventually become in Toronto gained real steam on internet message boards.

Mike Dubrick was the inaugural president of the Red Patch Boys. To him the internet was a powerful tool to help organize ideas and to create the atmosphere of "what was possible." One reason Dubrick was drawn to message boards was that none of his personal friends had any interest in soccer. On the message boards, he found like-minded people. He found a home.

Unless Canadian soccer fans had been to live games in Europe or South America, many had very little concept of what a true supporters' group could look like. The access online to information about supporters' culture worldwide changed that. "Because it was at our fingertips, it was really easy for us to say 'Why not here? Why not now?'" said Dubrick.

And Beirne was on board. He wanted to embrace supporters' culture within the club and to make it very clear that it would be the supporters who would carry the club's vision in the early seasons.

When the first seating map for tickets was released, there were the traditional stages and pricing, but one section of the seating map stood out: the entire 3,000-seat south end was coloured yellow and called the Supporters' Section.

"That's a phrase that is common ticketing nomenclature today," said Beirne. "In Canada, in 2006, it wasn't. It was a code. Diehards knew what it was, but nobody else did."

Much in the vein of the Südtribüne (the "South Bank," that some call the "Gelbe Wand," the "Yellow Wall"), at Borussia Dortmund's Signal Iduna Park in Germany, the idea was simple: economical tickets ($10 per game for a 17-game season ticket package) for fans who would support the club by standing and letting their voices be heard for 90 minutes straight.

It was the antithesis of the tepid atmosphere that Maple Leafs games at the Air Canada Centre had become known for.

Jack DePoe and the Red Patch Boys intended that their actions during a game should be responsive to what was happening on the field. They wanted to be spontaneous, but they also wanted to have use of what fans regularly see in Europe: "ultras," who use tifos (choreography), smoke, flairs, flags, and chanting.

"We wanted to take elements from all of those things we liked," said DePoe.

For the Red Patch Boys, they were simply trying to fill a void they felt among the fans of some of Toronto's other teams. "I never understood why that level of passion and culture wasn't here," said Dubrick. "It didn't seem like there was a good reason why it wasn't here. Even with the Leafs and Jays, it was there, but it wasn't organized."

Dubrick saw fans buy in very early on to the possibilities of what fan culture at TFC matches could be, because they wanted to replicate the support they saw while supporting other clubs on TV most Saturday mornings. "You're never as connected as the people who live there," said Dubrick. "Having the club here, you bridge that gap. The songs you're singing, they're about where you were from. I think that's what makes football such a special sport."

Dubrick personally felt he had something to prove. He wanted to show that the kind of fandom that many North Americans were in awe of, and many Europeans took as commonplace, could exist at a Toronto-based club. Which is why, early on in his time with Red Patch Boys, Dubrick made it the club's mandate to get organized and do TFC proud.

"We didn't have faith in MLSE to do it themselves," said Dubrick. "They reached out to us and they were quite open to say that they didn't have the knowledge that we did about the game."

Dubrick remembers Beirne coming to him and delivering a simple message: "You guys are the experts. You tell us how you want this thing to go down and we will, to the best of our ability, make this thing happen. And we'll sink or swim together."

Both the club and its supporters were venturing into uncharted waters.

Though the new team coming to town was playing the most popular sport in the world, they were also entering into a city that already had four major league clubs, one of which, the Maple Leafs, dominated the city's consciousness in a way that few clubs do, in any sport, around the world. So, in order to survive, both the new club and their supporters not only embraced an outsider mentality, they found that it was hardened in the face of naysayers. Early TFC fans, especially long-time fans of the Toronto Blizzard or the Canadian national team, didn't just support the club, they quickly embraced it as part of their own identities. Dubrick continued:

> That mentality of being disregarded, not being part of the
> sports tapestry of the city, not being welcomed very warmly
> onto the scene by the major sports figures in sports TV
> and so on — I remember in those early years, if you got

a mention on the radio, it was probably because we threw streamers on the field. It was never because Toronto FC did anything. It didn't help that the team sucked. In the early days, the only thing they had to talk about was these crazy fans.

Eventually, TFC would lean heavily on fans in their own promotional materials to bring the "All For One" mentality to fruition.

As people who loved the sport, we believed we needed to be passionate about it and show them what a great time Toronto FC could be and also show them that this is the most popular sport in the world for a reason. And that we deserve our spot on the Toronto sports scene just as much as other teams do.

An early promotional video tried to latch on to the idea of "All for One": that the most popular sport in the world could indeed unite Toronto. In the video, a ball is kicked from a classroom full of young children, to a shop of women selling traditional Indian dresses, down College Street, and onto a subway, before bouncing into a Little Portugal barbershop, then into a Bay Street bank, before finally landing in BMO Field.

"They [the hard-core fans] did a good job of selling the product in the stadium, not the product in the field," remembers Keay. "Without that strong supporter culture, nobody would have bought tickets."

It was, indeed, a very economical option for curious fans unaccustomed to the sport. Finally, the Blue Jays had regular competition from another sports team in Toronto. The Jays were finishing their first above-.500 season in three years, with high ticket prices accordingly, and the prospect of an affordable family outing on the shores of Lake Ontario became enticing. Being also able to see the downtown skyline, Lake Ontario, and Billy Bishop Airport (where new Porter Airlines had just started up in 2006), made for a welcome alternative to the cavernous Rogers Centre.

In spite of the many failed pro soccer teams in Toronto, including the Lynx and the Blizzard, supporters showed up early to buy season tickets.

Within 48 hours of season tickets going on sale, it became clear that fans did not want to see this venture fail like every other pro soccer team in Toronto.

And all of this was done without a lineup.

TFC had tapped into a mindset that longstanding fans of professional soccer franchises in Europe and South America understood: when a club becomes so ingrained in the psyche of the place it represents, that team can often go through long stretches of poor results but its fans will keep coming. The notion of fair-weather fans and clubs relocating to other cities isn't nearly as prevalent in European soccer culture as it is in certain North American sports and leagues. Beirne and TFC had found a group of supporters who not only understood that right away, but were ready to ingrain the new soccer club in Toronto.

On behalf of Red Patch Boys, Dubrick's original request to MLSE was 50 season's seats in section 112. There were only 25 people at the time in Red Patch Boys and each member wanted a pair.

What seemed like a small request went a long way with TFC. "It's not like the Leafs where there's a waiting list," said Dubrick. "When we asked for 50 seats, they were like, '50 seats? Amazing.'"

Dubrick and the rest of the Red Patch Boys helped develop fan enthusiasm before the first season even kicked off. The group's members would return from their own expeditions to support clubs around the world and talk until they were blue in the face about how fanatical the support over there was. And in doing so, they paved the way for future TFC support.

Dubrick has already seen children, who once stood with their parents in the south end on family outings, grow up and eventually move to sit in the more expensive seats. TFC had, deliberately and inevitably, created a loyalty program by allowing passionate fans the opportunity to express themselves fully, without the restrictions on chanting and physical objects that exist in many other arenas and stadiums in Toronto.

Beirne, relying on his experience with the Raptors, utilized some of the traditional ticket-selling methods, including offering incentives to those who purchased tickets on behalf of their companies. To anyone who bought tickets for their company, Beirne offered season seats in the south end for just $100, likening it to a fast-food up-sell. The club sold 900 tickets that way, but then realized they had put 900 spectators in among the hard-core fans who refused to let 90 minutes go by quietly.

Even though some people resented the language, having to stand, and the flags, Beirne and TFC didn't place any restrictions on how TFC fans could express themselves in the south end, even in the face of mounting pressure from high-end ticket-buyers. He wanted to continue to celebrate the "culture of football."

"It took some time for that to wean itself out," said Beirne.

Toward the end of 2006, TFC had become a phenomenon by MLS standards. By Christmas, they had sold 10,000 season tickets. When rumours of David Beckham's landscape-altering move from Real Madrid to the Los Angeles Galaxy began to look more credible, the club sold another 2,000 season tickets before the official announcement of his move. Early in January, when the move was confirmed, the club sold 2,000 more. With Beckham coming to MLS, many casual fans did not want to miss out on seeing him in the flesh. His arrival added an extra layer to the club's expectations. "This league is going to be bigger than we thought," Beirne remembers thinking.

With Beckham came the Designated Player rule, nicknamed the Beckham Rule, which allowed teams to sign notable players and not have their contracts count against the team's hard salary cap. TFC's first meeting as a league member was when the league as a collective decided to approve the DP rule. It was a monumental change, meant to increase the profile of the league, and would eventually have tremendous ramifications for TFC. The new club appeared to be entering the league at exactly the right time: just as the general public was becoming aware of the MLS.

Coupled with the addition of Beckham to MLS was Canada's hosting of the U-20 World Cup, with the Toronto stadium to host group stage and knockout-round matches as well as the final. The U-20 World Cup was probably FIFA's second-biggest property. The club ran a promotion that allowed those on the season-ticket waiting list to get first dibs at tournament tickets for games at BMO Field. Season-ticket packages also included an opportunity to purchase U-20 tickets.

The U-20 tournament is held in high regard by the world's soccer purists as a breeding ground for the future greats, rather as dedicated hockey fans in Canada and abroad view the World Junior Hockey Championships.

Despite not having played a single game in a league many of those purists were not convinced of, simply associating with the tournament provided TFC a relationship with the skeptics. "It was permission to talk to them," said Beirne, of the city's hard-core soccer fans who knew the U-20 World Cup was a chance to see the world's best budding players. "It opened a door that would not have been open otherwise."

Concurrent with these promotions, TFC had boots on the ground. They were casting their net wide and trying to create a brand and to distinguish themselves from their peers. With the club already having early roots in the pubs, Beirne wanted to establish a continuing presence in nearby Liberty Village watering holes. Starting in November 2006, the club hosted weekly pub nights in conjunction with Carlsberg to promote TFC and create the image of a hip sports team that young professionals could support. Beirne and TFC recognized that, having been born out of a small community of fervent supporters, those same community connections would have to inform their approach to building a brand. Spending time before and after matches in pubs, as fans would in Europe, was encouraged. If you were young, curious about soccer, and enjoyed hanging out in bars anyway, TFC wanted you. Eventually, TFC would bring their weekly pub nights to bars throughout the Greater Toronto Area, to announce player signings and continually to engage fans.

MLSE was sometimes seen as an unapproachable corporate monolith that cared only about their bottom line with their sports franchises. Now they were trying to bridge the gap between ownership and fans. Though MLSE had a product fans were interested in, the corporation first had to convince those same fans that they could be trusted.

Their chosen variety of methods would pay off: TFC had to cap season ticket sales at 14,000, just so there could be some single-game tickets left. By comparison, 4 of MLS's 12 existing teams had an average attendance of less than 14,000 per home game in the 2006 season. "We were shaking the tree and they fell out," said Beirne of the club's inaugural season-seat holders. TFC had tried to expand their reach beyond the hard-core fans to the merely curious. And it worked.

Dubrick understands that many don't like to give a corporation like MLSE credit very often, but he believes the corporation does deserve credit for the way it embraced supporters. "The way you treat your fans is more important than wins and losses," said Dubrick. "The clubs that embrace that are the ones that succeed."

With a fan base in place in 2006 and excitement starting to grow about the possibilities of what the club could become, TFC needed to move quickly.

For all of Beirne's enthusiasm, someone with more soccer knowledge was needed. After a few conversations with Peddie and Anselmi about possibly helping launch the club, TFC formally brought in Earl Cochrane as the club's first manager of team operations in July 2006.

Cochrane was an OUA All-Star defender at Carleton University and had briefly played in Malaysia and Japan afterward. He'd previously worked as director of communications for both D.C. United and the Canadian Soccer Association (CSA). During the build-up to the 2007 U-20 World Cup, he was part of a group travelling cross country to assess venues. The belief was that Cochrane's experience both with MLS and the Canadian soccer landscape would make him a valuable addition to steer the ship in the right direction. And Cochrane was needed immediately.

When he arrived, Cochrane found just two things at TFC: Beirne, and "a lot of ideas." Long conversations between him and Beirne at Toronto's Beaches Jazz Festival solidified some ideas on how and what the vision and branding for TFC would be.

Not long after that, the club's few employees literally pushed their desks together at 50 Bay Street and got to work. The first task? Balancing the obvious need for the club to turn a profit while ensuring that, according to Cochrane, "we weren't fake in any way."

> A lot of the time when you're beginning a franchise, you tend to lean on a lot of business metrics and you try to keep it afloat, but you sometimes forget to get the support staff around the team ready to try and kick things off. And that can take a long time.

Cochrane's early role was both dealing with the brunt of the naysayers and convincing those they had to convince that Toronto FC were going to play a vital role in the growth of Canadian soccer. Cochrane was bullish on the understanding that Toronto was a city that was "tailor-made for what we were about to do." Still, he remembers there were "hundreds" of detractors.

Many could think only of the A-League and its inability to capture the imagination of the soccer fans in the city. Cochrane wanted people to remember the late '70s heyday of the NASL (North American Soccer League) and how the Toronto-based franchise, Metros-Croatia, captured the 1976 Soccer Bowl in front of 25,000-plus fans in Seattle on the strength of a Eusébio free kick. Trying to remind a mass audience how one of the greatest players to ever lace up boots, just a year after having left Benfica, played for a Toronto-based club, turned out to be an exercise in futility.

"There had been a long void in the city," said Cochrane. "Most of the people were saying no because they didn't know what yes could look like."

The concerns came fast and hard, particularly from a group of people who still associated MLS with its terrifyingly strange early versions, in which shootouts occurred at the end of every draw and players had five seconds to dribble and score from 35 yards out.

Some people, according to Cochrane, worried that with Toronto FC would come cheerleaders, TV timeouts, and an equally terrifying "Americanized" version of the game.

The close relationship Cochrane and TFC established with supporters' clubs went a long way toward convincing casual fans that the club had the best intentions. But Cochrane's real work began with the Ontario Soccer Association.

Part of TFC's early vision, Cochrane said, was that they "*really* wanted to be seen as Canada's club." Some league restrictions, including a quota of Canadian players being required in the squad, would have inclined TFC down that route anyway, but, for Cochrane and Beirne, the ultimate over-arching goal would be, be it 10, 15, or 20 years down the line, to have an all-Canadian starting 11. "In some ways, the dream was built around that," said Cochrane.

With six million people within an hour's drive of the city that was "bursting" with kids who, in the right circumstances and given the right environment, could really succeed, Cochrane had to established connections with the Ontario Soccer Association.

It didn't begin well.

"There was a lot of apprehension," said Cochrane. Amateur clubs were standoffish, largely because TFC didn't have any sort of track record to back up what they were suggesting they would be able to do; namely, develop and promote local talent.

Some of Ontario's top soccer minds looked at players moving into a possible TFC academy as less about seeing them move up and more about simply losing them. It's a mindset that Cochrane wrestled with throughout his time with TFC. But, when the 2007 season kicked off, Cochrane was named TFC's first academy director.

"We realized an academy was something we need to be building," said Cochrane. For the next three years, he made it his job, among all of his other duties, to build the academy and to strengthen ties with local clubs. In doing so, he fought to legitimize TFC as a brand and a business.

Cochrane would eventually bring on Stuart Neely, who had experience with the CSA as technical programs manager, to be TFC's academy manager. MLS clubs were mandated by the league to have two academy teams at the time, and Neely was in part tasked with appealing to the Ontario Soccer Association and to local clubs for players to join their academy. Initially, TFC couldn't clearly communicate their direction for the club and how academy players would fit in, or even what league the academy teams would be playing in, largely because Neely himself didn't know. Neely knew that, in theory, an academy could provide a stepping stone to the first team. But, with little proof of this, the skepticism and the local clubs' unwillingness to release local talent to the TFC academy only grew.

The club's aggressive start-up mentality had claimed a victim: the pathway to the future for young, local players in a growing soccer market. "We were selling something we didn't know," said Neely.

Neely wanted nothing more than an opportunity to show the local soccer community that TFC could properly train players. And yet while fans of the first team would happily buy tickets to see an academy team play, as it was a product they could become invested in immediately, the local clubs and the parents of young players were not as eager to gamble. "What was missed was everybody in the same room at the same time to say,

'Here's what we're doing.' As much as that sounds like a small component, it's massive," said Neely.

Of course, MLS at the time TFC entered looked very different from the MLS you see today, whenever you're reading this. The growth of the league has been exponential. Teams back then had to run really tight ships, and academies often felt the crunch.

There were no training grounds in Toronto, of course. During one of their very first days trying to get the academy started, Neely and fellow coach Jason Bent arrived at Gate 4 at BMO Field simultaneously, eager to get to work — and were greeted by 98 Adidas boxes full of kits of all different sizes. With no one else to help on the administrative end, their first day on the job was spent unpacking boxes, organizing gear, and, with no TFC logos on any of it, tracking down a company to get the gear embroidered.

"Have you ever done this before, Jason?" Neely asked of Bent, who, it should be noted had spent seven years playing professionally and had earned 32 caps for Canada. Both broke out into laughter, but not before realizing they'd have to rent a van to get the hundreds of pieces of gear up to an embroider.

"We literally had three weeks to get that academy team together," said Neely.

Say the name Jozy Altidore in Toronto and you'll likely be met with a smile. Not only did the forward score a goal on a hobbled ankle that sent TFC to the 2017 MLS Cup final, he delivered yet again in the playoffs with the first goal, on his off foot no less, of that Cup final. And, just for good measure, he took the stage after the MLS Cup parade in an inebriated state, grabbed the microphone, and, with all the charm of your favourite barfly, professed "I'm TFC 'til I die" to an adoring crowd. In a city full of folk heroes that go by the names of Barilko, Gilmour, and the two Carters, Altidore is the man who can mystify fans with both his goal-scoring prowess and his bludgeoning charm.

What's often forgotten about Altidore is that the man who first introduced him to the professional soccer world became TFC's first head coach: Maurice "Mo" Johnston.

Johnston was head coach of the New York MetroStars at the time and had become convinced that the 16-year-old Altidore was worth taking a chance on with a second-round pick in the 2006 MLS SuperDraft.

Altidore would end up making his professional debut later that season, and, even as a teenager, made an immediate impact, scoring four goals in nine appearances across all competitions. Johnston had been fired from his post in New York by that point, but the former Scottish international still displayed enough of an understanding of MLS and the many intricate drafting and roster rules of a then evolving league to become a wanted commodity.

Johnston, 43 in the summer of 2006, had a past that stretched beyond MLS. Just as one might elicit a smile by asking TFC fans about Jozy Altidore, bringing up Johnston to either a fanatical Celtic or Rangers fan would probably elicit the exact opposite response: the prolific striker was the most well-established Catholic player to move from Celtic, a club with longstanding ties to the Catholic Church, to Rangers, a club that, up until that point, had an unwritten rule of not signing Catholic players. In 1989, after a brief stint in Nantes, Johnston became the first player to cross that great divide: Rangers signed him. The signing caused an uproar throughout Glaswegian soccer: Johnston was regularly referred to as "Judas" by Celtic fans, and faced hostility from within the Rangers organization and from fans all the same. Publicly, Johnston appeared undeterred, still scoring with great regularity for Rangers. Yet, throughout his time in Scotland, he wore so much of the pain of having broken allegiances on his own, while hardly ever seeking counsel about his decision.

Despite Scotland having won just four games in World Cup history, and one of those wins the result of a Johnston penalty kick in the 81st minute to seal a 2–1 win over Sweden, it became difficult for Johnston to remain in Scotland.

In 1996, he had moved from Europe to MLS and made more appearances with the Kansas City Wizards than with any other club in his career. Any return trips to Scotland would become sources of anguish for Johnston as he was met with calls of being a "Catholic cunt" from the moment he arrived in the Glasgow Airport.

The experience hardened Johnston and informed much of his insular approach in MLS. He never lost the gift of gab, and never shied away from digging deep into the league with an extended list of contacts, although when he became set on an idea it became difficult to convince him to change it.

And that suited Tom Anselmi just fine. He saw that MLS was looking increasingly inward instead of culling resources from Europe, and with Johnston's track record of selecting players who could succeed within the league and also his detailed understanding of MLS, Anselmi happily received the number of recommendations regarding Johnston for head coach.

From a soccer perspective, it was difficult for many at MLSE to judge his accomplishments, given that they themselves had none. But it was the right place and the right time to bring in someone with Johnston's confidence. With his high-energy approach, fuelled regularly by a Red Bull followed by a venti cappuccino every morning, his ability to spin a great yarn, and a career that gave him brand name recognition, the new club was sold. It was just over seven months until TFC would play their first game and, as is common in a start-up, they didn't have the luxury of an extended search time.

"Mo just ticked a lot of boxes for us," said Beirne.

Johnston was officially unveiled as the club's first head coach on August 22, 2006. And while MLSE provided Johnston with resources to add to his staff, early on it was just Johnston and Beirne in charge of filling out every area of the club. "It was literally hand to hand combat," said Beirne.

Johnston's charisma worked wonders for a staff that was trying to find their way. He wanted as many people as involved in non-roster decisions as possible, and he would go out of his way to make young staff members feel like they were valued by the club, including buying lunch for any staffer that would also go and fetch Johnston his lunch as well.

The short turnaround, and perhaps the continuous supply of caffeine, fuelled Johnston. No one could fault him for not buying in to the start-up mentality, even if it meant making decisions that appeared short-sighted. Johnston wanted to win immediately. "When you start from nothing, you don't have an end goal beyond being competitive," said TFC assistant GM Corey Wray, who began that first season as an intern with the club and has been with the organization ever since.

Johnston was going to help guide a franchise that had garnered much more support from their local fans than anticipated. Peddie remembers thinking of MLS as a "quaint" league, and it wasn't out of the realm of possibility that MLSE believed that their noted experience in the NHL and NBA would transfer over easily enough. But for all of Anselmi's experience with those two leagues, MLSE would have to understand how to make an MLS franchise successful in a much shorter amount of time. The league, with salary cap restrictions and a focus on cost containment, regulations on Canadian players, a supporters' culture unlike its counterparts in North America, and a league that was still finding its way meant that MLSE, according to Anselmi, was "just trying to keep up."

Concerns over Anselmi, and his lack of soccer background, essentially being handed the keys to this franchise were felt by some in the organization, including manager Earl Cochrane. "I think a lot," he said, of how much Anselmi's lack of soccer knowledge impacted the club early in their existence as they attempted to navigate an "insular, unique place" with its many rules.

Driven by the fans' enthusiasm and what a previous expansion team, the Toronto Raptors, had become, MLSE began dreaming big, immediately envisioning how they could grow to become one of the league's dominant franchises. Yet Cochrane's reservations persisted. "The types of managers you bring in need to have a belief in the way MLS runs things," he said, instead of simply believing "what happens in the rest of the world is better and that's what MLS should go for. That places you on the back foot right away. It was challenging."

The challenges TFC faced were not unlike those of a start-up company. What they lacked in experience, the club's early employees made up for in passion. Being awarded an MLS franchise late in 2005, the organization had a year and a half to get a team on the field. That sort of turnaround brought the need to think and act quickly. To put this in perspective, the ownership group that would eventually become Atlanta United FC were awarded a franchise in April 2014 but would not play their first game until close to three years later. And when MLS awarded Los Angeles their second team in October of 2014, the new Los Angeles Football Club would not play their first match until March 2018, almost three and a half years later.

Anselmi felt the crunch to understand the league and was overwhelmed by the intricacies of the sport and MLS. While nine out of ten start-up businesses fail, TFC were determined to turn the support they had from the mayor of Toronto and the ardent fans into a sustainable club. "All of a sudden, before you know it, you have this tidal wave of enthusiasm. So, instead of modestly dipping your toe into the water of the soccer business, we were trying to ride this wave of enthusiasm into something that we could control," said Anselmi. "We got overwhelmed with this incredible enthusiasm."

As predictable as coach Johnston was in his daily habits, he gained notoriety for wildly unpredictable early roster decisions. No one would be surprised if emotion got the best of him when building a squad. "He just wanted the team to be good quickly," said Wray. "And that was our attempt. We went all out in those first three years, but we fell short. And when that happens, then you have a roster that isn't very manageable in terms of the salary cap."

It wasn't just the salary cap: early MLS regulations stated that TFC must have at least eight Canadians on their roster. Given that the pool of available Canadian talent wasn't nearly at the level of their American counterparts, Johnston had to aim high out of the gate.

Using his connection to local soccer agent Barry McLean, Johnston called one of Canada's most reputable defenders at the time, Jim Brennan. The then 29-year-old had been logging regular minutes at clubs across England, including a successful four-year spell at Nottingham Forest after he became the first Canadian player to ever be bought by a club for over £1 million.

Brennan immediately refused Johnston's offer, but the coach persisted, trying to sell him on the promise of a new stadium and being a club's first-ever captain, but it wasn't enough.

"Who owns the club?" asked Brennan.

Learning of MLSE's ownership was enough to convince Brennan to agree to a meeting with the club. His contract was up at Southampton and he eventually came to his own realization: "Maybe it's a good time for me to come home … and play a few years in Toronto … in front of my friends and family. And then hang up the boots in my hometown."

Brennan was officially unveiled as the club's first-ever signing just over two weeks after Johnston was hired. But, even with the acquisition of Brennan, there was a growing feeling that the club was handicapped by both the salary cap and the Canadian-player restrictions. These factors only forced Johnston's hand, making him jump at every signing opportunity, sometimes without doing the proper due diligence on a player's background. Johnston's impulses planted the seed that would define TFC's rosters early on: constant turnover and often limited success.

"Because [the sports world] is so fast, he would jump on so many opportunities," said Wray. "But perhaps it would have been better for him to just slow down."

In total, 32 different players, including 13 Canadians, would make an appearance for TFC in their inaugural season. To Johnston, players became dispensable, with 10 of those players making five or less appearances that season.

For all of the enthusiasm off the pitch, TFC's inaugural training camp didn't exactly provide an auspicious start to the on-field product. The hodgepodge collection of players suffered from a variety of challenges, including having trouble getting accustomed to MLS rules, getting salary payments arranged, and of course, trying to come together as a group. "It was a logistical nightmare," said North York–born defender Marco Reda.

With BMO Field not yet fully constructed, players would be shuffled back and forth from different venues in vans. The majority of players lived out of their suitcases in hotels, or in the spare rooms of other players. Coupled with this instability was the variety of backgrounds that players had. There was a gamut of players — from local players on trial to those with semi-pro experience in Canada, to MLS players, and to those coming from the top leagues in Europe.

"It was something that I'd never ever been a part of before," said Brennan. "Sitting around, looking ... at a handful of guys with two hundred pro games under their belts. Other guys that had never been in a pro environment. I said to myself, 'This is going to be a tough one.'"

Johnston's coaching style was also more hands-on than many were used to. "He was probably one of the best players in training," said former TFC midfielder Carl Robinson. "He loved to join in."

Torn between both building the team and preparing the squad, Johnston struggled to run the kind of sessions that could prepare the team for the upcoming season.

Reda had just returned from playing professionally in Norway, where the training sessions were built on tactically preparing teams for what would be necessary come Saturday. Johnston's approach was simpler: never give the ball away and be physically tough to play against. "It was a lot of instinctual play from individual members, and that catches up to you," said Reda. "We were going against teams whose cores had been together for years. You can't play instinctually, because they're going to destroy you. And they did."

Adds goalkeeper Greg Sutton,

> They weren't the most tactical training sessions. It was more about competition. That's what he was looking for. We weren't preparing so much for what opponents were going to do. It was more about how we were going to compete as a team. Part of coaching is making sure your team is prepared, but making sure you understand what each different opponent is going to bring. I don't think we went over that in-depth enough on a regular basis.

Johnston could be forgiven for having more on his plate than your average MLS coach. Eddie Kehoe, TFC's first-ever goalkeeper coach, remembers sitting at breakfast one morning ahead of a training camp session when Johnston showed him a text message from a team representative: "Do you want the names on the back to go on an arc or a straight line?"

"Why the fuck am I getting asked this?" shouted Johnston.

"The way they showed their inexperience was they didn't put anybody in with [Johnston]," said Kehoe. "There was no one above Mo with any football experience."

That instability stretched into the first team. Players didn't know the other players and couldn't always trust their new teammates. With a lack of clear instruction from the coaching staff, few were sure of what their roles would be in the upcoming season. "We just weren't prepared from multiple angles," said Reda. "That's from Mo, down to the players. You can't say enough about chemistry and gelling as a group and having the trust of coaches and managers. So, from that end it was a bit of a struggle. Mo treated us as best as he could, but coaching isn't his calling card."

2

The 2007 Version of Viral, MLS 2.0, and a Complete Lack of Nuance

IN PAUL BEIRNE'S DOWNTOWN TORONTO office, there is an echo.

When you enter, there may or may not be a receptionist, and so when you peer around the many empty desks surrounded by exposed brick walls and see just a head or two typing away at laptops, you have no choice but to call out his name, lost in the woods.

"Paul?"

Your voice bounces off the walls, and you start to wonder what, if anything, is done in these offices.

"I'm back here," says the voice, before the warm, congenial smile greets you.

There are a few pieces on the walls that might tip you off as to what happens here: a framed Christine Sinclair jersey is one. But it's only when you sit down in the boardroom and Beirne brings two different beers out for your conversation is the world of possibilities of this new venture opened up wide for you to see.

Beirne, bespectacled and balding, isn't the picture of a former athlete desperately trying to stay in the game of soccer. Instead, he is the very image of the person you might see hugging the bar around breakfast on a Saturday, clinically looking at a game of soccer an ocean away and hell-bent on making the dream of sustainable soccer in Canada a reality. Yet, still, it is stories and narratives, not wins and losses that drive him. Beirne is trying to create something out of nothing, and he sees soccer as a sport that can enchant a curious audience.

It is 2017 when Beirne and I meet in the cavernous office of the upstart Canadian Premier League. When we chat, Beirne is the sole employee of the CPL and he is navigating the league around thousands of interested parties, and perhaps thousands more who are skeptical about what he is trying to accomplish.

I'm mentioning this only because very few people got to peek behind the curtain at how TFC launched their own ship, but their launch was similar to that of the CPL. "You could've kicked a ball from one end of the room to the other," said Eddie Kehoe of the club's wide-open early offices.

Sheer ambition drove the club in its early days, a start-up trying to navigate the waters of a field it had no experience in and using that ambition as an engine.

It really didn't matter that TFC flew to Carson, California, for their debut MLS match, armed with a ragtag collection of players that had limited cohesion as a squad and some with perhaps even less experience of competitive, professional soccer. It didn't matter that TFC dropped that game 2–0, including a Sacha Kljestan goal in the 88th minute (a name TFC fans would never forget). It also didn't even matter that 8 (8!) of TFC's starting 11 that day would not play for the club again after 2007, with some making just a handful of appearances for the club in their careers.

What did matter was that TFC were at the dance.

What sort of moves they could bust out were of little relevance. Professional soccer, led by a bona fide corporation with deep pockets that would not want to see this club fall by the wayside, had arrived in Toronto, and it would take a lot to wipe the collective smiles off the faces of those who had been waiting so patiently.

Two more drubbings, at the hands of the New England Revolution and the Kansas City Wizards, still without a goal scored, wasn't going to spoil the party ahead of the April 28 home opener.

Jack DePoe watched from the balcony of his Liberty Village condo on the afternoon of the home opener as thousands of people streamed toward BMO Field. He heard the chanting, singing, and stomping resonating up from many floors below. "It's just something you don't often hear at a Toronto sports event," he recalled.

And when he finally came through the stadium tunnel into the stands near his seat at BMO Field? "I felt this atmosphere wash over," said De Poe.

Months of planning and coordination from the early supporters' groups manifested in an electric environment that day. The sea of red and white was one thing, but a constant, almost surreal blend of organized singing and deafening cheering despite the biting cold created an inescapable buzz that provided a much-needed antidote to the assumption that all Toronto sports fans are a blasé bunch.

And it had even the most hardened of Europeans convinced that the supporters could provide a promising future in Toronto. "For the first time in a long time, I felt goosebumps at a game," said Johnston, in his post-match press conference.

Unfortunately, during the match, Eddie Johnson embarrassed the TFC back line with a quick sidestep for the lone goal in a 1–0 loss to the Wizards. The fact that TFC had set a record for dismalness on that day, creating the longest scoring drought to open a franchise's history — 360 minutes — was met with smiles and the fans' ability to act impulsively, not just in coordination, was evident. Hundreds spontaneously began to sing "All we are saying, is give us a goal!" to the tune of John Lennon's "Give Peace a Chance." To this day, Beirne can't help chuckling at the memory.

After the game, TFC's first overall pick in the 2007 MLS SuperDraft, Maurice Edu, was impressed not only by the atmosphere, but by the understanding that TFC fans showed on the day. "I think they're going to hold us to a high standard," he said, as he sat in his locker-room stall.

That comment foreshadowed the future of the club; but, in the meantime, a precedent had been set: even without positive results on the pitch, the fans in the stadium could become the narrative of the club's first season.

For all the fears that Toronto FC would not be able to unite a city divided by the fans' own soccer allegiances, the opposite was proving to be true. The cries of MLS being an inferior product could barely be heard amid the shouts of thousands of jubilant fans who now had a team of their own to support in their own backyard, and a loyalty that they could pass down to generations of fans to come.

But every generation needs a hero, and TFC were admittedly wanting for a hero through their opening four games.

To put it plainly, Johnston and TFC were desperate for goals. Johnston had recognized very early on that, with defenders Carl Robinson and Jimmy Brennan, the expansion roster would have a decent spine and could play long balls from the back and from the wings. But without anyone to finish those long balls, TFC were doomed.

So, Mo Johnston went to work doing what he did best: working the phones to produce a player almost immediately.

Danny Dichio had played for 10 clubs professionally throughout England and Italy and the six-foot-three forward had earned a reputation as a bruising, hard-nosed finisher. He'd once visited Vancouver on a pre-season tour with Millwall FC, and as he entered his early thirties, he sensed that his career in England was beginning to wind down. His wife had been born in New York, and North America had always intrigued him and his family as a place not just to end his career, but to continue living long after.

So, when Dichio began the 2007 pre-season training camp with the Chicago Fire, he thought he'd found a new club. Unfortunately, the haphazard nature of early MLS signings became evident. Fire management assumed that Dichio held a U.S. green card because of his wife's birthplace, and would therefore not take up an international roster spot. But there was no automatic green card, and Dichio would have to wait at least six months and possibly two years before he'd know if he could get one. Unable to sign the contract he was given, a frustrated Dichio sacked his agent and went back to Manchester. But there, when he checked his messages, he found calls from D.C. United and Toronto FC, both inquiring about his status.

There was an urgency in Johnston's voice that led Dichio to consider the option presented: Johnston said TFC could offer him a contract as an international immediately and, given how wide open they were at the top of the pitch and their lack of production early on, they wanted him to return to North America and jump into the lineup immediately. All too familiar with being bought and sold like a commodity in England, Dichio packed a bag and hopped on a flight back to Toronto, unaware of how he would change the course of the club's history.

Dichio had a track record of scoring goals, and some of his new team-mates knew it. Brennan, who had played against Dichio in England, would remember his giant bald head crashing into the box. TFC now had their first real attacking threat.

"That was a relief," said Brennan, of Dichio joining the club.

When he joined the club for the home opener, Dichio immediately redeemed himself to a sizeable portion of the fan base that had grown fond of Toronto-based athletes not afraid to show their brawn in the heat of the moment, including Darcy Tucker, Tie Domi, and Charles Oakley. Dichio was given a yellow card in his first game.

Off the pitch, Dichio's own transition was coupled with the constant state of transition he saw within the club. "Walking into a club that was just in its start-up process was exciting for me," he said. "There was a lot of disorganization at the beginning because no one had any idea about a lot of things, whether it be travelling to away games, organizing squads ..."

So Dichio opted to simply keep his head down and keep his end of the bargain, while the circus that was the inaugural season continued to develop around him.

Beirne had recognized early on that the club still had to take a few risks and deviate from some traditional soccer statutes if they were to earn new fans and, in a sense, create a fan culture all their own.

While the idea of sitting outside on hard plastic seats in bitter cold had become a rite of passage for many soccer fans in northern European countries, Beirne reminded MLSE that Toronto fans had not sat out-doors for any major event since the building of the SkyDome, and that the plastic seats didn't exactly lend themselves to a comfortable Saturday afternoon. The "most logical thing to do" was to partner with the Bank of Montreal, who were TFC's kit sponsor anyway, and create seat cush-ions with a handle. With the cushions stamped as being from the opening season, fans could bring them to every game for years to come with pride in their early fandom.

The idea was quickly bought and sold, but Peddie couldn't help briefly wondering if it was a bad one, as he walked through the BMO Field gates on that May 12. He did think a few of the seat cushions might end up on the field, but couldn't worry too much, as he, like the other 20,000 people who entered the stadium that day, were more preoccupied with hopes of finally seeing TFC's first-ever goal scored.

Early in the match, the south end's take on the Plastic Ono Band picked up again as TFC could not beat the Chicago Fire: *"All we are saaaying, is give us a goooooal!"*

Dichio had heard enough. He had developed one instinct throughout his career that had always served him well. Just go to the goddamn net.

In the 24th minute, Marvell Wynne simply lathered, rinsed, and repeated, and sent a long ball into the box from the right flank. It was on a hope and prayer, and after the ball took a fortuitous bounce over the Fire defenders, Edu sent Edson Buddle on a short run just wide of the goal.

Ask those in attendance that day and you'll hear the same thing: fans just *knew* the goal was coming. Now, revisionist history is a strange thing, but there's no denying that TFC fans had been toyed with long enough. The storybook version would have the fans rise to their feet as Buddle took a swing at the ball and fell hard to the bright turf as he crossed the ball in toward the centre of the box. In reality, the fans were already on their feet, as they had been since kickoff.

Dichio was marked by a Fire defender but used his size to push him off. He didn't know if Buddle's ball would be a shot or a cross, so he gambled half-heartedly and, in his words, "bumbled it in" as he fell to the ground, watching as the ball worked its way past Fire goalkeeper Matt Pickens. "It wasn't the sexiest goal I'd ever scored," says Dichio, laughing.

It didn't have to be. There had been nothing sexy at all about TFC's inaugural season so far.

Dichio, carrying the weight of the teammates who had jumped on his back, ran to the advertising boards behind the net and nearly broke his toe as he kicked them in excitement. The noise around him was, in Earl Cochrane's words, "overwhelming."

"We'd finally done it," remembers Dichio. "And now we can go and build off of this and get three points," he adds, ever the professional.

But before Dichio and the rest of the squad could concern themselves with building off the goal, they had to take cover. With no reason now to sit, there was no need for the seat cushions. In a spontaneous act of elation, a few fans' outright relief over finally seeing a goal at BMO Field caused them to throw their souvenir seat cushions onto the pitch.

"One of them flies," said Beirne, "and then in your peripheral vision, a snowflake flies by. And then, and it was a tangible three seconds, all start flying."

Beirne's not kidding. In the blink of an eye, thousands of the white seat cushions were hurtling down to the green pitch. "I think we're going to pay close attention to those Red Patch Boys," Garber remembers thinking.

The game had to be stopped and any employee on hand had to take to the field to clean up what may have been 10,000 seat cushions. "It was just something that was not on our radar," Beirne said.

"I think they're going to have to rethink their marketing strategy a little bit," then Fire head coach Dave Sarachan said, after the game.

Beirne laughs while recalling the afternoon, but the souvenir-seat-cushion affair was symbolic of TFC as a whole during that inaugural season. It was an idea that came together quickly, with little thought given to how it would affect the action on the pitch; and the fans took the idea, ran with it, and became the stars of the show.

YouTube was still in its relatively infancy at the time, so it went, in Beirne's words, "the 2007 version of viral." Clips of the goal, the bedlam that ensued, and the pitch covered in seat cushions began popping up on stations around the world. TFC were getting requests for comment from as far away as Japan. Cochrane's old friends from his playing days in Asia were sending him emails, curious about this strange phenomenon that had occurred at the stadium by the lake.

Among the many calls TFC received that day was one from the league office: MLS commissioner Don Garber, at least publicly, was not happy. His message was simple: TFC were never to give away seat cushions, or any sort of projectile, again. There were the standard legal concerns involved. But even as that conversation drew to a close, the league also could not contain their excitement. They let it be known that as dangerous as thousands of seat cushions being tossed in the air could have been, the attention it received worldwide was also a boon for the team and the league. "Before that, I'm not sure anything MLS-related got that much global attention or was as much of a spectacle," said Cochrane.

Fan support was quickly changing in MLS, and those changes were being manifested at BMO Field.

Beirne credits D.C. United's La Barra Brava supporters' group as one of the pioneers of unique, if relentless, fan culture within the stadium, but still, as he left his office the day after Dichio's goal, he realized that, regardless of what sort of results TFC would experience on the pitch, the MLS office and the rest of the world now recognized the tiny, upstart club, and one thing was clear: "TFC had arrived," said Beirne.

With that sort of fan support in the club's first few games, Beirne got even more enthusiastic about what the future could hold. "It signalled new era for soccer in Canada and MLS. From a cultural perspective, MLS had arrived."

Cochrane's gusto was equally boundless. For all the commentary from traditionalists who still, even after the roaring success and strong attendance numbers at the 1994 World Cup in the United States, believed that MLS was a castoff league, he began to see the club's image taking shape. "This is a fun city," he said. "This is a fun team. This is what MLS could be."

And the rest of the league did indeed take notice. That season, encouraged by the atmosphere at BMO Field, TFC hosted the entire ownership and management groups from what would become the Seattle Sounders. Representatives from clubs that would eventually become the Philadelphia Union and the Portland Timbers also met with TFC to experience the culture TFC had created. They all had the same question: How did you do it?

Cochrane were more than happy to share their best practices. "Permissible plagiarism," as he calls it. "We're only as strong as our weakest member," he would tell visiting clubs. His belief was that, although the clubs were opponents on the field, sharing information would improve the quality of the entire league. TFC shared strategic initiatives and advice on how to tailor-make them for their specific communities. And so much of what they offered involved the ideas that TFC had subscribed to since day one: don't pander to your fans. Respect the inherent soccer IQ that no doubt exists in major markets all over North America. And create an entertaining game-day environment that thrives on inclusivity.

And Beirne says the success that currently exists in markets like Seattle and Portland, with two of the league's most dependably engaged fan bases, can be traced back to what TFC was doing in their first season. "Their success was elevated because Toronto FC had done this stuff," said Beirne, of fan-engagement strategies TFC had from the beginning of the club's existence.

While so much of what happened during TFC's first season cannot be called successful, that they sometimes operated on the fly and were not afraid to see an idea and roll with it was ultimately contagious. The support TFC enjoyed early on became something of a tidal wave and no soccer fan in the city wanted to miss out. BMO Field had become a place to gather, a place to feel part of something for fans who missed out on the beginning of the Leafs and may have missed out on the beginning of the Blue Jays. Now they had a new team and a venue to call their own.

Being a "Day One" TFC fan is not worked into a conversation just casually: the pride in having been part of the creation of a team in a stadium that was theirs and theirs alone, in an already crowded sports market, is inherently palpable. "Nobody on their own decides to become a face painter. There's strength in numbers. There's joy there," said Beirne.

During that legendary game, Dichio would end up being sent off 20 minutes after the goal for engaging in a scuffle with the goalkeeper, Pickens. But that only further endeared him to fans who demanded the same passion out of their players that they exhibited in the stands.

As loud as the crowd was for his goal, Dichio remembers the fans reacting even more vehemently when he was shown his red card.

> I thought, "Wow, this is the first time I've gotten applause for being sent off. This crowd is pretty insane." They were embracing me for what I'd done for all my career. I wasn't the most gifted of players, but I worked my ass off for the team I was playing for.

TFC would win 3–1 on the day, but it is Dichio's goal and the seat-cushion shower that will always be remembered. Dichio has been immortalized with a song sung in his honour in the 24th minute of every home game since.

Dichio still calls Toronto home, coaching in the club's youth academy. How could he leave, after all? He'd fallen on his ass to score his first-ever goal, and TFC themselves had perhaps inadvertently fallen into the creation of MLS 2.0: a league that fans would not turn their noses up at, but one they could revel in and share.

As commissioner Garber says of TFC's early fan support and the creation of MLS 2.0,

> We had not yet embraced the hard-core supporter-driven soccer culture. We had not yet figured out the value of building accessible downtown stadiums. We had not yet figured out that in order to capture the value of being part of the world's game, we needed to have teams that were outside of the United States. And what better place to do that than [in] one of the most important cities in North America, the City of Toronto?

A win at home four days later against the defending MLS Cup champion Houston Dynamo saw that passionate support extend beyond BMO Field itself.

Greg Sutton had backstopped the shutout win and went with his wife to a nearby pub after the game for a quick bite. From the moment he walked in, TFC's open interest in getting fans into the local pubs before and after games began to show. The Red Patch Boys had set up shop at the crowded pub and, surprised to see Sutton come in, broke out into a spontaneous roar and followed up with a few of their new songs. The fan club found Sutton and his wife a booth, kicking the current tenants out of their seats, and sent a round of drinks Sutton's way. It was, in a nutshell, the club's supporters coming to life in 2007.

Sutton shared the tale with the rest of the club afterward. He understood that the players were being marketed, not as inaccessible stars, but as relatable people sharing in the journey of the club's first season.

"You understand how meaningful this is to people," said Sutton. "They live this. They don't just watch a game and go home. That was pretty impressive for me. That laid the groundwork as the identity for a club that stepped up."

Of course, the kind of results TFC garnered in May would end up being few and far between in that inaugural season. Those two games may have provided some false hope, and going 3–3–2 in their next eight games may have kept the haters at bay, but it was that third win, on the Fourth of July in Salt Lake City, that would be the last reason for the team and its fans to truly smile for quite some time.

Johnston's training sessions were focused largely on small-sided games, crossing and finishing. It was up to the team's veteran core of Brennan, Robinson, and Dichio to instill a sense of team spirit and to unify a squad from across the globe that lacked any sense of harmony. "There was no chemistry and camaraderie," said Robinson. "You have to build that."

Certain players took the idea of playing in Canada as a slight that left a sour taste in their mouths, which caused those three, who were more than proud to be playing in Canada, to dig their heels in even more. Brennan in particular took on an unofficial ambassador role, trying to convince many around and within the team of what success on the pitch could bring.

> There's so many soccer people in this country. It gets downplayed because people say "Hockey's the number one game," but when you look at it, there's more registrations for soccer than any other sport. The problem is we'd never had a professional team in the top league in North America. Finally, when you saw Toronto FC come, you could see people were starved.

Brennan was proud of how local fans, who had teams overseas but not a team to call their own, finally did come to adopt TFC, as did many first-generation Torontonians.

Robinson's leadership within the dressing room mirrored his own personality, as he bluntly directed players with the ruthless efficiency of a future coach. "I'm a firm believer that the best way to get the best out of people is to be open and honest. Get to know players and challenge them to be professional," said Robinson. He would remind players of his own motivations for coming to MLS and had the same expectations from them: "I didn't come here to have a holiday," he would routinely state.

Johnston, often equally as blunt with players, didn't always display the kind of communication skills necessary to properly usher a new squad built of largely spare parts into the league. Some players found him unapproachable and stubborn. "Mo was his own guy," said Brennan. "Mo did what he wanted to do."

Brennan was used to playing for coaches with specific demands and an authoritative coaching style, and, as captain, he was left to simply respect the coach's decisions. But still, as nine players were traded out of the roster early in the season, Brennan became increasingly concerned and wary about Johnston's role. One of these lost players was Buddle, the man who collected TFC's first-ever assist. Buddle would thrive with the Los Angeles Galaxy, scoring 42 goals in 87 league appearances from 2007 to 2010.

"There was a lot of things where you questioned it and said 'Are you sure this is what you want to do?'" said Brennan.

Johnston's true passion for working the phones led to the nickname "Trader Mo" being attached to him very early on during his tenure. Having been instilled into a winning franchise in New York and making the playoffs in his three full seasons with the club, he expected a certain level of success, and perhaps even a playoff berth, early on. "With Mo, he wanted success, but he wanted it so quick," said Brennan. "That's why there was a revolving door. If he was a little more patient, we might have had more success."

Defender Marvell Wynne arrived early in the season, and, while he understood fans wanting results immediately, he found it difficult to balance that need for results with the equally pressing need for the team to be built up and have, in his mind, "some sort of steady, common ground and ideas.... And I don't think that was able to be built upon at all while I was there."

With a variety of players and personalities on the squad, Johnston didn't step in nearly enough to create any sort of cohesiveness. No one could doubt his own ability on the pitch, but just the same, Johnston often had trouble teaching players what he might have picked up during his 20-plus years of playing professionally. "If Mo got pissed off and was having a bad day, he would take it out on the goalkeepers. His finishing was unbelievable," said Eddie Kehoe. The goalkeeper coach said Johnston would line up 10 shots, finish every one with no instruction to anyone nearby. "That's what you do, go do it," were Johnston's only words of wisdom.

In contrast, Carl Robinson might not have been the most athletically gifted player, but being so technically and tactically superb allowed him to properly educate younger players on the finer details of the game. Johnston, however, was referred to by many in the club as a street soccer player, unable to teach the necessary skills. "Mo didn't have the attention to detail to be a good coach," said Kehoe.

In the second half of the season, TFC would win just one match. This stretch included a horrendous nine-game goalless span, at the time an MLS record. Even having Dichio, a striker with top-flight experience, wasn't nearly enough to keep the team competitive. For as much as a striker can help with finishing, the club's dip in production spoke to the flaws of a hastily built squad. Johnston, constantly preoccupied with upgrading players on his roster, had overlooked the need to formulate a specific style of play, an identity for the squad to buy into and follow. "It was a disparate group of players put together with no rhyme or reason," Sportsnet's John Molinaro remembered thinking.

Dichio had become one of the mainstays of the roster, and surely had the kind of power and quality in the box that few other strikers in MLS possessed. But TFC's quality in their roster also became their Achilles heel of sorts. In the absence of a vision instilled from Johnson, TFC had just one course of action on the pitch: play long balls from every area to Dichio and hope for the best.

"With the squad that you've got, you're not going to play Barcelona football," said Brennan. "You have to play to the strengths that you have. We just found it easier to play the ball up to the big man and play off of him."

The slim possibility of scoring goals became the only unifying factor in a squad with players from many different backgrounds and styles. Without much time to adapt and create a plan, there was no other choice but to "kick the ball up to Danny Dichio and hope he would do something miraculous with it," said Wynne.

Dichio was used to receiving long balls and crosses during his time in England, so that approach suited him just fine, even if it didn't exactly make for long-term sustainability. And the small-sided games in training only allowed players to work on their own individual styles instead of team strengths. That lack of vision and inability to play in a composed way out of the back quickly became obvious to the opposition.

During an August 18 loss at home to Chivas USA, Chivas midfielder Jesse Marsch approached Dichio on the pitch and shared his thoughts on TFC: "You're so predictable. We just have to put two or three guys on you and that's our game plan."

"You're probably right," Dichio responded.

It wasn't just the squad that had been hastily built. Much of the infrastructure within the club, including their attempts to increase awareness via local media, yielded up and down results.

Michelle Lissel was the club's first head of media relations and had to battle with some of the many mainstream media outlets in the city for coverage. The media outlets were not sharing the passion that local fans had. When journalists did appear at training sessions, Lissel found much of their coverage to be repetitive, and to focus on the same handful of players. Very few journalists had an innate understanding of the game, or even any interest in the sport. "There were some journalists that were on the beat that could've cared less to be there," she said.

With MLS interested in generating as much coverage as possible, they adhered to the North American standard of access, in which dressing rooms would be open to media after training sessions and games. Many of the players from outside North America took time to adjust to this, especially given how banal many of the local media's questions sometimes were.

But it was Johnston who struggled the most with the inherent demands of the media. "Mo didn't like doing press, period. His experience with the media as a player probably wasn't a good one. It was hard for him to be trusting and let people in a bit more," said Lissel. He was a colourful-enough character with the media and would always indulge reporters with a juicy sound bite or two. He was rather like future Toronto Maple Leafs GM Brian Burke in how outspoken and quotable he was. Yet Johnston still frequently pushed back against Lissel in the hopes of getting some peace and quiet after training. "I got into the habit of not having the coaches read the press," said Lissel. "They'd get too worked up, and then they wouldn't want to talk to the reporters."

Sports journalist John Molinaro, for one, enjoyed an often-contentious relationship with Johnston as he would repeatedly grill him on the club's direction. "There was a complete lack of nuance with Mo," said Molinaro. "There were no clear goals for what they wanted to do."

That much became painfully evident as the season drew to a close. Brennan, Dichio, and Robinson were all 30 or older and, aside from the exceptionally talented Edu, who wasn't long for MLS anyway, there appeared to be little for the club to build on. With Johnston, building slowly was never an option anyway.

The club would clinch their final win of the season on October 4 against Johnston's former team, the New York Red Bulls. The winning goal came, perhaps unsurprisingly, as an own goal. Two more losses on the road set up a meaningless final game of the season at home against a strong New England Revolution side. Sitting on 24 points, TFC were already assured of finishing dead last in the MLS table. But that didn't stop a sellout crowd of 20,374 from showing up, fervent as ever, to mark the end of the inaugural season.

Even Revolution goals just before and immediately after halftime did little to suck the air out of the fans' sails. A few goals against couldn't break tradition, and Revolution midfielder Steve Ralston felt those fans' loathing when his corner kick attempt was delayed for several minutes and the fans coated him with red and white streamers.

The BMO Field crowd stood in adoration. What takes some clubs generations to manage, TFC had done in just one season: traditions, however hostile and self-indulgent, had been made, and were available to be passed down. "It's almost like you become 23 all over again," David Miller said of those early traditions. "I became a manic soccer supporter. And I just can't help it."

In the 59th minute of that season-final game, Collin Samuel got TFC on the board to cut the Revolution lead in half. The second half slowly clicked away, and, perhaps fittingly, TFC seemed destined to end the season as they had begun it on the pitch: by losing.

But, in added time, the soccer gods reminded those in attendance that they had a sense of humour and could dig a little deeper to find an ending even more fitting. Danny Dichio, who had missed the previous seven games with an ankle injury, came on as a late substitute. And, like clockwork, a long ball was sent in toward the top of the box. A TFC defender went up for the ball, but instead went ass over teakettle over the Revolution defender and landed embarrassingly on the turf. But he'd done enough to keep the ball alive and in the air. With one bounce, it landed near Dichio, who had his back to the net. His last-ditch effort might look painfully clumsy on the replay, but in turning and volleying the ball high in the air he gave it just enough sauce to send it bar down, and the team salvaged a 2–2 draw.

Dichio did as Dichio does, running to the south end to celebrate. It would be the final play of the season. Dichio had scored the club's first goal ever, and its last of the year. A strange but fitting end to an even stranger season.

One might not expect a draw on the final day of an otherwise miserable season to make many fans euphoric. That was not the case at BMO Field. Once the players left the pitch, fans took their place, quickly rushing to the centre of the pitch to keep the party going much longer than perhaps it should have. The same songs were sung by the same fans that had stuck by TFC all season.

There was nothing to celebrate, except for the fact that these loyal "Day One" fans had made it through the season together. "The way they packaged the game day experience and the way their fans stuck by them passionately, it was like they were watching Real Madrid," said Molinaro.

Much of the talk immediately after the season ended centred on how successful the team had been from a marketing and fan-engagement standpoint. In the MLSE offices, it was quickly acknowledged that Johnston could not continue stretching himself so thin with the double duties of head coach and general manager. Johnston agreed to step aside from the coaching position to focus on building a more competitive roster. Paul Winsper, who had worked with the club in a strength and conditioning role briefly in pre-season, suggested his former colleague at Newcastle United, John Carver.

Carver had served as caretaker for short spells at Newcastle and Leeds United and was thought to have the kind of traditional English sensibilities about the game that would pair him well with Johnston. Carver's initial reservations about working for Johnston were assuaged when Johnston assured him he would work strictly as general manager and his sole purpose would be to find players to Carver's liking. "Once we decided on that," said Carver, "it was all guns blazing."

Though Carver was certainly in need of a job and interested in his first head coaching assignment, he remembers exactly what originally attracted him to TFC in the first place. "I saw the fanatical fans," he said. For all of the influence the club would have on supporter culture throughout the league in the decade after, in less than a calendar year, a collective group of fans had already grown enough to impress the man tasked with leading the club.

That first season will never be remembered for TFC's results on the pitch, especially not by those who filled BMO Field every game, including the man at the top of the city's political food chain at the time. "It didn't matter that we were terrible," David Miller said of the 2007 season. "It was so much fun."

3

Being a Badass, Writing Shit, and Fighting over a Cookie

WEARING A RED TRACK SUIT for the first time in his life, John Carver walked along the side of the pitch during the first training session of the 2008 season, sizing up his new roster. The many wrinkles around his constantly furrowed brow grew deeper by the minute. He scratched his short brown hair and muttered a few curse words to himself in his thick Geordie accent. After having coached Premier League outfit Newcastle FC and Championship side Leeds United, he was eager to see what kind of players he now had at his disposal. With Marvell Wynne and Maurice Edu both away on international duty, he was shocked. He knew MLS would be a change, but he was dumbfounded by the standard of players he had in front of him.

"I thought to myself, what have I done here?"

Carver quickly went to Johnston to voice his concerns. And immediately, Johnston agreed: the squad required drastic improvement, so Johnston started working the phones to somehow turn shit into sugar.

TFC's second coach in as many seasons was not convinced he could immediately turn things around. He had, of course, come from a country in which the sheer popularity of soccer meant the resources dedicated to technical development of players far eclipsed Canadian standards. And because of the large number of Canadian players that made up those early training camps, Carver's hopes for the upcoming season quickly diminished.

In just over a full season, a concerning trend had been established with Carver's hiring that would end up defining TFC for so much of its existence. The club wanted too much, too soon, and chose the wrong method to go about trying to attain it.

Carver himself admits he knew "very little" about TFC when Johnston reached out to him. His research consisted of examining the "fanatical fans" on the club's website and becoming enamoured by the reaction to Dichio's first goal from the 2007 season.

The then 43-year-old was originally meant to take on the assistant coaching job for the 2008 season but once Johnston decided it was best he step down as coach, Carver was given the step up. With almost no understanding of the intricacies of MLS, from salary cap restrictions to international and local player allotments, not to mention the media requirements and standard of refereeing in the league, Carver had been on a flight to Toronto.

Carver had been craving the chance to have a club to call his own and the message he received from TFC management was that no one was too concerned about winning trophies too quickly. Carver had been sacked as assistant coach at Luton Town weeks earlier. Like those who came before and after him at TFC, he was lured by the possibility of greatness. "It was an opportunity for me to come into a football club," said Carver, "and build it from scratch."

His first order of business was modernizing the club with some peripherals that were being utilized in England: Carver took advantage of the financial resources available at MLSE and set up a sports science department, proliferated the scouting network, and began using ProZone to provide data analyses of matches.

Carver insisted on using video sessions to explain his tactics to the team and, since TFC did not have a proper, fully equipped training facility, he told the club to bring in proper catering after training to help some of the younger players who weren't on sizeable contracts and often didn't feed themselves properly. Whatever Carver lacked on the tactical side of the team's improvement, veteran players took note of how he worked to better organize the operation.

There was a general feeling throughout TFC and MLSE that in the club's first season they'd asked too few people to do too much. Carver was brought in not as a response to the club's play in the first season, but largely to take on the weight of the coaching role so Johnston could build the roster and the coaching assistants could better develop players.

Carver relied heavily on Johnston's extensive knowledge of the intricacies of MLS's rules and regulations. Johnston's "methodical and clever" approach to building a roster allowed Carver to focus on getting his players match-ready. Contrary to rumours at the time, Carver insists Johnston stayed out of his way. "He never interfered in any side of the coaching, any of the playing side," said Carver.

Instead, Johnston would simply check in regularly with Carver in terms of which type of players he wanted. Johnston would bring a handful of names to Carver, they'd break down video of the players together, Carver would then make a choice and allow Johnston to wheel and deal as he was prone to do. "If I didn't want them," said Carver, "Mo didn't get them."

And so, the 2007 roster was complemented with a number of free-agent signings. Canadian midfielder Tyler Rosenlund would become the first-ever Canadian player to score for TFC but would last less than a year with the club and make just eight appearances. French winger Laurent Robert was familiar to Carver from his time at Newcastle after featuring in five seasons for the club. Despite having played for the French national team, the free-kick specialist lasted less than a year with TFC and was waived before the end of the season. English midfielder Rohan Ricketts impressed early with his goal-scoring touch but was released the following season. The effect of the pressure on Carver and Johnston to produce immediate results was obvious. "A lot of guys had to put up right away," remembers Greg Sutton. "And if they didn't, they were gone."

Johnston also flipped draft picks in the 2009 and 2010 MLS SuperDrafts for Honduran midfielder Amado Guevara, who would finish his MLS career at BMO Field with an impressive nine goals in 46 games.

To continue to bring his players up to a higher standard of performance, Carver also hired Paul Winsper, who had been fitness coach at Newcastle United, to become TFC's strength and conditioning coach. Winsper had served as David Beckham's personal trainer in the lead-up to his debut with the L.A. Galaxy. Winsper enforced a strict regimen that punished players for tardiness, but with the larger goal of preventing the injuries that had derailed parts of the previous season.

Through pre-season Carver and Winsper worked together to create drills that would lean heavily on stamina and fitness, including small-sided games that forced quick, impulsive movement. Winsper also revamped the health equipment to make it more suited to his plans, which leaned heavily on a scientific approach. "We don't train muscles," Winsper told the *Toronto Star* in May 2008. "We train movement. You don't see anyone doing bicep curls. That's not the way we work here."

Winsper had a tall order. He insists that at the sport's highest level, the focus of someone in his position was more about getting players recovered than anything else. But what Carver found was that in MLS there was great disparity in quality and physical fitness between the senior professionals such as Dichio, Brennan, and Robinson and some of the team's younger players. The type of drills and conditioning exercises that Winsper would complete in the Premier League just couldn't be done with TFC's younger players.

"I enjoyed it because I had different problems to solve," said Winsper, very much summing up not only his but many others' roles within the club in those early days.

Despite everyone's best intentions, the club was still walking lambs to the slaughter. For all Carver's accomplishments, he knew of one way of doing things, having coached and played only in the United Kingdom before arriving in Toronto. Carver was not prepared for so much of what being in a league in just its 13th year of existence would entail, and for what a club that had been around for even less than that could hope to accomplish.

Nevertheless, Carver's immediate focus became less about developing the club tactically and more about toughening them mentally and improving their competitive spirit. With the club's leadership core of Brennan, Robinson, and Dichio having plied their trade in England, Carver's approach seemed to make sense through training camp. The Newcastle man would rant and rave at players but would also be sure to deliver hard, sometimes uncomfortable truths to his squad about their limitations, much in the way he had done in England. "The British boys were used to it, but the Americans weren't," said Robinson.

"He let you know exactly what he was thinking and exactly how he was feeling at that exact moment," said American forward Chad Barrett.

The early training sessions continued to be competitive as Carver pushed the squad to move beyond the previous season and stop thinking of themselves as a new club. Carver struck Barrett as a coach who "doesn't really believe in weakness," but believed instead in the English way of training: "getting stuck in, being tough, be[ing] badasses."

While Carver's training sessions were more detailed than Johnston's, they also focused more on individual strengthening and improving personal fitness. Tactically, Carver often employed a traditional defending shape in a 4-4-2, common among his generation of English players and coaches. This came at a time more variety was being employed in formations from teams around the world and more attack-oriented formations were in vogue. With more soccer being available on TV and online, young players were now able to study formations themselves and understand how to best utilize players in different positions. "It didn't," said Wynne of Carver's approach, "ring through."

One element Carver was never prepared for was the level of access that local and national media had in Toronto compared to his native England. It's a plight not uncommon to many international players and coaches, since access outside North America is generally restricted to a single incredibly structured pre-game press conference and quick, generally cliché-filled post-game interviews in a mixed-zone setting. But, as is customary in every major North American league, in the MLS reporters met teams after every practice and were allowed into the locker rooms after games.

Regardless of how protected some of the world's biggest stars were from the press within Europe's biggest leagues, the need to continually grow MLS begat the need to encourage reporters to tell as many stories from within the clubs as possible.

Carver, in particular, struggled with the access he had to provide, and with the consequences of having the media pick apart his every decision.

Broadcasters would request formal sit-downs with Carver ahead of games to discuss his starting lineup and to gather as much information as possible to be used during broadcasts. Carver pushed back, and TFC media relations representative Michelle Lissel had to step in. "They want me to what?" Lissel remembers Carver saying. "They want to ask me what?"

Lissel held regular training sessions with Carver about North American media, in an effort not to suppress his expressive personality, but instead to harness his ability to deliver great quotes and to keep the press corps interested in this new but floundering team. Yet, Carver still struggled.

Winsper had some wry fun with Carver's exasperation. The two would ride the GO Train in to training together from Oakville every morning, the two long-time colleagues flipping through the morning papers. Winsper would go out of his way to show Carver every negative detail that was being written about him, just to wind him up.

Winsper was valuable to the organization. He had taken on more than a fitness coach normally would. For example, part of his job in warm-up ahead of games was to get the squad physically, emotionally, and mentally ready. Then he would privately give Carver a pulse on the team, to help him prepare what kind of pre-game team talk to deliver.

And Winsper's influence within MLSE was growing, owing in large part to the way he was revolutionizing the team's training methods. But in mischievously winding up his friend, Winsper was also adding to the large load of stress Carver was carrying.

The day after a plodding 0–0 draw against the San Jose Earthquakes in July that saw TFC's winless streak reach four games, Carver sat in the BMO Field press conference room to address the media. His frustration over the intrusive media, combined with the team's poor play, came to a head, and the assembled media were to get a front-row view of his emotional side.

Carver was not without props to prove his point. Armed with a stack of local newspapers, Carver started by taking to task a reporter who had questioned the team's play and described the squad as "sluggish" on the day.

> I sit and wonder, why hasn't [Toronto's] hockey team won anything? Why hasn't the baseball team been successful lately? Because I'm coming from the outside and I don't know if you guys get your heads together because you don't like writing nice things. You just want to write shit.

He turned to his stack of newspapers and began reading deriding sections from articles critical of Toronto's other major-league teams. Carver's commentary could not have come at a worse time: the Maple Leafs had finished in last place in the Northeast Division in 2007–8, the Raptors were eliminated in the first round of the playoffs that same season, and the Blue Jays were falling short of expectations in 2008, eventually finishing fourth in the American League East.

"And I'm wondering if it's a knock-on effect to all the other sports," continued Carver. "Does Toronto want their teams to be successful? I'm asking you."

"I was standing there, thinking, *Oh boy*," said Lissel. "*Well, that's going to cause some problems.*"

Carver, for his part, believes he was being second-guessed for taking his players to a Toronto beach for training in the days before the game, though the same type of session — minus the extra effort required of players running through sand — would still have been conducted had they been on a pitch.

What Carver's blow-up at the assembled press did do was bring more attention to the team's trials that season. "I think [Carver] struggled at times, letting small details get to him instead of letting them go over his head and focusing on the bigger picture," said Danny Dichio.

The club did not yet have the mainstream appeal that the aforementioned other three clubs did, but a quote-laden clip like Carver's made for good highlight-show fodder, and the reason for the blow-up was always attributed back to the club's poor performances. At a time when the team was meant to be developing toward their first-ever time in the playoffs, their struggles were being broadcast for all of the city to see.

And it wore on Carver even more.

Carver was spoken to by some within the organization, but it was still hard to overlook his genuine desire to improve the team, misguided as it might have been. "He did take it so personally," said Lissel, who at times could not understand Carver's reactions to the negative press he received, considering the vast amount of negative press football clubs in England regularly endure. The more Lissel worked with Carver, the more she felt the personal attachment he had formed to the club in his first full-time head coaching position. "He did feel like everybody was out to get him and out to get the team," she said. "He cared so much. He wanted the team to do well."

Carver had bit off more than he could chew, and had trouble accepting his own limitations. "I wanted to make the playoffs in my first season," he said. "I realized it was going to be a tougher task than what I first thought."

He felt no pressure from those in management above him to get into the playoffs but instead took it upon himself to over-exert his influence on the club. Believing more in results than the process of improving, Carver employed heavy-handed ways that didn't always redeem him to players, and the passion he wanted to communicate became lost in translation. "John had his own ideas, as well, tried to get us to play a certain way," said defender Marvell Wynne. "But only a few players tuned in, not everyone at once."

Carver's rigidity and need to create a more competitive edge in his players spread down to restrictions he put on player's diets. Before one away game, any player with a sweet tooth went unfulfilled as there were believed to be no desserts available — until one table of players noticed that those at the coach's tables had cookies.

Once the table started to complain, Carver let it be known that nothing would come easy for the players, even at the dinner table. "He walked up to one of the tables, threw a cookie in the middle, and said 'You guys can fight for that,'" recalled Wynne.

Stunned glances were exchanged until one player took the cookie and threw it on the ground in disgust.

The progression under Carver was noticeable on paper, with the club improving on their point totals and overall goal differential from the previous season. With a convincing win over the David Beckham and Landon Donovan–led L.A. Galaxy and follow-up wins over Real Salt Lake and the Kansas City Wizards, the squad strung together the club's first-ever three-game winning streak through April.

By mid-June, they sat in a comfortable position at 5–4–2, with another win over the Galaxy included. On June 14, deep in the south end of the pitch, Rohan Ricketts corralled a loose ball on his own with his back to the net. As he turned, he quickly dodged around two separate Colorado Rapids defenders before roofing a shot in the back of the net. It was the final nail in the coffin in a 3–0 win over the Rapids that sent the fans into early summer delirium and shot TFC to 6–4–2.

But it would be one of the final few bright spots for the club on the season. They'd go winless in their next six regular season games and win just three of their remaining 18 games.

As the season dragged on to its inevitable end, outside of the playoffs looking in, Carver continued to take issue with something so many of the other veteran players did: the standard of refereeing in MLS. As early as March, Carver grew frustrated when a DVD sent to MLS officials show-cased his touchline behaviour. In May, Carver took issue with a fourth official and claimed the official had been "disrespecting" him.

During a tirade after an Earthquakes draw, Carver read an email from MLS's Joe Machnik, who was on the league committee that oversaw offi-cials. In the email, Machnik admitted that referee Jorge Gonzalez made two errors. "They've admitted to it! I've got it in black and white here. Now, if you'd asked me about the referee's performance [yesterday], I would have said that was sluggish," said Carver.

And while Dichio believed that everyone inside the TFC locker room was frustrated with the poor officiating within MLS, by constantly voicing his frustration, Carver's action may have had an adverse effect on the young players within the squad. "We needed someone to lead us and keep our emotions in check. And sometimes, some of the players followed suit to what [Carver] was doing. Sometimes he got too emotionally involved and that impacted the team at times."

Carver's emotional approach only gave licence to the team to spew their own anger toward referees. "If they get a sense that their head coach is doing it," said Dichio, "then they don't think there's anything wrong with doing it as well."

Carver's frustration continued as the club's late-season travel schedule wore on players. After the June 14 loss, TFC went a dismal 2–7–1 on the road. As they continued to lose players to international duty, the holes in their roster began to show. During a dreadful September 6 loss at home to Chivas, Carver was forced to use academy employee Rick Titus in the match. Titus had not played in MLS since 2002, but with TFC missing a total of nine players on international duty, Carver grew desperate. Titus was not paid for his appearance. Carver also called up Tim Regan, who was not playing but working toward a job in TFC's scouting department.

"The league allowed me to do *this*," said Carver, aghast because he could not bring in academy players (because that would have interfered with their amateur status, which would have affected their scholarship chances to prospective colleges). "It was doing our crowd a disservice because they were paying good money."

"That was when the head coach really earns his money," said Dichio.

Carver still can't understand why the club collapsed late in the season as they did. Losing Edu, the 2007 MLS rookie of the year, to Glasgow Rangers in August didn't help, nor did waiving Robert and defender Olivier Tebily. The quick fixes that Johnston and Carver had proposed to begin the season didn't just not pan out; they highlighted what a monumental task getting the on-field product would end up being.

"If you're chopping and changing it's very hard to build that team sense of playing with each other," said Dichio.

4

Legs Like Jell-O, a Miracle in Montreal, and a Complete Meltdown

IF WE'RE COMPARING CITIES, MILAN and Scarborough couldn't be more different. One is known as a capital for luxury brands, a place where upscale fashion is a way of life. The other is a hub for mini-malls full of knock-off clothing. One is the very epitome of Northern Italian snobbery, where bourgeois residents furrow their brows at what they have long believed to be their peasant-like neighbours to the south of the country, and the other is often perceived as a hotbed for gang violence.

Growing up in Scarborough, a short drive east of BMO Field, Dwayne De Rosario could never have imagined a city like Milan. The prodigious young talent knew from a young age he wanted to become a difference-maker on the soccer field, where he spent so much of his youth, but he struggled to figure out exactly how to do so.

At 14, he was offered a five-year contract with Italian club AC Milan. It was, in retrospect, as rare an offer and opportunity as a Canadian Hockey League club recruiting a 14-year-old from Italy.

After a brief visit to Italy's fashion capital, De Rosario couldn't neglect his inner "street kid," as he told the *Guardian* in 2011, and opted to return to Scarborough. If he was to make that aforementioned mark, it was to be done closer to home. So, at 18 he signed with the Toronto Lynx, then playing in the A-League. At the time, De Rosario understood this was the only local option for a professional player in Toronto, but he was still left unfulfilled. Even as a teenager, he had the attacking presence to excel beyond what the A-League could offer.

Less than a season later, De Rosario was on a plane back to Europe, this time to the German city of Zwickau, an hour's drive from the Czech border. De Rosario would spend two seasons with FSV Zwickau in Germany's second and third tier. Again unsatisfied, he returned to North America to log time in the second tier of America's pyramid with the Richmond Kickers.

Still, his star was rising with the national team, and as a 21-year-old, he was named to Canada's Gold Cup squad that, in 2000, shocked this side of the soccer world with a win over Columbia and their first, and only, Gold Cup title.

Not long after, Canadian coach Frank Yallop brought De Rosario to MLS and the San Jose Earthquakes and his career, perhaps finally, began to flourish. He would win two MLS Cup titles with the Earthquakes and would be named a finalist as MLS MVP in 2005. De Rosario didn't just score, he did so prolifically, twice being awarded with MLS goal of the year and also scoring the golden goal to give the Earthquakes their first-ever MLS Cup.

De Rosario had finally found his element. When the Earthquakes moved to Houston, De Rosario won two more MLS Cups, including his second MLS Cup MVP award. He'd vaulted into the conversation as one of the most talented ever to come from Canada and also had firmly established himself as one of North America's best.

And, all along, he kept a close eye on the developments in his hometown. "To know that Toronto was committed to MLS was a dream come true," said De Rosario. "It was a boost to the sport not just in Toronto, but in Canada."

While De Rosario's Houston Dynamo were celebrating their finish atop the Western Conference standings, Toronto FC coaching and management were trying to figure out how to follow through on their original plan and get into the playoffs in their third season. There was a common understanding: the backbone of a strong team was in place and Robinson, Dichio, and Brennan had figured out how to steer this new franchise. Still, management and coaches needed to also accept what was missing: a game-changer.

"We knew that," said Carver of the club's hole in the roster. "If you want to challenge for the top position, you have to have someone to score goals."

At the end of the 2008 season, Johnston and Carver sat down to identify players that could fill that need. It was a short conversation. De Rosario's name leapt off the page, along with Amado Guevara, who was identified as the type of player that would provide De Rosario with the necessary service.

With TFC having just finished second in average home attendance in the league, even with very little on the field to show for it, the opportunity to come home and play for loyal fans and an ambitious project was the focal point of Johnston and Carver's sell.

The memories of BMO Field and TFC were fresh in everyone's minds during negotiations. De Rosario and the Houston Dynamo had visited BMO Field late in the season and, in front of a sellout crowd, the home side had held the Dynamo to a 1–1 draw on the strength of a stunning left-foot strike from outside the box by Marvell Wynne.

"Everything was right to get Dwayne," said Carver. "I don't think Mo had too much work to do."

And MLSE understood it was necessary to go after a player of De Rosario's capabilities and price tag. "We were ahead with where we thought we'd be," said Beirne. "It made sense to invest in players."

While TFC was still ultimately owned by a pension fund at this point, the bottom line still ruled the day. To TFC ownership, an investment in star power would help drive returns, regardless of De Rosario's contract. In 2008, De Rosario earned $325,000, which was at the time in the upper echelon of MLS contracts.

Bound by salary cap concerns, Houston agreed to a trade in December 2008. TFC shipped out young defender Julius James as well as allocation money. The move was propelled by the club's desire to become one of the league's pre-eminent franchises.

"You go back to the type of city that Toronto is," said Cochrane. "We always viewed ourselves as one of the big four markets in North America. We knew at some point that was going to happen. In many respects, the plan was about building a solid team, a group, and then, when the team was ready, to infuse it with a Designated Player."

When De Rosario was finally unveiled as a TFC player in January, 2009, the forward was signed to a four-year contract at $357,000 the first year, the 11th-highest salary in MLS. Though he was not considered a Designated Player, with De Rosario's salary came expectations that the local boy embraced.

De Rosario felt it was imperative not just to bring success to Toronto, but to "change the mentality" within a club that, in De Rosario's mind, "wasn't breeding success." He had, after all, never *not* made the playoffs, and immediately began convincing those around him that a win should be expected in every match.

It was an audacious approach, but one that had indeed been to some extent lacking, and it was what made De Rosario so elemental to the club at the start of the 2009 season.

TFC travelled to both Florida and South Carolina for training camp that year, and from the start, spirits were high. "Especially with Dwayne's arrival, there was a lot of optimism," said Sam Cronin. Cronin was the club's first pick in the 2009 MLS SuperDraft, being chosen second overall. The highly touted holding midfielder from Wake Forest University had met with many teams that held high draft picks in the 2009 draft, though, surprisingly, not with TFC.

Carver and Winsper's relentless and combative training sessions, with a heavy focus on repetitive 1 v 1, 3 v 3, and 7 v 7 drills, were a tough initiation for Cronin. "That was a complete ball buster," said Cronin, then 22. "It was almost like boxing. My legs were like Jell-O afterward."

By trying to build strength and capacity within players, and specifically in their legs, Carver and Winsper were hoping to spark that elusive competitive spirit. "I was nearly throwing up after sessions," said Cronin.

Lost in the planning, once again, were the tactical nuances that other teams utilized in favour of what Cronin called a "roll-your-sleeves-up mentality."

Without much of a clear tactical plan for how TFC would dominate possession and build up their attack from the back of the pitch, it became evident as early as pre-season that De Rosario would be expected to take the team on his back.

As such, De Rosario's determination to win emerged as early as training camp when he didn't take kindly to people not giving the same effort he did. If a player, regardless of his stature in the club, wasn't finishing passes with the same amount of effort that De Rosario was putting in, he'd let them know.

And, likewise, if De Rosario missed a pass, he wouldn't simply shrug and try to get the next one. He'd wear his disappointment openly, telling those nearest to him that he had let his teammates down.

By the time TFC returned from training camp and the regular season was set to begin, the expectations De Rosario and the club had for themselves had spilled over into fans and the media.

Before the season, *Bleacher Report* predicted that "this could be the year that 'The Reds' finally make the playoffs and compete among MLS's elite."

A 3–2 win in Kansas City followed by a 1–1 draw in Columbus were a promising start, but old troubles emerged again as TFC scored just one goal over their next two games, both at home, and then dropped a 3–2 result in Dallas.

When the club returned to BMO Field on April 22 for a date with Chivas USA, already desperate to right the ship, 2004 MLS MVP Amado Guevara notched his third of the season to get the club back in the win column.

From the outside, now at 2–2–2 on the season, all signs pointed to TFC getting on the right track toward their goal of reaching the playoffs. Off the pitch, though, the stress of his time in Toronto had reached the boiling point for John Carver.

TFC was about to continue the worrisome trend that had become part of the club's narrative.

Alone in his office, Carver felt the weight of the future of the club on his shoulders alone. What few in the club knew, however, was that, early in 2009, both of Carver's parents had become ill. As their only son, Carver also began wearing the weight of responsibility to be near his parents, even if, as he knew, it would mean the end of his time in Toronto. His wife was happy in Toronto. The club was finally showing progress. But the loyalties of a Geordie run deep, and as both of his parents' conditions grew worse, he felt overwhelmed by accountability to his family. Carver made a seemingly rash decision that came as a shock to many: he was leaving his post as TFC coach, effective immediately, and returning to Newcastle.

It was his loyalty to TFC and the manner in which he had cared so deeply for the club that endeared him to many within the organization. But it was that same loyalty, to his family, that caused his time as a Red to end abruptly.

One day before TFC was set to host the Kansas City Wizards at home, the club announced his departure.

Publicly, he simply said he was leaving "for personal reasons." "I have worked with some top international players in my time, and we've got some here in Toronto, but this group is the best bunch of guys I've ever worked with," Carver said in a release at the time. "I also want to thank the fans. They are some of the best without a doubt and I hope they keep supporting this club for a long time to come."

Looking back, Carver said leaving TFC so quickly has become his only regret in life. "Maybe I should have sat back a bit," he admitted. "I made a hasty decision. Maybe I should never have done that."

Inevitably, with TFC now about to have their third bench boss in just over two seasons, the whispers about the state of the club off the pitch grew louder and infiltrated the place the players called home. "You wonder what's going on behind the scenes," said Sam Cronin. "It's jarring to the locker room."

But the season schedule would not allow players time to absorb a change on the touch lines. Despite De Rosario calling the change "devastating" to the locker room, saying that he'd "never experienced this before in my career," TFC had to line up against the Wizards in less than 24 hours. And they'd do so with Chris Cummins, Carver's previous assistant, occupying Carver's seat. It was almost impossible for players to focus on the task at hand, given the constant array of rumours floating around the dressing room.

Cummins had a past relationship with Carver and it was Carver who had asked him to join him as his assistant just after the start of the 2008 season. Cummins was a coach in the truest sense of the word. He believed it was his role to teach players, rather than to direct them. After 11 years spent at various roles within Watford's academy, including having found and developed Manchester United mainstay Ashley Young, Cummins had travelled overseas for his first coaching role with a first team.

As an educator, he took more of a docile tone and approach than Carver. He would take time to explain his methodology to players in an attempt to raise their tactical awareness. His attention to detail and openness to feedback from players about his tactical approach and his training methods redeemed him to many, coming after a coach who had relied more on brute force to get his message across. "He understood the way to talk to players and how to get feedback," said Dichio. "He'd go over sessions and get feedback from players. That was a new way of planning from coaches."

Cummins was the first-ever "man manager" at TFC. De Rosario believed that concept of man management is the "most important thing to understand at the pro level.... Once you have the guys buying into your beliefs and you have the guys playing for you, no matter your system, you should have a successful recipe," he said.

Cummins had very little time to plan for his first game in charge, so it was no surprise that against the Wizards TFC looked very much like they had all season, grinding out a 1–0 win on the strength of a Dichio goal from deep inside the box that came off a cross. Dichio ran through the pitch, waving his right arm in can-opener motion. Intended or not, it was hard not to chuckle at the symbolism: rotation, rotation, rotation — that which would become TFC's pattern for so long.

Cummins's third game in charge would be the club's first in the three-team Canadian Championship. After falling to the Montreal Impact in the inaugural tournament the previous season, there were enough quality additions to the lineup in 2009 that winning their first-ever trophy felt like a reasonable goal for the club.

A round-robin tournament, with each team playing their opponents in a home and away series, would determine the winner.

It was fitting then that Kevin Harmse, a defensive midfielder from Vancouver, was the difference for TFC in their opening game of the Canadian Championship with a third-minute goal to seal a 1–0 win. One week later, Chad Barrett scored to lead TFC to a 1–0 win over the Impact.

The Impact would then go on to lose their next two Canadian Championship games without scoring a goal, effectively eliminating themselves from contention and putting the Whitecaps in the driver's seat. A 2–0 loss to the Whitecaps in Burnaby meant TFC were still in contention with one game left in Montreal, but with a Mount Royal–sized hill to climb: they needed not only a win, but a win by a four-goal margin.

TFC was largely written off by the Canadian soccer community, but on the bus ride to the Saputo Stadium in Montreal, if anything, that lack of pressure ended up influencing some players in a positive manner. "It frees up the players to just go out and compete," said Cronin.

That liberated mentality actually began to instill a belief that the club could pull off the impossible. That belief only got stronger when they learned that the Whitecaps would be at the game, presumably expecting TFC would not pull off a lopsided victory, and the Whitecaps could pick up the Voyageurs Cup in person.

"That just pissed all of us off, knowing they were there," said Brennan. "They shouldn't have done that."

And if that added any fuel to the fire, the visitors' locker room was then ready to explode when the Impact's team sheet was released before the match: with a vital league game to play soon after, and the team themselves having no chance of winning the Canadian Championship, the Impact had decided to field a roster based largely on bench and reserve players.

The Reds saw a championship for the taking. It would be one of Cummins's first real tests as manager, so he kept his pre-match talk short and sweet: "Go out and express yourselves," he told the group.

No one took that more to heart than De Rosario.

After the previous loss to the Whitecaps, De Rosario was "pissed off" at his team and angry at himself. He had put his foot through a cooler when he arrived back in the dressing room. The Whitecaps and the Impact were inferior teams that TFC should be rolling over. Over the next two weeks, De Rosario had studied tape and was overwhelmed by how unlucky the team seemed to have been. "I was losing my mind trying to figure it out," he said.

And so, minutes before he took the pitch, he excused himself from the team and went into the bathroom. De Rosario was alone with his thoughts, and the expectations of a city weighing heavily on his braided head of hair. He looked deep into his brown eyes in the mirror and, stone-faced, told himself that he'd have to take the team on his back.

You have to do this for your city, he remembers telling himself.

De Rosario walked back into the dressing room. "Regardless of what happens," he announced, "we're winning this game."

Full of confidence, TFC took the pitch.

"I thought we were all fucking crazy, to be honest," said Dichio, laughing.

And just 24 minutes in, they saw their hill to climb get even bigger.

Impact defender Stephen DeRoux played a ball into the box and Peter Beyers tried to corral it for a shot. TFC defender Nick Garcia immediately fell to the pitch, and with a clumsy, half-hearted challenge, tripped up Beyers. A penalty kick was awarded to the Impact.

"Is this the beginning of a disaster for Toronto FC?" wondered Gerry Dobson on the broadcast.

Tony Donatelli converted from the spot, and what was a four-goal deficit quickly became five.

Oh, shit, De Rosario said to himself.

De Rosario couldn't help recalling a similar situation he'd been through when he was with the San Jose Earthquakes. Against the L.A. Galaxy, in the 2003 Western Conference semifinals, De Rosario and the Earthquakes found themselves down 4–0 on aggregate just 13 minutes into the second leg. Against all odds, the Earthquakes would come back to score five goals in 75 minutes to take the series win.

"It's just part of the process," he remembers telling himself. "Just keep grinding."

And he did.

Off a corner kick in the 29th minute, De Rosario knocked in a goal with a bicycle kick. On any other day, he might have celebrated the highlight-reel goal for what it was. Instead, he turned and ran back to his half.

Ten minutes later, De Rosario collected a long cross and fired a low, hard shot past Impact goalkeeper Srdjan Djekanović. He clenched his fist and again ran back to his own half.

At halftime, up 2–1 but still in need of three goals, Robinson spoke up and leaned heavily on his experience of how momentum had shifted games he'd played in England. "If we get one goal after halftime," he proclaimed, "they will wilt."

As a halftime substitution, Cummins turned to Chad Barrett, whose terrible luck had epitomized TFC's goal-scoring struggles. He would log 2,069 minutes that regular season, the most of his career, but up to that point had scored just three goals and had been the butt of fan frustration.

Four minutes after half time, De Rosario got the benefit of the doubt from the linesman and streaked past a high Impact back line to knock home his third. Cronin looked at De Rosario and saw "a different animal and a look in his eye." It was turning out to be a performance from De Rosario that Cronin believes defines him and was a microcosm of him as a whole. "He was a madman," said Cronin.

As the minutes ticked away, the mentality within the group did not falter. Brennan kept shouting instructions from the back, demanding those around him keep driving forward. The belief that they could pull off the win had not wavered. Even Dichio was starting to believe. "If you don't have that belief, you're behind the eight ball," he said.

In the 68th minute, Amado Guevara lined up to take a free kick, with all 11 Impact players between him and the net, desperate to hold on. His curling kick found its way past Djekanović and the squad's possibility of beating the Whitecaps really came into focus. As a group, they ran back to their half with little in the way of celebration. "It was a real showing of how strong a team mentality can be," said forward Chad Barrett.

"The 11 best players on the field were wearing red that day," said Cronin.

With less than 10 minutes remaining in regulation, TFC earned a corner. Guevara sent a high ball in to the far post. With 10 Impact players inside the box, Barrett still strolled in untouched and his header made it 5–1.

"Have they done it?" asked an incredulous Dobson. "They've put it in!"

The section of TFC supporters erupted in delirium. It was the first time in club history they'd scored five goals in a game. "It was one of those team moments that, as a Toronto supporter, they probably lost their minds. And we did as well," said Barrett.

The team's emotion was difficult to contain.

"Tactics didn't really play a part," said De Rosario. "It was just a desire to win."

In an effort to protect the lead and clog up the pitch, Cummins immediately instructed the squad to move to a 4-5-1 shape. As added time started, however, there was no slowing TFC's momentum. Fuad Ibrahim sent in another long cross that Barrett, touched to Guevara. One quick sidestep around a defender and Guevara sealed it.

At 6–1, the Miracle in Montreal was complete. At one end of the stands, the Whitecaps were left stunned. At the other end, an emotional De Rosario leapt up and was swarmed by TFC supporters.

After Brennan lifted the Voyageurs Cup, De Rosario took the first trophy in club history back to the stands and raised it in front of the travelling section. It was the first step in delivering trophies, and ultimately success, to his hometown club. And the lure of AC Milan was now very far away.

"It's one of the craziest games I've ever been a part of," said Barrett.

And even the club's hardened veterans, who have seen it all and have since graduated to the coaching ranks in MLS, agreed.

"It will never, ever," said Robinson, "be repeated."

Less than a week after the Miracle in Montreal, TFC returned home to a hero's welcome. The scheduling gods had blessed the Reds with a date against the lowly New York Red Bulls, who had won just two out of their 16 regular season matches to that point. They'd just come off a five-game losing streak and were ripe for the taking.

Earlier in the season, TFC had signed the once-promising Argentinean forward Pablo Vitti, on loan from Independiente, to help the goal-scoring drought that had seemed to plague the club since its inception. Vitti had become something of a journeyman, moving between three different Argentinean clubs in six seasons, with a loan spell in Ukraine, as well. He had been the difference-maker in a 1–0 Independiente friendly win over TFC the previous season, and now, against the Red Bulls, he finally scored his first goal for TFC with an awkward header.

In one-off pink kits to support the Canadian Breast Cancer Foundation, TFC doubled up with a De Rosario goal to send the Red Bulls home with a 2–0 loss. It would be the first of a six-game losing streak for the Red Bulls en route to a cataclysmic season in which they managed just 21 points on the season, good for seventh-worst in league history.

TFC appeared to be headed the other way, losing just two of their seven matches following the Canadian Championship. The club's first-ever playoff berth began to look like a very real possibility.

Changes were afoot at BMO Field as well. Before an August friendly against Real Madrid, a temporary grass turf was laid. In what would ultimately be a test run for the field's complete conversion to grass ahead of the next season, the field held up when TFC welcomed the "Galaticos," a team that had spent €261 million that summer alone, and included Cristiano Ronaldo. Ronaldo did his part, entertaining fans with a 19th-minute strike. At the end, it was arguably the best TFC fans could ever have felt after a 5–1 loss.

By early September, TFC began to stumble again, going goalless in three road games and seeing their record slip to 8–9–7. Eight of the league's 15 teams would qualify for the playoffs, and it had become obvious to management that De Rosario could not handle the heavy lifting on his own. A further injection of talent was needed, and TFC didn't have to look far.

Julian de Guzman, a Toronto-born midfielder who was voted the Canadian Soccer Association's 2008 male player of the year, was out of contract with Spain's Deportivo La Coruña. He had been offered another contract by the Spanish club, but with a balance still owed to him, in part because of the global financial crisis, de Guzman began looking elsewhere.

Offers from Wigan in England and PSV in the Netherlands were on the table, but didn't excite the 28-year-old. Still, as he continued to wait through the summer, training with his former German club FC Saarbrücken, the contract offers that did come in for de Guzman began to drop drastically.

So, when his agent reminded him that TFC had approached him after his strong performance with Canada at that summer's Gold Cup, de Guzman started to think realistically about going home.

TFC's offer wasn't just good, it was historic. They were offering the midfielder the club's first-ever Designated Player position, under what was still then commonly referred to as the "Beckham Rule." Such a player could be compensated handsomely with a contract that would not count against MLS's strict salary cap.

At the time, de Guzman had no idea what a DP was, but once the club flew him out to tour BMO Field in early September, he felt the strong urge to return home. Of course, his contract, which eventually became $1,910,746 per season, didn't hurt, either. It was a move that came together very quickly, and, in retrospect, perhaps was not the most well-thought-out attempt to salvage TFC's 2009 season.

De Guzman had excelled as a defensive midfielder, one whose impact on the game is not often seen on the score sheet. With Deportivo, de Guzman had scored just once in 97 total appearances. And yet he was sold to TFC fans as the type of player who would feature prominently in their attack. Many within TFC's management expected de Guzman to play as a number 10 and contribute goals whenever possible. Some who were in a position of influence during the signing had never watched any of de Guzman's matches before offering him a contract, as he was offered performance bonuses for goals, something he had rarely produced in his career.

The irony of the de Guzman signing was only compounded when Mo Johnston forced Danny Dichio, still a source of goals for the club, to retire to make room for de Guzman in the team's financial budget.

And de Guzman felt that pressure immediately. "To sell that to fans who want the team to do well and expect the local boy to do well, it was really tough," he said.

De Guzman became acquainted with the rigours of MLS's travel schedule immediately as he was on a flight across the continent for a date with the L.A. Galaxy on September 19. Even as he boarded the flight, de Guzman knew he wasn't match fit. But that was of little concern to a team that was desperately trying to sneak into the playoffs. "That was my taste of what playoffs meant. It was pretty much like promotion and relegation in Europe," said de Guzman.

A 2–0 loss in Los Angeles only intensified the emotions within the club. With just four matches left, there was a growing sense of tumult.

"It was a new pressure for us with only a couple of games together as a team and it's do or die. I feel, maybe, around that time, we weren't solid as a unit to compete in such important matches. We knew we wouldn't have enough time to prepare. But we had enough quality individuals on paper. We just weren't prepared. We needed more time to prepare for moments like that. You almost need a full season," said de Guzman.

Two draws against the Chicago Fire and the San Jose Earthquakes were cobbled together before a win at home against Real Salt Lake. With just one game remaining in the regular season, TFC's playoff fate was in their own hands. They would travel to East Rutherford, New Jersey, for the final MLS game at Giants Stadium and a date with the Red Bulls. Having long been eliminated from playoff contention, the Bulls were playing simply for fleeting pride. The forecast was simple: a win in New Jersey would send TFC into the playoffs for the first time.

In Toronto, Michelle Lissel began preparing for what felt like the inevitable. With just one win needed against a historically poor team, TFC looked bound for the playoffs. That would mean extra media attention and a new marketing campaign, so Lissel got to work and hoped the squad would hold up their end of the bargain.

Heading into Giants Stadium, it had become clear that the squad itself was feeling the weight of the most important game in club history. They were without Carl Robinson, sidelined for the season and back in Wales recovering from a knee injury, and they desperately missed that calming, veteran voice.

With the playoffs on the line, no one could accuse TFC of not being concentrated on the task at hand. Instead of focusing on their collective goals, however, as kickoff ticked closer, too many players became focused on their own individual goals for the match, and that concentration derailed their shared thrust.

"It got too much in our heads, I believe," said Marvell Wynne.

Cummins insisted on trying to take the pressure off the players. He was his typical relaxed self before the game, offering little more than the facts in his pre-game talk. "We have a chance, let's go for it," said Cummins, reminding players that "if you want something to happen, this is what you have to do."

But Cummins didn't exactly help ease the tension in the dressing room. Before the game, Cummins made the switch to an attack-minded 3-5-2 formation, different from the 4-4-2 they'd utilized all season. The switch brought curious looks within the locker room. With a 3-5-2, TFC's wide players would have to become more involved than they had all season.

TFC were met by wind and what would eventually turn into a torrential downpour that caused a delay to start. The pitch itself was a travesty:

the lines and logos of the NFL field were an eyesore. Rookie goalkeeper Brian Edwards, playing in just his third game for TFC, manned a goal area with a dark blue *GIANTS* underneath it.

And just two minutes into the match, Edwards saw some quick movement through the middle of the pitch as the Red Bulls' first attack of the game began. Juan Pablo Angel quickly sliced through TFC's midfield with a deft pass and Red Bulls forward Macoumba Kandji found himself with a clear look at goal. He sent a low shot past Edwards.

What originally looked like a given for TFC now seemed strangely far away. For a team that had tried to be prepared, they looked anything but early on. "There's only so much time you can play with destiny like that," said De Rosario.

Chad Barrett looked around the pitch after Kandji's goal and sensed the deflation. "It just seemed like everyone just lost that fight after that first goal."

That first goal was just the beginning.

After Chad Barrett was subbed off because of injury, TFC threw up a series of lazy clearance attempts in the 33rd minute. Despite being surrounded by TFC defenders, Angel put another shot past Edwards from distance.

"It was just a methodical ass-kicking," said Barrett.

At halftime, TFC sought respite from the rain. But inside the dressing room, there was absolutely no sense of pushback. Cummins believed at that time that if he put too much pressure on them, he'd lose them. So, while Cummins did his best to again remind his team of the facts, namely that they'd scored more than two goals in a half before, everything he said fell on deaf ears. "Sometimes you've got to dig in and show that real character, that real fight to win the game," said Cummins, adding that while there were some in the dressing room who had that big-game experience, the younger players and their lack of mental fortitude was sinking the team. "I just felt there wasn't enough belief," he said. "We could have shown a lot more desire. I don't think there were enough characters."

De Rosario decided to step in and try to motivate the young squad. He saw a team that, with all due respect, had not won many important games on their own and were crumbling under the weight of expectations.

"Toronto's one of the few places where there's pressure actually felt in MLS," said Barrett. And it was up to De Rosario to remind players that they could succeed.

"I felt like I was a therapist," said De Rosario. So, as he implored players to perform better and pointed out specifically where they needed to improve, he also pushed some farther away. "Some players took that to heart," said Cummins of De Rosario's halftime talk.

Any TFC fan hoping for another miracle was quickly grounded after the second half started. Edwards couldn't contain an Angel shot from wide on the wing in the 62nd minute.

"We got a bit tight as things were slipping away," said Sam Cronin. "Maybe that made it worse."

Seven minutes later, Edwards ran out into no man's land to try to intercept Kandji. He simply sidestepped a jumping Edwards before tucking home his second goal into an empty net. Matthew Mbuta doused TFC's open wound with salt with a converted penalty kick in added time.

For all the experience that did exist on the team, few had seen such a depressing locker room after.

De Rosario quickly called out his teammates. "I want to see more heart on this team," he told the *Globe and Mail* reporter after the match. "How do you teach that? You tell me. I could have come in here and kicked everything down, but what's that going to prove? I've done it many times and there's been no response. Been there and done that."

With the wound still fresh, Cummins told the assembled reporters that there was a good chance he wouldn't return for the 2010 season. He added that management had made promises to him that hadn't been kept.

So, when Cronin, just a rookie, noted after the match that TFC needed a "culture change and a psychological overhaul," the team's veterans agreed.

"You don't even need to look at the video or highlights to know that there was a complete meltdown," said Barrett.

Three days later, Cummins was relieved of his duties as TFC coach and on a plane back to England. With his wife and children still in the U.K., the pull to return home was too great. "There wasn't much point in staying," he said.

Also, it was a handy way to avoid the tire fire that was growing in and around BMO Field. Losing had become accepted, and that mentality had seeped into every corner of the club.

Johnston acknowledged, at the end-of-season media availability, that he could "absolutely" understand the growing fan frustration, including that of those who were calling for him to be fired. But he stayed on in charge, eager to right the wrongs of the 2009 season, one that can be distilled into a single dismal performance on an equally dismal day in New Jersey.

De Rosario's wife has since told him that "sometimes things happen." But for a man who has replayed the sequences of events of that game over and over, his retort stays the same: "No, they don't."

"That's a game you want to forget," said Barrett.

Unfortunately, TFC could not. Three seasons into their existence, there was very little success to speak of and the club's reputation as a sad-sack franchise was now firmly established throughout North America. Change was inevitable, and perhaps welcomed. But the overreaction to the loss in New Jersey, and the many new faces that would come as a result of it, were not.

5

The Dictator, the Frustrated Star, and a Fateful Trip Up North

"Difficult."

"A dictator."

"Hard-core."

"He didn't really want to be buddies with anybody."

These are just some of the ways that Predrag Radosavljević was described by those who worked near him or played for him.

It didn't take long for TFC to try to wash away the awful taste of the end of their 2009 season. On November 19, 2009, the man better known as "Preki" was hired to be the club's fourth coach, as they prepared to enter their fourth season.

It wasn't as if Preki hadn't had some previous success. The Serbian-American had played 28 times for the American men's national team, is the only player to have won the MLS MVP award and be crowned the MLS scoring champion twice (1997 and 2003). He was an MLS Cup champion as well, having won with the Kansas City Wizards in 2000. He was named MLS Coach of the Year with Chivas USA in 2007.

His mandate with TFC was simple: toughen up the team that wilted in the final game of the 2009 regular season. "I can't promise you that we're going to win tomorrow but we'll win soon because we're going to have a committed group on the field," said Preki, when he was announced as head coach at a press conference at BMO Field. He had left his previous job at Chivas USA just a week earlier, after three seasons as coach.

Johnston promised that Preki would bring discipline and his work ethic to the club, though it was impossible not to question how that would have differed from Carver's approach. Tactical discussions again fell by the wayside.

He hinted at his vision for a hard-working club early on.

"Things will be different. How different? You just have to wait and see," said Preki at the news conference.

Now, when many are asked about Preki, they don't associate him with his past accolades; they associate him with the results that stemmed from that aforementioned "different" approach that he took with the club on the pitch and the overhaul that came with it.

"That," Peddie told Sportsnet in 2016 of Preki's hiring, "was a fuckin' disaster."

In the aftermath of the loss to the Red Bulls, TFC management was torn. Some believed that the likes of De Rosario, de Guzman, Cronin, Robinson, Wynne, and Brennan were still a strong-enough core and that all that was needed for success on the pitch was some simple tinkering to the roster and additions that could complement a specific tactical structure and formation. Those that argued for tinkering also pointed to the fact that Cummins had changed formations in that final game: if a clear tactical vision were adhered to, for an extended period of time, the results would follow.

Cochrane was leading this charge. In the days after the loss, he felt the hurt that a loss of that magnitude can bring. But he was also one of the first to assess what went wrong — beyond the notion that the team simply lacked unquantifiable virtues such as mental toughness.

"It probably hurt too much," Cochrane said of the loss, admitting that many within the club immediately overreacted to the loss in New Jersey.

"If we had found a way to just roll that disappointment in 2009 into 2010, instead of blowing it up, things might have been different," said Cochrane.

And on the other side of the argument were those who believed that, in Cochrane's words, "blowing it up" was necessary to destabilize a sense of complacency within the squad. To them, that TFC did not show up on the pitch when it mattered most was symptomatic of a pervading attitude of contentment among the club's stars. They had had everything handed to them and there was no one within the club to keep them in line: they needed a taskmaster.

Cochrane tried to reason with the hawks, arguing that the team's salary cap situation meant some high-priced pieces had to be moved out, but the club's core was enough to build on.

Ultimately, those who viewed a roster overhaul as necessary won the argument and Preki's hire meant massive changes were afoot. The overreaction would be televised.

One element of that argument, misguided or not, was that the club had to do everything in its power to keep BMO Field full. TFC had struck gold from their inception with their rabid and intelligent fan base that drew envy from around the league. Those first three seasons, without much in the way of results on the pitch, saw the club continuously market their fans in the stands as part of the TFC game-day experience. Win or lose (though probably the latter), fans were still guaranteed one of the better sporting atmospheres in Toronto. And to some in management, a roster overhaul was necessary to keep those fans in attendance.

With an average home attendance of 20,344 in 2009, TFC ranked third in MLS. They were the only team in the top six of that metric to not make the playoffs. There was a concern that while TFC had been blessed with tremendous crowd support, those same vocal and intelligent fans also expected a winner in the immediate short-term to justify their attendance. That was an alarming factor that, ironically, drove many ill-advised decisions.

Future TFC president Bill Manning and then president of 2009 MLS Cup champion Real Salt Lake remembers TFC as a franchise in constant confusion, and that no one around the league knew who was calling the shots within the club. And that went down to the coaches and players.

Around this time, Manning shared a conversation with Paul Beirne.

"At Real Salt Lake, we wanted to have what TFC had with their crowds and Beirne said they were trying to build what Real Salt Lake had on the field," said Manning.

Believing Preki was the man to get TFC to that level, he was given the keys to the castle at the end of 2009.

And immediately, he was shocked at the state of the club. After his first few days on the job, he began questioning the many people he believed were simply "hanging around" the club, collecting paycheques but not contributing to the development of a winning soccer culture. "If I knew what kind of disaster the club was," said Preki, "I never would have taken the job."

With Johnston in Scotland for Preki's first day on the job, he asked Beirne to deliver him spreadsheets on the club's salary cap situation heading into the 2010 season. Upon first glance, Preki hit himself so hard on his own head that he left a bruise. "What have I done?" he asked himself aloud. Secretly, Preki began to think that he wouldn't last the year. He knew he'd have to be the fall guy for the many roster moves that inevitably had to be made.

There were 19 players on the TFC roster when Preki took the job. He implored anyone who would listen: "I had 24 in Chivas and I was under the salary cap, they [TFC] had 19 players and they were $1 million over the salary cap."

Preki began shedding contracts and talent early in 2010. Three of the club's top four earners in 2010, excluding de Guzman and his DP contract, were gone in the space of a few weeks. Amado Guevara and Pablo Vitti, despite the obvious talent that each possessed, had their options declined and were not brought back to the club. Each had earned just over $300,000 in 2009.

Carl Robinson, who had become a fan favourite despite his slumping 2009 season, was shipped to the New York Red Bulls for draft picks, clearing the Reds of another $300,000 in salary.

Two stalwarts on the back line, Adrian Serioux and Marvell Wynne, who combined for 47 MLS regular season appearances in 2009 and together earned just over $290,000 in guaranteed compensation in 2009, were respectively traded out within two weeks of each other. In return, TFC received two third-round draft picks in the 2011 MLS SuperDraft and defender Nick LaBrocca, who had earned $72,500 in 2009.

Matt Gold and Efrain Burgos Jr., the two players selected with the acquired draft picks, would make a combined five MLS appearances for Toronto FC.

"When you don't have the tools, you can only go so far," said Preki of the outlook within the squad heading into the 2010 season.

And while Preki believed the changes he made to the roster were born out of necessity to manage an awful salary cap situation, others saw his moves as exacerbating an already tenuous situation at the club. "When you look down a roster and say, 'I don't want this guy, I want that guy,' you can't do that in MLS in one fell swoop," said Cochrane.

Preki was moving with blinding pace early on, having little regard for the feelings of those around him and following up on the promise he made at his opening press conference: he said he wouldn't "blow the smoke up anybody's butt."

Julian de Guzman didn't know much about Preki when he arrived at TFC or even when Preki was hired to fill the head coaching vacancy. But when Preki was brought on board, de Guzman received the same text message from multiple former players: "Good luck with the running."

And as pre-season commenced in Bradenton, Florida, and Walt Disney World in Orlando, Preki got to work ensuring his players were fit for the season with training sessions that he felt would properly prepare them for the long, grinding MLS season.

Early on, balls were nowhere to be seen. Even for a team that often lacked tactical awareness in the previous season, Preki believed the key to revitalizing this group would be exhaustive, endurance-based exercises in the sweltering Florida heat.

"At that moment, you find out who the real men are and who thinks it's hard to train for one hour and twenty minutes," said Preki, observing that he made his players run "a little bit." "Of course it's hard, but games are hard," he said of his training sessions. "If you're not going to train hard, you're not going to play hard." He acknowledges that some of his veteran players probably didn't like his methods, but believed that a team's star players should always set the tone in training and games. "It was easy for them before I got there, I think," he said.

Preki also noticed what he believed was an alarming trend: though he had planned on giving Canadian players every opportunity to succeed and to find their way onto the first team, they did not display the work rate he wanted. "It was difficult for me to accept. That's one thing I always saw with some of the Canadian players: they're talented guys, but they don't want to work hard," said Preki. He points to Canadian forward Ali Gerba, a prolific goal-scorer with the Canadian national team who had been signed by TFC the previous summer.

When Gerba showed up to training camp and Preki saw a player who he claimed was "50 pounds overweight" and was being lapped twice by goalkeepers on the field during runs, Preki had to cut him loose that summer, even if it didn't sit well with Gerba's fellow Canadians.

De Rosario called Preki's pre-season approach "devastating."

As difficult as the training was for TFC's veterans, Preki claims it was just as difficult a time for him. Whenever players like De Rosario implored Preki to take his foot off the gas, he would just ask for more from them. "'The way you conduct yourself, the way you show these young guys, that's the way we're going to go,'" Preki recalls telling his veterans. "Unfortunately, that never happened."

Almost immediately, the pushback against Preki's intense training sessions began. His single-minded approach rubbed many players the wrong way. "I've never done so much running in my life during pre-season," said De Rosario. While he understands that there are different philosophies with regards to training, the fact that De Rosario had never experienced this type of training caused him to seek out Preki personally. "This is too much," De Rosario would implore his coach, as there were veteran players feeling the toll of training camp at a time when their bodies should simply be re-energized.

One of these players was Brennan, who was dogged by rumours of a rift with Preki throughout pre-season. At 32, time had caught up with the first-ever player signed by TFC. He officially retired after the club's first 2010 regular season game, a 2–0 road loss to Columbus Crew, to take the job as assistant general manager to Mo Johnston. And while he vehemently denied the rumours of any conflict with the new coach, saying then that he had "great respect" for Preki, it was impossible to overlook the impact that Preki's pre-season had on Brennan.

"I did pre-season, (but) I just didn't feel right, I thought my body was a bit tired and I didn't feel like I did every other season," he told the assembled media at a news conference on April 7, which, coincidentally or not, was not attended by Preki. "I remember saying to my wife, 'I've gone through three coaches now.' I thought I was ready [to go]," Brennan said of his decision to retire.

The constant turnover had bothered Brennan, as well. He remembers growing frustrated with having a new coach and a new plan every season: "Sometimes the door was revolving a little too quickly. In the beginning stages, I would have liked to have seen more building.... A five-year plan; let's build slowly and gradually, so that you build a good, decent squad."

With Brennan now in the front office, Johnston resumed adding to the roster. At the press conference, Johnston said Brennan's retirement meant the club was now $60,000–$70,000 under the salary cap. Less than a week later, Johnston attempted to bolster the club's back line by signing three defenders: Latvian Raivis Hščanovičs, Russian Maxim Usanov, and Canadian Adrian Cann. Combined, those three defenders earned over $287,000 in compensation for the 2010 season.

And while all three started in TFC's back line at BMO Field for the home opener, it was De Rosario who again did the heavy lifting during the April 15 match, bagging a brace in a 2–1 win over the Philadelphia Union.

Fans could have been forgiven for rooting for De Rosario more than for any other player on that day: he was the only player left from TFC's lineup for their 2009 home opener, just over one year earlier.

In the eyes of his players, what truly hindered Preki was his inability not just to connect with them on an emotional level, but to educate them about his on-field vision. Preki himself was never one who had to have instruction. Born in the former Yugoslavia in 1963, Preki emerged as a player who had high standards for himself and equally rigid standards for those around him. He presented a hardened exterior, confirming every assumption about players coming from the Eastern Bloc. There was no doubting his own abilities; there was a time, after all, when Preki could have been considered the most talented player in MLS.

But with those abilities came an alarming lack of patience.

Very early in his final MLS season, a 42-year-old Preki was still suffering from a dislocated ankle and had been sent to play rehabilitation games with the Kansas City Wizards reserve team, an assignment Preki didn't take lightly. "Why do I need to fly 10 hours to get to these games?" Preki told the *New York Times*. "If you're in your twenties or thirties and coming off an injury, this is great, but not in the last year of your career. They are great for younger players, but I have played one thousand games. I don't need them."

Upon arriving at TFC, that same man, intolerant of anyone who could not *immediately* perform at the level he demanded, was not exactly welcomed with open arms by his players. Preki had ideas, but even if his disciples wanted to learn from Preki, he did not always display the ability to get his message across. "He held his players to a very high standard," said former TFC forward Chad Barrett. "He expected players to get things right away. I don't think his character really matched what Toronto was going for. He wasn't what the city needed."

Cronin found Preki to be very regimented and meticulous, a man who knew exactly what he wanted. Entering just his second MLS season, Cronin, too, saw that it was difficult for players to form a relationship with Preki. Like many of the younger players on that squad, he wanted to crack Preki's exterior and form a relationship with the coach. But Preki had concerns other than making friends: he had to keep his pre-season on track and maintain control of a club with his veteran players already showing dissent.

If Cummins was a teacher and eager to utilize a democratic process to ensure all voices within the squad were heard, Preki was the type of coach that many in a democracy fear. He was an authoritarian. He didn't appreciate challenges from players who had earned control in the club previously. "He wanted complete domination," said Cronin.

Soccer was progressing and around the world, players of quality were recognizing the impact they had on their respective clubs, and, as a result, wanted to be heard more than ever before. Globalism had led to increased tactical awareness in players. Eyes were being opened to different approaches to playing the game. And it was no different in the TFC locker room. But Preki came from a different time and place, where the coach's voice reigned supreme. That may have appealed to Anselmi, but not to the players. "If you would make a suggestion, he would immediately slap it down," said Barrett. "He felt like his input was the most important."

And that didn't sit well with De Rosario. After being shut out in the season opener in Columbus, De Rosario went on a tear, scoring goals in five straight games. Six games into the season, he had scored six of the club's seven total goals.

After a May 29 3–1 win on the road in San Jose, during which De Rosario scored another two goals, TFC finally sat above .500 with a 5–4–1 record. Hope sprang eternal, as was common early on in TFC seasons. But if your star player and your coach aren't on the same page, it's only a matter of time before the wheels fall off.

"He was in competition with me the whole time," said De Rosario. Then 32, De Rosario's impeccable MLS resumé didn't exactly resonate with Preki. De Rosario would repeatedly request updates on Preki's vision for the club tactically and any suggestions he'd offer would be met with the opposite response.

Communication was never part of Preki's skill set, nor was that required. As the summer approached, he still adhered to his mandate: harden a team that was viewed as mentally soft after their meltdown to end the 2009 season. But in doing so, he also alienated some of the players he needed most.

Barrett calls Preki the strictest coach he's ever come across. For all the accolades Preki amassed during his playing career, he was now coaching in a time when players required more personal attention. "It wasn't so much like a player-coach relationship, he almost wanted a father-son relationship where he expected you to give him the respect he's amassed over his career," said Barrett. "You pay him his dues as a player, but as a coach he hadn't been around long enough and coached long enough to understand that you can't just push everybody. Everybody has a different personality and you have to key in on that. You have to bend it so you're not affecting that person, that player, so that you're not making him play underneath what he can."

By late May, one suggestion kept creeping up again and again from the players: with the upcoming World Cup and a three-week break in the MLS schedule, they needed a rest from Preki's intensive approach.

At 5–4–2 heading into the World Cup break, TFC had climbed to sixth place in MLS, their highest position all season. The growing sentiment was that they'd earned the break, having risen to Preki's demands and also playing their best soccer of the season.

Anselmi took Preki out to lunch at a downtown steakhouse, commended him on his job so far, and asked him if he wanted to make changes to the roster. Preki said no, acknowledging that the squad was in a good spot and more roster changes would interrupt the progress they'd made. For a fleeting moment, many in the squad were happy.

Until Preki told the squad to pack their bags. They were headed to Nottawasaga Inn Resort, over an hour away from Toronto, for another training camp. And if it was to be anything like the pre-season camp, there would be little time spent at the spa. Players were exhausted and frustrated but now hit a boiling point. Once in Nottawasaga, they were outright refusing to buy into Preki's demands. "That was the straw that broke the camel's back," said De Rosario.

Informal players-only meetings all reached the same conclusion: Preki's philosophy now meant nothing. The remainder of the season would not see the most attuned performances. The ship was calling for a mutiny. "I didn't know what to do," said an exasperated De Rosario.

When the club returned to action on June 26 against the Galaxy at home, they looked lifeless in a 0–0 draw. They continued to fall in the standings, managing just one win in six games after the break.

"They didn't want to change things because they were comfortable," Preki said of the squad and their reluctance to adapt to his methods. "Losing was okay for them. Everybody was getting paid."

So Preki and management flipped the switch on earlier feelings that all was going well, and used de Guzman's connections to bring over Spanish forward Miguel Angel Ferrer Martinez, better known as Mista, as the club's second-ever DP. Mista was teammates with de Guzman at Deportivo and had previously won two La Liga titles with Valencia.

But at 31, Mista was a shell of the player he had been in Spain. He would make just nine appearances and not once could he do what he had been brought over to do: find the back of the net in MLS regular season.

"When you leave Europe, you're so used to things," said de Guzman. "And they have to adapt to things quick. Mista was signed in the summer and we needed him to perform right away."

The signing didn't sit well with De Rosario. For all of his early season success, few players saw their fortunes turn like his after Nottawasaga.

De Rosario would not score again under Preki. The secondary scoring would dry up as well. For the rest of his time with the club, De Rosario saw TFC score more than one goal in a game just once.

Wins at home against Colorado and Chivas USA that summer became the outliers. TFC's position in the standings dropped drastically as the losses piled up. Entering the September 11 home match to last-place D.C. United, Preki had started to feel the tide turning against him. He started Canadians Nana Attakora and Adrian Cann (who together earned $105,342 for the season) as his centre-backs. While he had seen results, from these two young players in particular, through the late summer, starting them was part of his campaign to get better players.

While Preki had continually gone to management in the late summer to ask for more resources to secure better players, he was not getting public support in the media from TFC management. Starting these two was something of an act of defiance, in an attempt to showcase just what cards he'd been dealt with by the club.

TFC held United up until Branko Bošković swung a free kick into the box in the 81st minute. The ball fell comfortably to former TFC defender Julius James, who was given more than enough space by Attakora to turn and fire a shot past TFC goalkeeper Stefan Frei.

When it became apparent that the Reds would be sunk 1–0, not just by the last-place team in MLS, but by one that would finish as the eighth-worst team on points all-time, boos rained down from the home crowd.

After the match, Preki didn't hold back on his assessment of the home side, admitting that that loss was probably the low point of their season. "Apart from Dwayne's individual effort in the first couple of minutes I felt we didn't have any legs," said Preki, referring to a spectacular run and a shot that had bounced off the far post. Even Preki saw that the group lacked the energy that, ironically, he might have drained them of. "We looked tired."

As was his custom, he believed the group underperformed. "I wouldn't say we didn't show up, but a couple of guys could have given more. I will leave it up to you to figure out which ones," he said to the assembled media.

It had always been Preki's plan to simply survive his first year in charge, in the hope that in his second year TFC's salary cap would open up enough for him to find the players he needed. But as management continued to have more faith in the opinions of the club's star players than in Preki's, he felt his time coming to an end.

Scathing, harsh, blunt, and frustrated. It was a post-match press conference that perfectly summarized Preki's approach to TFC. Fitting then, that it would be his last.

Three days later, Preki walked into Anselmi's office. He was relieved of his duties, along with general manager Johnston. Preki simply stood up, shook Anselmi's hand and walked out with barely a word.

"I wasn't given a chance," said Preki, "to finish the project I had in mind."

Anselmi would eventually tease the assembled media with rumours of the players' revolt. "What we had seen over the last several weeks was the team was heading in the wrong direction, but it was even bigger than that. The situation was not right, that's the best way I can describe it," said Anselmi.

De Guzman echoed his sentiments to the media, complaining of how many in the club would head into matches unable to express themselves in a way they would like to. As he said at the time,

> Not even just players, speaking on behalf of pretty much the entire staff, you'd feel the environment not 110 percent positive the way a club would need to be if they want to be successful at any level of this game. Being able to express yourself and feel free on and off the pitch meant a lot, and that's something that was missing in the group with Preki being involved.

With the playoffs out of sight, many were happy to have washed their hands clean of the failed Preki experiment. It would be almost three years before Preki would land another coaching job, this time in the USL. None were more pleased than De Rosario, who, in his first game after Preki's dismissal, took TFC on his back and bagged another brace in a 2–1 win in Houston, now with former assistant coach Nick Dasovic at the helm on an interim basis.

Dasovic's plan was simple: "Just right the ship. Don't let it sink."

Even with the season all but lost, just keeping the club treading water might be an insurmountable task.

TFC returned home for a late September date with the surging Earthquakes. Though many had written off the Reds from playoff contention, De Rosario believed otherwise. He was inarguably the team's franchise player, and the frustration of another wasted season, coupled with all the duties that come with being one of the few voices of reason in the locker room, was evident even as he was finding the back of the net.

At $443,750, De Rosario was earning more than all but eight players in MLS in 2010. But his salary was still far less than the $1.7 million de Guzman and the $968,736 Mista were pulling in as Designated Players.

Down 2–0 to the Earthquakes in the 66th minute, De Rosario stood unmarked on the corner of the box, blatantly calling for a pass. When it came, he put one touch on the ball and chipped it over goalkeeper Jon Busch with all the effort of a Sunday league player but with world-class quality.

He turned to the BMO Field suites and, instead of his standard "Shake 'n Bake" celebration dance, began to mimic signing a cheque with his right hand.

De Rosario didn't just want to get paid; he wanted everyone to recognize something: he was doing more at TFC than just scoring goals. Quietly, De Rosario had become frustrated with the amount of work he was doing counselling players, paying for team dinners when the club wouldn't pony up, being the go-between with the dressing room and management during Preki's reign, all while still producing at an incredible rate. "What else do you want me to do?" he would ask of a splintering management group. "I'm the only one that's waving this flag here."

After management continued to put off De Rosario's request to be made a DP and then after further promises that his designation as a player could eventually change, De Rosario decided to make his anger public. "I was sick of being put off," he said. "It was disrespectful."

If it was De Rosario's intention to let fans into the world he was living off the pitch, his goal celebration succeeded. "This was the first time that all the dysfunction was out in the open," said Sportsnet's John Molinaro, then with CBC Sports.

It didn't take long for the club's loyal fans to voice their displeasure with the terrible season and the turning tide as well.

With word that season ticket prices would be increased the following season by 30 percent with no results on the pitch to speak of, and no big-name signings being made, a group of fans unfurled a banner reading "ML$E: ONLY $EEING DOLLAR IGN" with others complementing the banner with handmade "$" signs, as well.

After two road matches (and two losses), TFC returned on October 16 for their final home match of the season.

TFC started off by stepping in it with a message on the stadium scoreboard reminding fans to renew their season tickets. Finally, the crowd spoke up; this time with a raucous chorus of boos. (The following week, season-seat holders received an email from the club admitting they had "screwed up" by increasing how many games were part of 2011 season ticket packages. Cochrane remembers it as a case of "counting chickens before they hatched.")

The club would eventually state that Anselmi would be thrown to the wolves and meet with supporters in a series of town hall–style meetings to hear their complaints. But during the game, the crowd of 18,084, sparse by the lofty standards fans had set throughout the first four seasons, had no interest in talking. They produced what was a shadow of the vibrant atmosphere BMO Field had become known as. The most vocal Supporters' Section sat on their hands and purposefully refused to engage in the very singing and chanting that the club had long marketed. The silent protest against the climbing ticket prices and another lost season produced a lifeless stadium that felt more akin to the vibe at the Air Canada Centre during a Leafs game that those fans prided themselves on moving away from.

"ALL FOR MONEY," and "ACTIONS NOT WORDS," read banners.

Heading into added time with a 2–1 lead, it looked as if the squad would give their fans something to smile about. With the club already having been eliminated from playoff contention, there was nothing to play for but pride. But the Crew added salt to the wound when an Eddie Gaven corner kick was sent into the TFC box in the second minute of added time and Crew goalkeeper William Hesmer, having sprinted out of his box to add an extra man, found the ball at his feet, and, with all the time in the world, smashed home the tying goal. He was just the third goalkeeper in league history to score, but he didn't exactly receive the recognition a goalkeeper normally would for that kind of feat. Never before in club history had the boos rained down as loud from the crowd.

That anger carried over two days later during the town hall meetings. Fans gathered in a BMO Field lounge to hear Anselmi, Beirne, Cochrane, and Brennan speak about their plans for the club, if only for a hot minute. Once the floor was opened to those in attendance, the club's plan to lather them up with free beer backfired: the fans were livid, and spoke without hesitation.

"That's when the fireworks would go off," said Rollins.

For more than four years, they had bought into the idea that TFC were a club they could call their own, would support with a passion all their own, and would be rewarded for their faith (and financial investment) with a winning product.

It was a Catch-22 by the lake. Fans had finally gone all-in on the soccer team they craved in the city, because that team's ownership had the kind of resources to keep it afloat. But it had ultimately become clear to those fans that those resources were not being utilized correctly. At the top of the list was the club's inability to properly utilize the Designated Player rule by spending larger sums of money on players who would perform adequately.

"Football supporters are not rational," said Beirne. "Nobody expects them to be."

Tears flowed. Anger spewed over.

"There was nothing we could say that could make them happy right away," said Beirne.

Fans would come with a laundry list of questions and literally throw their list of questions to the floor, instead staring the assembled executives directly in the face. Representatives from fan groups would transcribe every word said for accountability. An older gentleman began speaking, but, too choked up by the emotion of supporting a losing club, needed his son to finish for him.

"The supporters' groups started to believe their own hype back then," said Rollins.

And TFC management knew who had all the leverage in these meetings. "We had to pump ourselves up full of humility before we walked into the room. We were going to wear all this stress and sadness," said Beirne. He would routinely have to look himself in the mirror and tell himself, as well as Anselmi, Brennan, and Cochrane, how important it was to listen to the fans, to let them finish their entire sentences, and avoid canned responses.

This was only made that much harder for Beirne, who felt he had to swallow his own personal pride. "For most of us, we felt this was beyond our scope of responsibilities, but there was no one left," said Beirne, of the decision to sit in front of fans.

He'd return home after, equally as frustrated. Yes, TFC weren't winning. But the notion that ownership was not doing everything in their power to create a winning club got his back up. "I remember feeling, 'Fuck. What are they asking from us?' We built the stadium. We converted it to grass. We built the training ground. We brought in arguably Canada's best player. That should have ticked two boxes: Designated Player and Canadian player. Good lord, what do you expect?" said Beirne.

It was the Designated-Player discussion that Beirne was willing to concede on. By the end of 2010, almost everyone within the club understood that asking the right questions about the team's style of play would be moving forward, and by not surrounding de Guzman with the right players, they had not set their first-ever DP up for success. Even before the town hall meetings, management knew a focal point of the off-season would be finding, and properly vetting, new DPs.

The town hall meetings caused some within the organization to argue that MLSE's budgeting schedule knocked TFC down the totem pole and caused a certain lack of interest in the club at the highest level. MLSE's fiscal year revolves around their basketball and hockey franchises and ends in the summer, which is exactly when TFC is at the height of their mid-season. It became apparent that a more dedicated staff was needed to keep TFC accountable on all fronts, instead of just relying on the whims of some prominent management figures. A TFC-specific yearly budget would also be required.

Expectations had changed within the club. The Mo Johnston era had been marked by a sense of exhilaration from fans at just having their new club and optimism about where they could be headed. But the overwhelming sense Cochrane got from fans now? "Prove what you got," said Cochrane.

The four men regrouped and realized that, however briefly, they had lost sight of how to treat the vital group of people who had helped launch the club.

TFC management had failed to support the fans' long-term dreams, and had been treating problems with band-aid solutions. Even Anselmi would admit that it was TFC's fans who had "owned the narrative of the market" up to that point.

As the 2010 season came to a close, management left with egg on their collective faces. They now had to figure out how to best clean it off.

"When things weren't going well, they let you hear it," Anselmi said of fan anger during the town hall meetings. "And they had every right to."

That MLSE were "trying their best" was, after four seasons, not good enough for the fans. What was needed was an injection of managers who better understood the game and could supplement the organization's own desire to win with practical know-how in the soccer world.

TFC had depended on their fans to keep them afloat with consistently strong attendance numbers and passion unrivalled in the league. They banked on the fans' high soccer IQ. But with the passion beginning to fade, management was now pressed to take action and match that same soccer IQ in their own roster and personnel decisions.

"I would take solace coming out of those meetings," said Beirne. As painful as it was to be the subject of such vitriol, he still walked away with a strange sense of resounding reassurance: "Holy shit, we matter to people!"

6

Ajax Culture, German Influence, and Starting from Scratch

SINCE 2008, WHEN HE JOINED the Toronto FC academy, Ashtone Morgan had waited for his opportunity. Growing up in Toronto, the soft-spoken full-back had always dreamt of playing professionally, not abroad, but in his home town. In his childhood home, Morgan would decorate his walls with collages of magazine photos of locally born players, including Dwayne De Rosario and Julian de Guzman. He eschewed the world's most talented soccer players in favour of those who would have the most impact in his own area code.

At 16, Morgan looked past the fact that the academy did not have its own dedicated training ground or a prestigious history to speak of. Instead, he saw TFC's academy, still a work in progress, as the next best thing for a young Canadian and an opportunity for those young players to improve and continue to move up the ladder.

So for two and a half years, Morgan quietly went about his business at the academy, plying his trade under academy mainstay Jason Bent and a rotating cast of first-team coaches, each of whom showed some interest in the club's academy products, but never enough to be worthwhile.

Since the club's inception, the focus for every first-team coach had been to satisfy an increasingly frustrated fan base and to produce results almost immediately. The long-term development of local products was never front-of-mind for the first-team coaches.

Still, Morgan remained hopeful that, one day, a first-team coach would recognize the talent in the academy, itself a product of an increasingly diverse city that was growing less attached to hockey and baseball as participation sports and more invested in the world's most popular game at the grassroots level.

When Morgan first heard the news in early January 2011 of yet another change at the top of the coaching ranks, he paid little attention, given that this would be the fourth first-team coach since he joined the academy. But when word came down on what new coach Aron Winter's focus would be with the club, Morgan's ears perked up. Winter, after all, was coming off three years coaching Ajax Amsterdam's first academy team. The Ajax academy wasn't just respected, but could arguably be considered among the world's best, having developed the likes of Johan Cruyff, Dennis Bergkamp, Frank de Boer, Marco van Basten, and Wesley Sneijder.

And Morgan's coaching staff wanted to replicate that success in Toronto.

"The long-term goal is we start to feed into the academy, the academy starts to feed into the first team.... If you look at all the models in world football — Ajax, Barcelona, Manchester United — that's the way to go. And because of the salary cap, we can't go out and buy million-dollar players, so we've got to produce our own talent," said Paul Mariner during the coaching staff unveiling. Mariner, a former England international and recent coach of Plymouth Argyle, was assigned the role of technical director, rounding out the coaching staff with former Ajax youth team coach Bob de Klerk.

Morgan couldn't help smiling. The world of international soccer was already trending younger and it wasn't unusual to see teenagers getting regular first-team minutes around the world. He'd had a sniff with the first team in October 2010, looking strong in the final CONCACAF Champions' League group stage game, despite not having a professional contract at the time. He was lauded for his speed and defensive abilities on the flanks, and when it came time for TFC to travel to Antalya, Turkey, for TFC's first-team training camp, the club's new coaching staff had taken notice: Morgan, by then 19, was invited to come on the trip. In total, four academy players were invited to Turkey.

In Turkey, during a long and gruelling pre-season, Winter and de Klerk worked to implement and enforce Total Football, a style in which outfield players could theoretically switch positions with ease to dominate the course of play.

For an attacking full-back like Morgan, Winter and de Klerk's approach was a godsend. The new coaching staff not only had an established plan for a first team that had been writhing in instability, but it was a plan that could be imposed all the way down to the club's youth teams. "As a young guy coming up, that was the best education in football for myself and for the other guys, to learn that Dutch system," said Morgan, shaking his head and smiling. "Some of the older guys might have been set in their ways, but for a young guy coming up, this was the best information I could ever receive."

After a successful camp, Morgan signed with the first team in March and made his MLS regular-season debut in TFC's second game of the season, a 2–0 win over the Portland Timbers at BMO Field.

While TFC had local products leading the first team to open the 2011 season in De Rosario and de Guzman, the club's new coaching staff wanted to ensure that there would be players from the city to carry the torch for years after. The feeding-in of locally developed players would be vital, given that both Total Football and Winter's demands on his first team for a level of professionalism never before experienced at TFC were already starting to wear thin on veteran players.

But young Canadians like Morgan would go on to factor heavily in Winter's time at TFC. True, it was yet another change at the top of the club, but at least for those expected to raise the standard of play in the long term, it was a welcome one.

"We loved it all," said Morgan, still smiling.

The end of the Preki era couldn't have come soon enough for Toronto FC, but with his departure another reality had to be acknowledged: the club still did not have an individual at the top of the food chain with a sophisticated knowledge of the game. Management had succeeded in building a brand based on a passionate fan base, and the business end of the club was also rapidly improving thanks to the unwavering support of those very fans. But a true identity that could stretch from the top to the bottom of the club was lacking.

Mo Johnston's penchant for working the phones and the instant gratification he received in trying to improve via trades meant few players stayed long enough to establish significant influence within club culture. And that same revolving door saw coaches enter and exit just as frequently, meaning there was a sense that nobody was truly in charge at Toronto FC.

Tom Anselmi recognized that the club needed help in establishing a long-term plan. Ever since MLS had awarded MLSE the franchise in October 2005, Anselmi had felt as if he, and many within the club, were constantly scrambling to keep up with not only the day-to-day running of the club but also the demands of running a reputable franchise. MLSE had only a little over a year and a half from being awarded the franchise until its first MLS game.

But TFC had started quickly, and interest had grown quicker than many could have imagined. With such a rapid rise, many roster and hiring mistakes had been made by management trying to capitalize on that interest. By the end of the 2010 season, and with the outrage that fans had expressed during the town-hall meetings, Anselmi was ready to admit that it was time to seek help with the vision of the club.

"We started from scratch," said Anselmi. "We were behind the eight ball, trying to understand that culture, how it needed to interface with the way we worked and the decisions we made."

Anselmi reached out to Tim Leiweke for help. Leiweke was serving as president and CEO of Anschutz Entertainment Group, and, as the owner of the Los Angeles Galaxy, had overseen arguably the best team in MLS up to that point, with two MLS Cups and three league titles. Not only did Leiweke have a track record of success, he had the Rolodex to match.

Leiweke suggested getting in touch with Jurgen Klinsmann. The former German striker had gained international repute not only for being one of the best goal-scorers of his generation but also for managing a young German squad to a third-place finish in the 2006 World Cup with an aggressive approach based largely on creating offense. His holistic methods weren't without their detractors, as Klinsmann had drawn the ire of many in the German media by going against the grain in player selection, tactics, and availability in a federation that was largely dictated by tradition. Klinsmann had stepped down from the German national team almost immediately after the World Cup, then had a turbulent spell at Bayern Munich, marred by disagreements with the club's board of directors, that lasted less than a full season.

Anselmi's first offer to Klinsmann was that he become the club's general manager, which he refused, perhaps sensing that the overhaul within the club was a long-term project and that there were still major coaching opportunities on the horizon for him. A compromise was reached: along with his consulting company, Soccer Solutions, Klinsmann would advise in a consulting role to help reorganize the club's infrastructure.

Immediately, Anselmi and Klinsmann developed a relationship focused on understanding how to integrate the city of Toronto and its soccer talent and history, the TFC brand, and finally the club's pre-existing leadership in a way that could determine what type of leadership the club should employ moving forward. "Who does TFC want to be?" Klinsmann asked of TFC management. He wanted to be sure that the answer would be all-encompassing and a frame for the club's development. Immediately, those in the first meetings with Klinsmann wished they had hired him after he'd stepped down from the German national team in 2006.

Contrary to what some had feared, Klinsmann did not suggest a complete overhaul of the club's infrastructure. Instead, he wanted to build on certain elements already established. In particular, the academy. "Jurgen was very complimentary of the direction we were going in. He believed that the academy was one of the places we had success. He thought they should continue to invest into it, dig deeper into the community and mine the potential talent," said Cochrane.

To continue to develop that talent, Klinsmann suggested MLSE pursue Aron Winter to take the lead in developing the academy as a means for long-term success. There was a general understanding among MLSE and club management that properly building the academy was going to take time and would not produce the immediate results TFC had been lacking. But the names that the Ajax academy had developed were too prominent to overlook.

With Klinsmann's advice, and his suggestion of Winter, himself a former international who had played in two World Cups, TFC was finally taking an overtly ambitious approach to *building* their team, and calls of MLSE misspending within TFC were being silenced. "When you say Ajax, you get it," said Cochrane. "The club buys in."

Selling Winter on TFC wasn't as easy. Winter knew nothing about the club when MLSE approached him. But their sales pitch was interesting. They presented the club's newfound philosophy, the one focused on youth development, and were clear that they wanted to "make a difference" within the city's soccer community. Winter stressed it would take three to six years before they would see the results of a youth-oriented system, which felt like a lifetime considering the club's relatively young existence, but MLSE was on board and Klinsmann offered his support with future endeavours. Everyone agreed: attractive soccer was needed, regardless of how long it would take.

"For me, it was important that the philosophy of football, to play nice football and to invest in their own youth department was something that encouraged me to come," said Winter.

There was a common understanding that everyone within the club now had and would adhere to: Mariner would serve as Winter's lieutenant in terms of player acquisitions and de Klerk was Winter's assistant who would enforce the club's coaching philosophy. A 4-3-3 formation, typical of Total Football, would be played from the first team down through the academy to develop a sense of continuity. Training camp was to be largely focused on one element of the game: passing. Adhering to the traditional Dutch approach, players would work through single passing drills for two hours at a time, to improve the team's ball movement.

Winter also brought a stern approach to the team's routines, enforcing dress codes, regulating meal times, and dictating that players could begin eating only once the entire team had arrived. While younger players bought in to the new approach, that was more in line with Europe's more prominent clubs, the rules drew the ire of older players. Early in training camp, tensions began to simmer between MLS veterans and the coaching staff.

Management appreciated the changes, and soon MLSE followed up on their end of the bargain, approving a $17.6 million investment in a new training ground dedicated solely to the club, weeks after Winter's hire was announced. The club followed up by announcing plans for a third academy team, stating once again that they wanted to eventually build an academy structure down to U-7.

Neely had been plugging away with the club's academy program, having successfully bridged the gap between TFC and local clubs. They'd continued to train at a variety of locales in and around Toronto, including Lamport Stadium. Not only had Neely and Bent played a vital role in developing the players that Winter was planning to utilize, Neely had helped arrange a program where players could train and play with their club but TFC would also put on training sessions five days a week and have local players train whenever they wanted as long as it didn't overlap with their own club's requirements. This approach allowed Neely and Bent to help build rosters for the following seasons.

But with first-team success still the priority, Neely and Bent had been able to operate largely undisturbed by club management. That meant as the two men were pushing the academy to local clubs, they were also cooking meals for players in the empty visitors' dressing rooms, doing Costco runs for mass amounts of groceries, and doing the team laundry, "unbeknownst to the MLSE and TFC staff," according to Neely.

So wide was the separation between the first team and the academy that when Winter and de Klerk arrived, they were surprised to see so much less of a proper infrastructure between the academy and the first team than they believed should have existed in a professional club.

Said Neely, "It didn't sink in," to the incoming coaching staff — not only how far behind the academy structure was compared to European clubs, but also how far the current academy had come under Neely and Bent.

As players were quickly jetted back and forth between the academy and the first team, and the instructions on how to run the academy went through an overhaul, the changes became too much for Neely to handle. He left the club and the academy structure in Winter's hands.

"My head was spinning," said Neely. "I didn't know which way was up."

The new coaching regime continued to put their own touches on the club by signing three Dutch players brought in on trial during training camp, including promising young forward Nick Soolsma. Four academy products, including Morgan, were signed under the MLS Homegrown Player Rule.

Perhaps lost in the shifting focus toward youth development was the status of the club's star forward, De Rosario. After he publicly requested a pay raise the previous September, there had been little discussion with MLSE regarding a new contract. The constant turnover within TFC had forced De Rosario to consider his options elsewhere. He had had the management's blessing, including that of Klinsmann and Cochrane, to travel to Scotland late in 2010 for a trial with Celtic. He'd earned the praise of Celtic manager Neil Lennon, and now, with yet another coaching change at TFC, his patience with the club was wearing thin. "It wasn't like I wanted to stay," De Rosario said of Toronto FC. "I wanted to go."

So when word got back to Celtic during De Rosario's trial that Winter wanted him to return to the club, even though he'd been given the club's permission to stay in Scotland for as long as possible, De Rosario became incensed. Some believed De Rosario himself was undermining Celtic. "You can't just sneak in here," De Rosario would tell those around him in Scotland. "That's a no-brainer."

With De Rosario still under contract to TFC, Lennon and Celtic had to bow to TFC's demands and ask him to return to Toronto for pre-season. Despite having received regular training during TFC's off-season, De Rosario found himself being asked by Winter to return, not for games in the regular season, but for pre-season practices.

"This is a complete joke," said De Rosario, frustrated that Winter could not see the bigger picture that included both his potential future with a top-flight European club and TFC's own revamped approach toward a younger roster. "After Preki, now this?"

De Rosario asked both his agent and MLSE if a return would mean a pay raise. He was told that it wouldn't, but that he needed to return to help deliver results for the first team and to continue to usher in the club's crop of young players. After repeatedly telling his agent that he would not return, De Rosario had to bitterly accept that his dreams of returning to Europe were over for now. The club's revamped structure and more promises of stability meant little to De Rosario, and the constant turnover that had changed the course of the careers of countless lower-level players would finally claim the best in TFC's short history.

Two games into the regular season, De Rosario was shipped out to D.C. United for two players who would stay in Toronto for only one season and a first round pick in the following year's draft. De Rosario would end up leading MLS in scoring that season en route to winning the MLS MVP award.

"I was exhausted, I was over it," said De Rosario. "This was not what I'd imagined when I came to Toronto."

After the win against the Timbers, TFC would win just two more matches before July, effectively eliminating them from playoff contention yet again.

Still, with more draws than losses at the halfway point of the season, some within management believed the season could be salvaged and that an injection of big-name talent would help the club and, as was always a concern, keep a restless fan base at bay.

Management turned again to Klinsmann as well as Winter and the relationships they'd fostered in Europe. Tasked with the responsibility of finding players to bolster the club, Winter believed that the club had to recruit players who had played at top European clubs and wouldn't find his rules to be such a drastic change. New Designated-Player signings would help Winter only if they would buy in to the philosophy he and de Klerk were working toward and would help speed up the development of the club's younger players.

Torsten Frings fit that bill. Klinsmann first made contact with the midfielder from his 2006 World Cup side. Frings had showcased versatility across the pitch as a box-to-box midfielder and could easily fit into Winter's 4-3-3 formation. And having played for Werder Bremen, Borussia Dortmund, and Bayern Munich over 14 seasons, as well as for two World Cups and two European Championships, by that point, the 34-year-old could enforce a standard off the pitch that young players could adhere to. Winter wanted Frings to be "an example for everybody" and finally convinced him to join TFC.

Winter knew a forward was needed to finish Frings's work in the midfield and turned to Danny Koevermans, whom he'd crossed paths with during his short loan spell at Sparta Rotterdam. Koevermans had stretches of being a prolific goal-scorer, including 24 goals in 29 games for Sparta Rotterdam in 2004–5 and then 22 goals in 31 games with AZ Alkmaar two seasons later. Winter knew Koevermans was going to be out of contract at PSV Eindhoven when he first began calling him in the spring, but Koevermans informed Winter that he'd given his word to Birmingham City FC, who had just been relegated from the Premier League to the Championship, that he would eventually sign with them.

Koevermans was sitting poolside during a holiday in Spain when his agent called him and told him that Alex McLeish, the Birmingham manager who had recruited Koevermans, had just resigned from his post. Knowing full well that a new manager would bring in new players and might not put much value in the possible addition of Koevermans, the then 32-year-old immediately circled back to Winter's original offer. The lure of TFC was less about titles, and more in line with what also had drawn Frings to MLS. "We want adventure," Koevermans said to his wife. "Let's go for an adventure. Let's see if we can make Toronto work."

A week later, Koevermans had signed with TFC and they now had the maximum three DP's in place. That these signings reinforced the belief that MLS was a league for players north of 30, unable to compete at top leagues in Europe, and simply looking for one last paycheque was irrelevant: the addition of Frings and Koevermans was a coup. They were the first DPs that TFC signed on the potential of a city they'd never lived in, but had been told was a world-class destination. Both De Rosario and de Guzman were from the city, and they returned both out of familiarity and a desire to pay back the soccer community they'd grown up in. And before those two, TFC had shown no semblance of order when recruiting players, relying simply on Johnston's whims and whomever he was sold on that particular day.

For the first time in franchise history, TFC had awoken to the possibilities of what being located in one of MLS's most attractive markets could bring. They homed in on the fact that both Frings and Koevermans wanted "an adventure," and pitched Toronto as a place that could provide both safety and stability for players with families, and the entertainment and diversity that younger players generally crave.

It was the beginning of a shift toward Toronto being thought of less as a stopover and more as a place where additions could put down roots for good. Bob de Klerk, for example, has never left Toronto, and Winter continues to voice his allegiance to the city, repeatedly assuring me that he would return if the opportunity presented itself.

Not long after, basketball star DeMar DeRozan, though likely showered with promises of fortune south of the border, embraced the city when he re-signed with the Raptors, proclaiming "I am Toronto," and speaking of his desire to make everything Toronto has to offer better known. And Maple Leafs coach Mike Babcock has consistently spoken about the elation he and his players feel when the club wins in Toronto.

Winter's may not have been the first group in Toronto to sell the city to athletes, but they were the first to do so within TFC. Some within management realized that if they could not change the perception of the club immediately, it would be best to sell players on the city and let their own happiness with their living situation dictate their performance on the pitch.

"Once I got to the city, I was admittedly drawn to it," said full-back Warren Creavalle, who was shocked to be traded from the Houston Dynamo to TFC in 2014. "It's Canada's New York. There's just a lot going on in the city. A lot of different things that everybody can enjoy. It appeals to a wide spread of people."

Years later, Sebastian Giovinco would fall in love with the city and decide to stay despite possible offers to ply his trade as the best player in North America elsewhere. And Victor Vazquez played with a liberated conscience en route to a MLS Best XI spot once he settled in Toronto and realized how happy his family could be in the city.

"I'm so, so happy that I had my time in Toronto," Koevermans stresses.

Koevermans realized very early that for him and his family, it would be, in his estimation, the "best move I ever made."

When Frings and Koevermans both finally suited up for their first game with TFC, they were struck by just how high a hill they had to climb with the team. They were the only players over 30 in the starting 11, and Frings in particular was struck by the youth and lack of experience in the squad.

"I had a clue that Toronto FC was on the very beginning of a good way. They had the idea to professionalize everything; they had good people in their jobs. Even if the team on the squad was very young and just in the beginnings," said Frings.

Frings lined up in the central midfield role in the 4-3-3 formation and was largely expected to act as a general, directing traffic and instructing a still-learning squad on their positional assignments. The 1–0 loss at home to FC Dallas was his first taste of what it meant to be a veteran on a young, rebuilding squad that at times probably belonged in the classroom more than it did on a pitch.

Koevermans would score in each of his next three outings, even if the club was unable to find a win in any of those three matches. He was doing the heavy lifting up front, eventually scoring an incredible eight goals in 10 MLS appearances that season, while the rest of the squad tried to put together the pieces in the back of the pitch. "The team just was too young in age and experience. And the quality was not on the level needed for the idea," said Frings, of Winter's vision of Total Football. "But if you want to reach something big in the future you have to start with it one day. To reach the later goals you needed this all, including the drawbacks."

Three wins in August and September were not enough to salvage the regular season. TFC would put MLSE's patience surrounding the rebuild and investment in youth to the test right out of the gate, finishing on 33 points in 34 games, good enough for third from the bottom in the league.

Sustained success in the league was likely never going to be possible early on in Winter's rebuild. He was far from establishing a reliable starting 11 and, for as much raw talent as there was present, consistency and cohesiveness within the squad was also far from being established. "We were a bunch of nomads thrown together," said Terry Dunfield, acquired by TFC from the Whitecaps in July of 2011.

The rebuild meant Winter could focus his efforts on finding success in shorter tournaments, and once the MLS season began to go south, that success began to manifest itself in the Canadian Championship. The four-team semifinal tournament, with just two MLS clubs, was a fitting opportunity for Winter to experiment with his lineup against weaker opponents with a larger payoff, an appearance in the CONCACAF Champions League, on the line.

TFC easily disposed of FC Edmonton in the semifinals, even with 18-year-old Oscar Cordon, 19-year-old Joao Plata, and 22-year-old Tony Tchani in the starting 11 of the first leg.

All three featured in the first leg of the final, as well, as did the 23-year-old Nick Soolsma, which produced a 1–1 draw against the Whitecaps. Plata's emergence was perhaps the most promising. The Ecuadorian forward had been loaned out from LDU Quito to MLS in order to further his development and was the sixth-last pick in the 2011 MLS SuperDraft. Winter saw tremendous possibility in Plata, the type of player that he could possibly centre a rebuild around.

And Plata provided reason for that faith during the second leg with steely nerves as he buried a low penalty past Joe Cannon to equalize the score. Mikael Yourassowsky would add the crucial second goal to put TFC up 3–2 on aggregate and deliver their third Canadian Championship in a row. With the win, TFC gained entrance into the Preliminary Round of the CONCACAF Champions League, and Winter didn't plan on pulling in the reins on his younger crop of players at all.

Plata singlehandedly toppled Nicaraguan side Real Esteli in the first leg of the Preliminary Round, bagging a brace, including a picture-perfect bending free kick, in a 2–1 win. The second leg was equally as favourable and TFC gained access to the group stage to start just weeks later.

Two losses in their first three games of the group stage backed the club into a corner. With the top two teams in the four-team group set to qualify, TFC's future in the tournament looked bleak. A 1–0 win against Panamanian side Tauro was a start, and a surprise 1–1 draw against a strong Mexican side, Universidad Nacional, set up a must-win against FC Dallas in Texas in the final group-stage match. Both clubs were 2–1–2 through five matches and the winner would go through to the quarterfinals.

Koevermans scored a classic TFC goal in its messy efficiency, swinging at a rebound from in close to open the lead. It was a promising start, even if TFC's track record of holding early leads wasn't great. Enter Plata, who was not burdened by memories of past failures by the Reds. A perfectly timed run left him open to bury the crucial second goal. His shimmying celebration near the net was eerily similar to De Rosario's, as was his goal-scoring prowess. In the 81st minute, Plata poked the ball away from FC Dallas full-back and future TFC acquisition Jackson, and darted in on his own before stopping short and making two Dallas defenders look incompetent with another low rifle of a shot.

On the road, against the odds, TFC had secured their first-ever spot in the CONCACAF Champions League quarterfinals. "I think that Plata, of course, he makes two goals, but I think everybody played well. We're a team, we battled, we created a lot of opportunities and gave nothing away," Winter said after the game. Credit was given where it was due: TFC didn't crumble with the stakes high, as past squads had. Despite the lack of success in the league, 2011 provided a healthy dose of optimism. Young players had bought into Winter's revamped code of conduct within the club, and once they had a full season with the club, TFC's newly acquired veterans would be able to exert even more of a positive influence on the club's young future.

Winter, delivering one of his final press conferences of the season after the win in Dallas, had every reason to be optimistic. "I think that this is a good step," he said, "for the future."

So, too, did Morgan. He would make 22 appearances in 2011, the fifth-most of any defender, while being easily the youngest of that bunch. It was during CONCACAF competitions that Winter truly leaned heavily on Morgan and the young defender found his way: his eight appearances in the competition were the most of any defender and tied for the most of any player on the team.

What Morgan gained wasn't just practical experience that he could utilize down the line. It was a sense of belonging in his hometown team and one that had been sorely missed within young players in the club up to that point. He's stayed with TFC longer than any other player in club history.

Though the results might not have been as desired, at least the black cloud Preki had cast over Canadian players within the club was gone. "You don't always have to go overseas or go to the draft to pick players up," said Morgan. "Over the years, we've showed that if you trust us, we can reward that trust you have in the Canadian player. We do what we do for the younger kids behind us."

Not only was Toronto FC learning how to best utilize a young crop of talent within the city for the first time, they were beginning the process of passing those experiences on. Even today, Morgan has not forgotten his roots in the academy. He'll continue to take time after first-team training sessions to meet with new young academy players and to speak to them at length about what's needed to climb the ladder to the first team. Despite having opportunities to play elsewhere and perhaps to receive more minutes, Morgan wants to be what De Rosario and de Guzman were for him: a connection between those bedrooms, littered with magazine cutouts, and BMO Field.

"Toronto is my home," Morgan told me in September of 2017, while discussing his time at the TFC academy. "I take pride in being a home-grown player. I'm doing it for the local boys."

7

The Realm of Comedy, the Nightclub in Houston, and the Worst Team in the World

THINGS STARTED DIFFERENTLY FOR TORONTO FC in 2012, which is to say that the club was preparing for their sixth season in franchise history with the same head coach that they had to begin the previous season, a franchise first.

For a brief moment in the winter of 2011–12, it appeared as if TFC were finally walking on stable ground with their coaching staff. And there was reason to be optimistic, as Aron Winter and Bob de Klerk's possession-based style of play and cohesive 4-3-3 formation seemed to be making inroads during the club's CONCACAF Champions League play. Many teams from Latin America prefer a similar possession-heavy, attacking approach, and in mimicking this style of play, as opposed to the physical, grinding approach taken by some MLS squads, TFC sought success.

The early CONCACAF returns had been poor, as TFC had lost two of their first three games in less than a month in the group stage. It had looked again like a Canadian Championship would mean very little against some of the more seasoned outfits, including Mexico's UNAM, who pasted the Reds in the 4–0 win in Mexico City with all four goals coming in the first half.

But the latter half of the group stage had seen a more well-rounded TFC come into form, as they won two of their final three matches and produced a gutsy 1–1 draw against UNAM at BMO Field. With 10 points in the group stage, TFC were headed to the Championship round for the first time in their existence.

Several players from the 2011 and 2012 squads believed that, as the team wasn't getting results in MLS, the club's focus began to shift toward garnering success in the Champions League.

But Winter, having played for clubs, including Ajax Amsterdam and Inter Milan, that regularly played both in their league and in European competitions, thought the club should be achieving results in both. "That was a little bit strange for me," Winter said of the team's poor league results to end the 2011 season, "because the games we were playing in the Champions League, we were playing well."

Once again, TFC benefited from the deep pockets of their owners as the team chartered their flights for CONCACAF games and provided players with comfort and luxuries off the pitch to ensure they were fresh to perform on it.

And with TFC in the Champions League quarterfinals for the first time, MLSE tried to catapult their success into a broader appeal within the city. Before the 2012 MLS season kicked off, TFC were drawn against the Los Angeles Galaxy for the quarterfinals. With the first leg on March 7, the decision was made to move the game away from Lake Ontario and BMO Field into the over 50,000 seat Rogers Centre.

BMO Field was not winter-proof and, much like a cottage, all the pipes at the stadium were exposed. It would have been impossible to have turned on the water and not have freezing water, burst pipes, and, essentially, no way to serve food. Then there were the fire-suppression systems, which required fair weather to pass inspection. So TFC moved the game to Rogers Centre, a stadium known for its cavernous feel. The conditions might have made the open-air BMO Field unsuitable at the time, but with a closed dome and artificial turf, the move to the stadium ahead of TFC's biggest game in franchise history undermined the efforts they'd made to create an authentic experience not unlike that in European stadiums.

And as to be expected, not everyone was thrilled about the decision.

Irish international striker Robbie Keane was critical of the "plastic pitch," saying before the match: "I think these days, it should be grass pitches. I don't think it's good, injury-wise. I think it can be dangerous. So it is a shame that we're playing on it."

In terms of international intrigue, it was TFC's biggest game to date. And the fans treated it as such. It was a coming-out party in a way, for a club that up to that point had been defined less by their success on the pitch and more by the energy created by loyal fans off it.

And while BMO Field sits just three kilometres from the Entertainment District that is home to the city's Maple Leafs, Blue Jays, and Raptors, it was still light years away from the large-scale impact those three clubs have had on the city's popular conscience.

TFC games at BMO Field might have offered the kind of engaging and energetic sporting atmosphere that Blue Jays and Maple Leafs games could not, but that didn't stop TFC's being looked upon as just a representation of fans on the fringes of mainstream sporting culture. Being based in Liberty Village was both a blessing and a curse for TFC. They had the benefit of being thought of as a neighbourhood club held closely by young professionals with plenty of disposable income, but were still unable to get through the door of the house long occupied by the aforementioned top three clubs.

"Maybe we're headed in the right direction?" Anselmi remembers thinking after he saw how well the ticket sales were going, for the first leg of the Champions League quarterfinal. It turned out to be a coming-out party for TFC fans.

An unseasonably warm day, with a high of 16 degrees and a low of just 12 at kickoff saw fans flood the downtown streets in the walk to Rogers Centre to welcome David Beckham, Robbie Keane, Landon Donovan, and the rest of the Galaxy.

Midfielder Jeremy Hall, traded to TFC in the off-season, was ineligible to play because he had suited up for FC Dallas (also in the CONCACAF Champions League) in the previous season, but he still made the walk from his downtown hotel to the Rogers Centre and felt engulfed by the support of those nearby.

After kickoff, Terry Dunfield felt the "incredible" support from the 47,658 fans in the sold-out Rogers Centre carried them through against a Galaxy side that had won the Supporters' Shield and MLS Cup in the previous season. It was the largest attendance for a TFC game.

Red streamers painted the royal-blue seats and would eventually cover David Beckham when he took corner kicks. "Our Stadiums, Our Rules" read one banner. "Let's Fight Together and Make History" read another. Supporters' groups had showed up en masse, quickly transferring the energy normally present at BMO Field into the otherwise cavernous dome, despite sitting much farther away from the action than usual.

"We were running on adrenalin," said Dunfield.

It showed.

A strong starting 11, featuring a healthy Koevermans and Frings, made an immediate impact. Frings placed a corner kick perfectly into the box and, after a brief deflection, Ryan Johnson roofed a volley past Galaxy goalkeeper Josh Saunders. Johnson ran to Frings in the corner, turning 360 degrees as he leapt in the air and kicked the corner flag on his way down.

"Now," asked Sportsnet colour commentator Craig Forrest, "can Toronto FC build on this?"

Less than five minutes later, they did. And again, it was Frings leading the attack. The German swung a long cross in from 40 yards out that found the head of an unmarked Luis Silva. It was Silva's first professional game after being selected fourth overall in the 2012 MLS SuperDraft less than two months earlier.

With one bounce, another ball had found its way past Saunders. A look of ecstasy appeared on Silva's face. He stopped and crossed his chest in disbelief. Winter's philosophy of giving young players opportunities with the first team looked like it was paying off.

Eventually, the Galaxy would get one back after some typically atrocious defending left Galaxy midfielder Mike Magee alone inside the six-yard box for a quick tap-in off a cross.

And in what had been a hallmark of much of TFC's early years, poor defending came back to haunt them late in regulation time. Beckham swung a corner kick into the six-yard box. Despite TFC having two defenders on the goal line behind goalkeeper Stefan Frei and another six between the original header, Edson Buddle, and the net, they could not clear the late challenge. Donovan tucked home the tying and crucial away goal.

While Beckham had been critical of the game's being played on artificial turf, he was impressed by the atmosphere. After the game, he said,

> It was great. I'm glad the game was staged here. Obviously I knew it was a bigger stadium and I knew these fans would fill it out. I think the streamers were a terrible idea during the game. Before the game, a great idea. Little bit difficult taking corners like that.... Obviously the fans saw their

team score two goals, I'm sure they didn't like seeing us score two goals. Overall it was a great atmosphere to play in.

Koevermans added that he thought BMO Field should be made bigger or that the club should always play at the Rogers Centre to take advantage of the larger crowds, and Beirne called it a "milestone" for the club.

There was still work to be done, however.

The following week, TFC travelled to the Home Depot Center in Los Angeles and were greeted by a fraction of the number of fans from the previous week. Because of an agreement between the Galaxy and the university housing, the Home Depot Center limited attendance to just 7,500 on games not played on weekends.

The 7,500 that were allowed into the stadium witnessed the biggest upset in TFC history. On the strength of a Ryan Johnson header and Nick Soolsma banging in a Johnson cross in the 67th minute, TFC knocked off the Galaxy 2–1 to become the first-ever Canadian squad to reach the CONCACAF Champions League semifinals. After each goal, there was a near-palpable sense of surprise from Sportsnet commentator Gerry Dobson.

But, as for Winter, his sense of confidence was growing. "We played like a team. We won like a team," Winter told the *Toronto Star* post-game. "And, we made history."

Now over a year into his tenure as TFC coach, Winter was starting to see early returns of his vision, or, as he commonly refers to it now, his football "philosophy."

When Winter first arrived, he felt some of the players he acquired could fit into the system he wanted, while most could not. Still, he didn't think it would be a problem, because he knew he could build a strong roster if he were given the time to do so.

By the second year, he was beginning to grow satisfied, despite the team's lingering injuries. Winter, like many on the team, saw that TFC's style of play wasn't altogether poor, but their lack of goals was hurting the team.

So, when the opportunity to go after those goals presented itself, Winter jumped at it, even to the team's peril.

On the pitch, Winter wanted to keep the ball and attack with poise and purpose.

And in the semifinals, TFC drew Mexican side Santos Laguna, who had finished fourth in the first half of Mexico's top flight in 2011 and would go on to finish in first place in the second half of the season. TFC held their own against them in the first leg at BMO Field in a 1–1 draw. The game was marked by a stunning Miguel Aceval free kick and, after the final whistle, an all-out brawl in front of the TFC net after an infraction involving Ashtone Morgan.

The brawl, and the two red cards handed out to two Laguna players, meant even more eyes were on the return leg. On the strength of some sound ball movement, TFC jumped out to a 2–1 lead in the first half in the Estadio Corona. Despite defender Ty Harden misplaying a long through ball seconds before the first half ended that led to Herculez Gomez's second goal of the half, TFC still held the crucial two away goals heading into half with a 2–2 scoreline.

But Winter wanted more.

Had TFC sat back and eventually kept that scoreline, they would have walked through to an unprecedented CONCACAF Champions League final. And, regardless of the result, getting into that final might have shown his detractors the merits of Winter's approach.

Instead, he went for broke.

With the entire squad gassed after playing two strong games so early in the season, Winter looked at the squad's drenched brows and still insisted they needed more goals and needed to press more. It was a rare sign of aggression from the normally thoughtful and rational manager. Perhaps recognizing what this squad was on the verge of and eager to put his stamp on the team, Winter insisted on a heavy press.

This aggressive approach didn't sit well with some of the players, including Terry Dunfield. "I even said to him at the time, 'Are you sure that's what we want to do, just looking around at the body language of players,'" recalled Dunfield.

Sure enough, as TFC went out and began pressing and could not keep an organized defensive shape, Santos Laguna quickly found holes in TFC's disorganized back end: de Guzman couldn't recover quickly in the box and made a clumsy challenge that resulted in a converted penalty attempt in the 56th minute. Seven minutes later, Aceval strangely decided to put his head on a soft cross in the box that could have been played off his chest or by his goalkeeper just a foot behind him. Instead, the ball took a bounce off Aceval's head and onto his hand. Juan Pablo Rodríguez converted his second penalty in the space of eight minutes.

"And so now it has all come apart for Toronto FC, and what a disappointing thing that is," said Dobson on the broadcast.

TFC were eventually sliced apart and allowed four goals in the second half. "If you're not organized," said Dunfield, "it's game over against a team with the quality like that."

Dunfield remembers the crowd being as intimidating as any he's ever played in front of in his 17-year career. The excitement of the local crowd only added salt to the wound.

"That's when our season was over," said Dunfield. "That was a difficult one to swallow."

TFC would return home to Canada to find their next league fixture just three days away against the Impact at Olympic Stadium in Montreal. It was the first MLS meeting between the two clubs. The Impact were an expansion team that season and understandably eager to make an impression on their rivals from down the 401.

What they got was a deflated TFC side that looked like a shell of the squad that had gone deep into the CONCACAF Champions League. Impact midfielder Siniša Ubiparipović found the back of the net in the 18th minute before Andrew Wenger doubled the Impact's lead in the 81st minute. Koevermans added a goal in the 88th minute, but it wasn't enough: TFC were now 0–4 to start the season. It was the first time they'd gone 0–4 to start a campaign since their inaugural season.

But for Koevermans and TFC, their early season struggles were only just beginning.

Koevermans had been signed by TFC to provide the bulk of the goals for the club. With eight goals in 10 appearances, he'd done so in 2011. But the 2012 campaign felt different for Koevermans early on.

Like many on that squad, Koevermans attributes their poor form in the league to the focus they'd placed on the Champions League. "It was kind of annoying," he said, "how we couldn't win in the league."

And what began as annoyance eventually festered into the kind of disgust and emotion so rarely seen in North America's often stoic professional athletes.

TFC would lose all four league matches in April to move to 0–7 after two months of play. It wasn't hard to imagine TFC missing the playoffs yet again, and it wasn't even summer.

Koevermans bluntly describes the 2012 season: "Terrible."

Some inside the dressing room believed they were level with other teams, but the veterans understood how far away the team actually was from contention.

Attendance was 18,364 at BMO Field for the May 5 match against D.C. United, the lowest of the MLS season so far. TFC lost yet again, this time 2–0 after allowing two second half goals. Frustration was evident on all fronts. "I couldn't believe it," said Winter, of the team's early season form.

Cochrane remembers an overall "malaise" creeping through the organization and felt the club were going down a path that didn't appear to "have an end to it."

Two weeks later, the team travelled south to RFK Stadium to again play D.C. United. Any hope that the two-week break might have allowed TFC to hit reset was lost in the very first minute, when De Rosario headed in a perfectly placed Branko Bošković free kick.

De Rosario ran to the corner to perform his trademark slow shimmy celebration dance. It was his fourth goal of the season, which was only two less than TFC had scored as an entire club up to that point.

Cataclysmic defending from TFC again reared its ugly head as De Rosario was allowed to stroll, unmarked, into the box and easily tap in his second goal of the game in the 43rd minute. To add salt to the wound, De Rosario turned and ran back by goalkeeper Miloš Kocić, shaking his finger.

Koevermans would convert a long de Guzman free kick from just inside the half in the 71st minute, but his effort, once again, wasn't enough. On the strength of De Rosario's two goals and a third from Hamdi Salihi, D.C. United would send TFC to 0–9 on the season.

An outsider might have appreciated the irony of how De Rosario, whom many believed to have been underappreciated by his former club, was the one effectively hammering the nail into TFC's coffin. But Koevermans had no time for poetic speculation after the match.

"When you're playing nine games and you're only losing, all your frustration is coming," said Winter.

Not a lot was said in the changing room. Bad luck had played a part, but there was only so much energy for the young club to expend through both league and tournament play. What should have been an opportunity to grow in the early part of the season was instead a lesson in how to stretch young players too thin.

"What could you say, really?" said Dunfield.

Sitting in his stall, Koevermans wanted to say something. The veteran was angry, largely at himself, for not being able to score more. He let out his frustration in typically blunt Dutch fashion, saying TFC were "setting a record as the worst team in the world."

The comment may have come from an honest place of genuine frustration, but it took the entire franchise by surprise. Koevermans's statement went viral and was picked up by websites around the world. After the early season high of the CONCACAF Champions League, TFC had returned to being the butt of jokes in North American soccer. And Koevermans's comment set off a firestorm within the club.

Torsten Frings was furious. "'Why the fuck would you say that?'" Koevermans said Frings asked him, reminding Koevermans that he was an experienced player on an inexperienced team.

"Torsten, he was killing me," said Koevermans. "And I can't say that he was wrong."

Winter wasn't as angry, but did share the frustration. "I could never understand why he said that," said Winter. "He was one of the guys who could understand that we were playing well."

After the comment, Koevermans genuinely thought it would go relatively unnoticed. He defended himself to Dunfield as they drove to training from the Beaches. "But we *are* the worst team," he said.

Soon, the comments were picked up by the BBC's website. "It brought even more spotlight onto our situation," said Dunfield. "And even more pressure that no one associated with the club needed."

At a training session three days later, Koevermans doubled down.

"Name me one team in the whole world that is 0–9," Koevermans said at BMO Field. "That's what I was referring to — that there is not one team in the world who has lost nine times in a row."

Canadian defender Adrian Cann didn't agree with the thrust of Koeverman's comments. "It kind of bothers me," he said after that training session. "I can say we're the worst team in the world, but it's harder to say we're the worst team in the world and do something about it. Actions speak louder than words."

For Koevermans, part of his frustration stemmed from the fact that he was unable to always back up his comments with words. He was frequently battling injuries and believed he wasn't able to help TFC to his full potential. And his comment still haunts him. "It was the worst mistake I ever made," said Koevermans, who was not used to playing on a losing club.

Winter would not let his veteran off so easily. In the second leg of the Canadian Championship on May 23, de Guzman was sent off with a red card in the 57th minute. Koevermans had been banished to the bench and immediately stood up, assuming he'd be brought in to provide support after the loss of one of TFC's veterans.

But Winter shot him a nasty look.

"Okay, I understand you," Koevermans said to himself and he returned to his place on the bench. TFC would end up winning the 2012 Canadian Championship 2–1 on aggregate over the Vancouver Whitecaps, but it was still little consolation to Koevermans and the floundering Reds.

At BMO Field, people were shouting at Koevermans. "Fuck off! Get out of here!" Koevermans remembers hearing. It was, in his estimation, one of the worst weeks of his life.

The eyes of MLS returned to TFC on May 26 when they hosted the Philadelphia Union at BMO Field. Once again, attendance had dropped, this time to 18,227.

Before the game, as a means to spark his squad, Winter told the team that any player who did not log 45 minutes would also have to suit up for TFC's reserve team after the game.

"'How can you do this before a game?'" Koevermans wondered.

He was not chosen for the starting 11.

At halftime, TFC and the Union were scoreless.

"I was so stressed out," said Koevermans.

At the half, Winter still refused to bring Koevermans on. Koevermans knew he'd have to spend time on the reserves. The prospect terrified him. "That was the one thing I didn't want to do anymore," said Koevermans. "Because in Holland, sometimes when you don't play, you play with the reserves, and I know that I couldn't go back to the reserves. When you're young, you can play with the reserves. But when you're old, it's so annoying. When I got injured, I loved playing those games. But when you're fit, those games are just horrible."

Midway through the second half, with the game still scoreless, Winter finally called Koevermans in.

Still, the BMO Field crowd reminded him of their disappointment. Koevermans remembers hearing a fan call him an asshole the moment he stepped up off the bench.

"Please let me do something nice," he thought to himself as he stepped on the pitch.

The minutes crept away and it looked as if TFC would remain winless to start the season.

But after a Soolsma cross, Koevermans found himself with the ball on his feet inches away from the goal and Union goalkeeper Chris Konopka. He tucked it home and immediately leapt into the crowd.

All of his sins were briefly absolved. "I've never felt better than at this moment," said Koevermans.

The Koevermans goal was the difference, and with a 1–0 win, TFC stood at 1–9 to start the season. But the excitement, as it so often was that season, was short-lived. "We got back into the locker room, everybody's excited, clapping hands, cheering," said Koevermans, "and the coach comes in and said, 'All the players who didn't play are going to play with the second team right now. And still, we have to score more goals.'"

Playing to just a few hundred people after the first-team game, Koevermans and the TFC reserves mustered a 3–2 win over the Union reserves. Like most of the season, it was a humbling experience for the veteran forward.

"You can't refuse," he said, "it's your job."

CONCACAF World Cup qualification meant a three-week break between the May 26 win and TFC's next league game on June 16. The break was meant to be a time for reflection for the TFC coaching staff to figure out how to begin to uphill climb to get their season back on track.

Winter understood that MLSE had been growing more and more skeptical of his approach with every loss, but figured the win was enough to keep his bosses at bay through the break.

The break meant Winter could refocus his efforts on building the TFC academy and developing young, local players. Winter had always wanted his players to be students of his, and students of the game. He believed that losses should not get in the way of development.

"I was trying to create a real football environment," he said. "That was a change for the guys to adapt to."

Winter felt confident enough in his role that he had stopped trying to convince those above him of the merits of his work. That he had started a 19-year-old Doneil Henry and 21-year-old Ashtone Morgan, both products of the TFC academy, and 20-year-old 2011 MLS SuperDraft pick Joao Plata in the last game was proof that his plan to develop young players was on track.

But behind the scenes, in the eyes of MLSE, the poor results with the first team overshadowed any improvements in development.

Midway through the nine-game losing streak, de Klerk received a call from his agent, Edo Boonstoppel, instructing him to meet with Tom Anselmi at Hotel Le Germain in Toronto. Informed that MLSE weren't satisfied with Winter's results, de Klerk was told there were two options moving forward: either Paul Mariner or de Klerk himself would become head coach to see out the 2012 season.

He was torn — de Klerk knew that Mariner's vision was the antithesis of Winter's but also wanted to remain loyal to his old friend Winter. His true interest was continuing to develop TFC's academy, so he made it clear that he would take on the head coaching job only on an interim basis, and that he would want to return to the academy at the end of the 2012 season.

Others within the club also wanted to promote academy coaches Danny Dichio and Jimmy Brennan as assistants and see Winter moved to president of the club to assuage the continued concerns that Anselmi didn't have the necessary soccer knowledge. Academy director Thomas Rongen's name was also thrown into the hat as possible coach, provided Dichio and Brennan would serve as his lieutenants.

With many possible replacements jumping over each other to be considered, Winter continued to take the risk and stay on in the head coaching job but would appoint Brennan as his assistant.

The politics of the job had become a focal point. "This has nothing to do with football and developing players," de Klerk remembers thinking.

What was missing was a central tenet that would run throughout the entire club. Every person in a position of power had their own vision of what could make TFC successful. And, in the end, that collective desire for TFC's success resulted in its downfall, as few could get on the same page. "Everybody needs to be one unit," said de Klerk. "You need to have the same people, with the same philosophy and the same vision."

Former staffers felt the relationship among the coaches was "always awkward" and that bringing in a number of different people with different visions "did seem at odds with the Ajax way." The original intentions of Klinsmann and Anselmi were quickly deteriorating in the face of another lost season with the first team.

The squad were given, much to their surprise, a few extra days off ahead of their return to training. By the time the players came back to TFC ahead of their June 16 match in Kansas, Winter had been informed by MLSE that his time with the club was up and that Mariner was being appointed head coach.

The firing left players unsure of where they stood. A new manager meant new personnel preferences. As had been the case with TFC throughout their entire short existence, more turnovers seemed likely.

"As a player," said Dunfield, "you're playing for your future."

"If they had more patience, maybe I would succeed also," said Winter.

He believes Anselmi was being informed by Cochrane and Mariner and that they influenced his decision. "Maybe I was too innovative," said Winter, still convinced of the vision he sold the club on before his hiring.

Corey Wray, then director of team operations for TFC, and Mike Masaro, the head of media relations, were preparing to leave the team hotel in Houston on the morning of Monday, June 18, to grab a coffee. They were abruptly stopped by a member of the hotel's front desk staff, who needed their immediate attention. The hotel had been receiving calls all morning about the whereabouts of a TFC player. Nick Soolsma's girlfriend had become furious that he had not returned her calls and, suspecting that he was out on the town and perhaps not remaining completely faithful, she had begun calling anyone and everyone associated with him.

When Soolsma did finally return his girlfriend's call, he didn't exactly reassure her that he had a wholesome evening. He told her that he, along with two other TFC players, had been arrested for public intoxication outside of Club Escobar, a Houston nightclub.

Already incensed, Soolsma's girlfriend could not contain her anger. Instead of allowing the club to become aware of the arrests and handle the news themselves, Soolsma's girlfriend decided to sully his name and call every newspaper in Toronto that would answer the phone.

With the *Toronto Sun* having already reported the arrests, Wray went nuclear and got to work on the kind of situation few team ops directors ever want to deal with. With very little information, Wray began calling every branch of the Houston Police, while Masaro began handling the multiple calls from media with questions of their own.

Wray found it difficult to get much concrete information from the Houston PD and was growing even more exasperated before a team member walked by and casually told him that Soolsma, Luis Silva, and Miguel Aceval, the three players in question, were currently in the hotel gym as part of a planned workout session, as if nothing had happened.

Wray burst into the gym and unloaded. "It was one of the scariest times for the players," said Wray. "I was furious."

Furious not at the players for blowing off some steam at a nightclub, but incensed at how they handled the situation. That teammate Julian de Guzman posted bail for each of the players ($267 US each) as a sign of solidarity mattered very little. All year long, TFC management had had a giant storm cloud hanging over their heads in what had become a historically bad season. Wray didn't want to chastise the players for having a night out. There was even infrastructure in place to handle arrests within the team, but that the players had not followed protocol incensed Wray, and sent an already disconcerted season into the stratosphere. The players, and TFC, continued to be the butt of jokes on social media.

Paul Mariner's new approach to the team had apparently planted a seed in the minds of the players. Now, whatever it was was bursting into bloom.

When Mariner had first entered the dressing room as head coach, it was before a training session and with very little fanfare. He informed the squad that he was going to establish a leadership group: Dunfield, Frings, Koevermans, and Frei. After Winter's heavy hand in controlling the TFC dressing room, the onus of responsibility now fell onto the players.

"He said he was going to need us to stabilize the changing room," said Dunfield. "He instilled a belief that we could get ourselves out of this."

Mariner had gone right back to basics, reverting to a 4-4-2 formation and ensuring that every player knew exactly what his role was, in and out of possession. He believed in playing a traditionally English style of play, with quick wingers and a reliance on crosses to set up scoring chances.

Training sessions became less about passing and meticulous movement of the ball and more about instilling a competitive spirit in the squad. "Dump it forward through the channels and get after it," Jeremy Hall remembers.

Yet for all the changes on the pitch, what really caught the players' attention was Mariner's different approach to the rules that governed them off the pitch.

One of Paul's early messages was that he expected players to be professional, and that he was going to relax the rules. Gone was the requirement that players wear the exact same outfits, and gone were the shared eating times. "It went from super tight," said Hall, "to loose."

And it hadn't taken long for the relaxed rules to be taken advantage of.

The 2–0 loss away to Sporting Kansas City had been Mariner's first game as head coach. The following day, Sunday would be a day off for the team with, strangely, no curfew on the Saturday. When details of Aceval,

The Supporter Section in BMO Field's south end.

All We Are Saying, Is Give Us a Goal. TFC fans finally got what they were asking for in the team's fifth game of the season.

Seat cushions litter the pitch after Danny Dichio scored TFC's first ever goal in the 24th minute of the May 12, 2007, match against the visiting Chicago Fire.

Danny Dichio, TFC's first hero. Supporters still chant Dichio's name in the 24th minute of each home game.

Supporters gather pre-game in nearby Liberty Village before travelling en masse down to the stadium, chanting and waving flags.

Canadian star forward Dwayne De Rosario became TFC's all-time leading scorer in regular season in his three plus years with the club. He was traded in 2011, but returned to Toronto for the 2014 season. He remains a team ambassador.

© Amil Delic. Used with permission.

With his acquisition touted as "The Bloody Big Deal," English striker Jermain Defoe was to be the centrepiece of a club that had fans just begging for a championship.
© Amil Delic. Used with permission.

A change of coaches at AC Roma may have facilitated the acquisition of midfielder Michael Bradley before the 2014 season. He was named team captain in 2015, and his leadership both on and off the pitch has inspired the team to become one of the best in MLS history.

© Amil Delic. Used with permission.

Greg Vanney became Toronto's ninth head coach in seven years when he was brought in with 10 games remaining in the 2014 season. In his first full season as coach, Toronto FC qualified for the post-season for the first time.

American striker Jozy Altidore was signed ahead of the 2015 season and would bring his size, speed, and scoring ability to the TFC attack.

© Amil Delic. Used with permission.

Another piece of the puzzle. Italian striker Sebastian Giovinco joined the team in early 2015. He made an impact immediately, winning the MLS Golden Boot, Newcomer of the Year Award, and MVP Award. He surpassed Dwayne De Rosario as TFC's all-time leading scorer.

TFC reached the MLS Cup final in 2016, only to lose in penalty kicks to the Seattle Sounders after playing to a 0–0 draw. Fans were understandably disappointed, but the best was yet to come.
© Amil Delic. Used with permission.

Canadian-born forward Tosaint Ricketts. MLS Cup Final, BMO Field, December 10, 2016.
© Amil Delic. Used with permission.

Thanks to the success of the TFC academy, the future looks bright for Canadian-born players like Jonathan Osorio.

© Amil Delic. Used with permission.

The MLS Cup was finally raised in Toronto after a 10-year wait.

The team celebrates in front of the hometown fans after winning the 2017 MLS Cup.
© Scott MacKenzie / vftss.com. Used with permission.

Silva, and Soolsma's arrest began to trickle out on Sunday morning, it was almost difficult not to laugh at how far the season had spun out of control.

It was later reported by the *Toronto Sun* that the players had had an opportunity to leave the scene outside the nightclub, but had refused: "When officers attempted to handcuff one of the Reds, 'one of [the players] ran and so the officer ran and took him into custody,' the spokesman said.... Silva was later reported to have been the player that attempted to flee on foot — something that could have elevated his misdemeanor charge."

"I just told the players about the following day [of training]," Mariner told the Canadian Press after the arrests. "I just thought that they would respond to that. And most of them did. But it looks like we had — well, I'm not going to use the words that just came into my mind, but some people chose not to be on their best behaviour, let's put it that way."

Throughout the 2012 season, TFC had continued to lose games largely because of the players on the pitch. The club was undergoing a rebuild under Winter and that many couldn't master the intricacies of the 4-3-3 Total Football system was a vital element in the team's lack of success.

But with the arrests, it was looking more and more likely that TFC would now continue to lose games because of what was happening *off* the pitch. And that only made the possibility of winning seasons down the line even harder to imagine: the growing sentiment around MLS was that TFC's dysfunction was far deeper-rooted than had been realized, and that no one knew who was truly guiding the ship. "It was fuel to the fire at that point," Hall said of the team's quickly declining season. "People were looking at us as pushovers when TFC came to town. And this only added to it."

And though Winter was no longer employed by TFC, he remembers feeling angry when he heard the news. "How is it possible that in the first game after I quit," he asked, "players were arrested?"

Eventually, Mariner would get his first win in charge of TFC, a 3–0 drubbing of the Impact in Montreal. The Reds would pick up two more draws after that, meaning Mariner had lost just once in his first six games as head coach.

"With a new gaffer," said Koevermans, "you just go for it."

A compressed summer schedule saw TFC play an outlandish nine league games in just over a month after Winter was fired. In the process, while battling exhaustion, Koevermans tore his ACL against the Revolution on July 14. He was ruled out for the rest of the season soon after.

Paul Mariner consoled Koevermans after the injury, giving what Koevermans called "the warmest embrace I've ever had" in the dressing room. Slowly, a bond was beginning to form between the new coach and his team.

Hall remembers Mariner having an open-door policy with his players and being very honest and blunt. Some of TFC's younger players weren't getting a lot of love for minutes because, in Hall's estimation, "It was more about needing to win now."

Wins over the Whitecaps, Revolution, and Rapids capped off that nine-game stretch.

"The resilience of these boys," said Mariner after the 2–1 win at home against the Rapids, "is off the charts."

TFC had never had a four-game win streak up until that point. And they'd have to wait much longer for it to happen again. The win against the Rapids would be TFC's final win of the season. They would close out their 2012 MLS campaign with four draws, 10 losses, and many, many wounds to lick.

Any evidence that TFC were indeed cursed could be, in an almost scientific manner, dissected and traced back to inept management decisions and an inability to allow a coach's vision to be played out in full. But by the tail-end of 2012, with another MLS season lost, star players still on the injured list, and fan frustration continuing to mount; it was hard not to believe that even the supernatural was at play for the beleaguered franchise.

But Toronto FC were again, almost curiously, riding high in the CONCACAF Champions League. Drawn into a group with Salvadoran side Águila and old foes Santos Laguna, TFC came flying out of the gate with a 5–1 drubbing of Águila at home. To make it out of the three-team group, TFC needed to finish in first place. And that began to look possible late in their second match, at home against Santos Laguna.

In the 68th minute, Quincy Amarikwa drew TFC level with the strong Mexican side, 1–1. A draw would've put them in good standing for the return leg until the aforementioned supernatural had its way with the long-suffering TFC fan base.

As Santos Laguna built up their attack from the midfield in the 84th minute, a black cat darted across the BMO Field pitch and ran between goalkeeper Freddy Hall and the net. Play continued, but, under the dark auspices, things quickly got worse.

Daniel Ludueña scored for Santos in the 90th minute and Cándido Ramírez piled on with a goal in added time. In a few minutes, what had looked like a favourable result disappeared as TFC gave up three away goals and saw their hopes for progressing out of the group stage vanish.

And it was impossible not to question the work of that black cat.

"Everyone in the press room was like, 'What the hell? How is this happening?'" said journalist Armen Bedakian. "This stopped being a jinxed team and went into the realm of comedy."

TFC would not make it out of the group stage of the CONCACAF Champions League that year, ending their run with a 1–0 loss away to Santos Laguna on October 24.

Four days later, away against the Columbus Crew, TFC would sputter out of the MLS season with a 2–1 loss.

With 23 points in 34 games, TFC would finish dead last in MLS. They would give up an astounding 62 goals on the season, the most in MLS. "I've never had a season like this," midfielder Eric Avila told the Canadian Press.

During the October 6 1–0 loss at home to D.C. United, with a recorded attendance of just 15,281, some fans wore paper bags over their heads in protest of MLSE and their lack of soccer vision. But it was during that October 6 visit from D.C. United that Tom Anselmi began his exit from TFC.

Kevin Payne, then president and CEO of D.C. United, was in attendance at BMO Field and met with Anselmi during the game. "We were two friends discussing his issues with TFC," said Payne. "He was looking for a solution."

Payne had established himself as one of the premier executives in MLS. He had two stints as president and CEO of D.C. United, from 1994 to

2001 and then again from 2004 to 2012. The club won four MLS Cups during that time and Payne could be considered something of a visionary in the early days of MLS.

The futility of the 2012 season was not lost on Payne. "Even from the outside, it was pretty obvious their roster was a mess," he said.

What struck Payne was how, as president of MLSE, Anselmi had so much more on his plate than just running TFC. And at the end of the club's worst season to date, it became obvious to Payne that Anselmi needed help.

> I did think that TFC seemed to suffer from lack of [a]
> coherent plan. It seemed that they had changed direction
> a number of times and there wasn't a lot of consistency in
> their approach. Tom was looking for someone with a great
> deal of experience and success in soccer. He originally just
> called me for recommendations. The more we talked, and
> I don't remember which one of us said it first, it became
> evident that what he was looking for was someone with
> my type of experience.

Part of what appealed to Anselmi about Payne's plan was that he wanted to bring some of the spotlight *off* TFC. Anselmi liked that Payne "wanted to retreat, not be as bold." By building better off the pitch and not making big name splashes in the overseas signing market Payne could temper expectations surrounding the club and then could properly meet them.

In short, the club was frustrated at how this MLS venture had continually gone off the rails, and that frustration led, in part, to the original discussions with Payne. MLSE liked the fact that Payne had a proven track record in the league, even if it meant dialling back the hopes of a club already starved for success.

The discussions to have Payne come in were relatively quick, and he was eventually unveiled as president of the club on November 28. "The only constant in life is change," said Payne at his press conference, immediately speaking in the kind of vernacular that TFC supporters would understand. "I believed the club needed to create a culture and a way of doing things internally," he said. Payne recalls a commonly used motto at

D.C. United that he tried to bring to TFC: "Do a better job today than you did the day before."

He tried to bring that mentality to TFC: "I wanted to create a mentality that we would never rest until we established TFC as a standard for excellence within the league."

But not everyone bought into the plan. The CBC published a scathing piece, calling TFC's continued attempts to trot out new solutions to the continued problem of poor results "so played out."

"I'm not so cynical to think that Toronto's hiring of Kevin Payne to front its soccer operations as president isn't a solution of sorts — it is — but I'm not foolish enough to think either that this can yet be declared a way forward," wrote the CBC's Ben Rycroft.

> Payne is one man. He is one man in an organization that took six full seasons of losing to discover that they needed to hire a president who knew a little something about this game called soccer.
>
> Yes, Tom Anselmi was the de facto president for most of those years, but as he has admitted on a number of occasions, it has been a "learning process" for them. Which, if you're trying to decipher press-conference-speak, means "lost in the woods."

Even Paul Mariner admitted that it was time for the club to, yet again, rebuild: "Absolutely," he told the Canadian Press after a late-season training session when asked about the prospect of a rebuild. "We've asked too much of the young players, to learn on the job. Then when we started to get hit by so many key injuries to key players, it's very, very hard for them to continue."

In failing to stick with a unified vision, or even create a sense of unity among top-ranking employees, TFC took a step back at a time when they should have been progressing.

As much as the 2012 calendar year began with a sense of stability for the club, the year drew to a close with many more questions than answers. And it was looking less and less like fans had much more patience to hear the answers anyway.

8

Pep Guardiola in Waiting, Surprise at Just One Point, and the Two Tims — Leiweke and Bezbatchenko

JOHN MOLINARO COULD ONLY SHAKE his head. He was sitting in the press conference room of BMO Field, as he had for countless other personnel unveilings, with each one bringing a new sense of hope. As one of the very few reporters who had covered the team since their inception and was still grinding out stories about them and their seemingly endless stream of losses and personnel turnovers, Molinaro had had a front row seat to every turn, sometimes inept, Toronto FC had made in franchise history. And he had tried to give every single move a fair opportunity.

But every man has his breaking point. And on January 8, 2013, the normally calm and reserved Molinaro hit his. For all the seven coaches that had manned TFC through its six seasons, he'd never seen one that both had never coached professionally before and was unsure when he would even join the team.

It was all he, and perhaps others around him, could do not to laugh when new TFC president Kevin Payne welcomed Ryan Nelsen as the club's eighth head coach. The 35-year-old New Zealand–born defender had been a mainstay in the Premier League with three different clubs, including the one he was then still under contract to, Queen's Park Rangers. Early rumours of Nelsen joining TFC as a player had been welcomed, but when Payne informed Molinaro and the other reporters that, given his current contract as a player at QPR, the club were "not sure when he'll join us," skepticism gave way to exasperation.

Even though Payne pointed to the hiring of Piotr Nowak in 2004, who had no coaching experience but would go on to win the MLS Cup that season, as proof of his eye for talented prospective coaches, the well of good will had finally run dry.

"They were making it sound like he was Pep Guardiola in waiting," said Molinaro, still shaking his head years later at the hiring of a coach without any coaching experience.

Payne had originally been hired as the club's first-ever president with the intent of developing a standard of excellence within a club that had been marked by losing seasons and turnover. He lauded Nelsen's leadership skills, having captained D.C. United, Blackburn Rovers, and the New Zealand national team at the 2010 FIFA World Cup. But with TFC's training camp set to begin in a matter of weeks, and their regular season beginning in two months, both of which fell within the QPR regular season, it was hard to see this move as a step in the right direction.

A year earlier, TFC had been preparing to enter the season with a coach who had managed arguably Europe's top academy. And yet despite Payne having preached a more low-key approach to building a successful club, his splash-down had alienated many fans and reporters who were already bewildered by the humiliating 2012 season. "It's a huge gamble, as TFC have done the rookie coach thing a lot, never with any great success," wrote Duncan Fletcher of the TFC blog *Waking the Red*.

TSN soccer analyst Jason de Vos called it "without a doubt, the most bizarre coaching appointment ever made in Major League Soccer."

For his part, Nelsen was always very interested in coaching and wanted to "dip his toe in" to see if he even liked the profession. He had been offered assistant coaching roles in Europe but eventually came around to Payne's offer, the only one extended from the club, of the coaching position. Nelsen had experienced success with D.C. United and had been part of the MLS Cup run in 2004.

"Do you continue to develop as an assistant or do you just grab the bull by the horns?" said Nelsen.

Some of the team's veterans remained optimistic. "He had the right attributes as a player that you think could translate into coaching," said Dunfield.

Nelsen felt he understood the league, its players, and how to turn around an MLS club dealing with the intricacies of the salary cap. QPR had offered him an extension on his contract, but, at 35, mentally he had already moved on from the idea of playing.

He was ready for a new challenge. And despite the confusion of when that challenge would actually begin, he could not be faulted for a lack of ambition. "You could tell with TFC that you had to roll your sleeves up and that it wasn't going to be pretty," said Nelsen. "And that was the fun part of it. I liked that it was a real turnaround."

Once he arrived and started training sessions, Nelsen established himself as a player's coach. Understanding the life of a player, he worked to treat every player under him with equal and unbounded respect. He would routinely bring every player, not just veteran players, into video sessions.

Training sessions were built heavily on playing and competing, even if they lacked technical precision at times. To unleash his own competitive edge, which he was still battling to quell in light of his recent retirement, it wasn't uncommon to see Nelsen jump into drills and small-sided games. "And he was one of the best players," said goalkeeper Joe Bendik, who had arrived at the club before the season.

Players stood in awe of him and his working on the pitch, instead of directing from the sidelines. It was clear to the team that Nelsen was still very much a player.

"I couldn't believe how soft and silky he was," said Dunfield. "I thought he was a big centre-back that just hit the ball."

Nelsen quickly established a typical English 4-4-2 formation for the club and wanted TFC to sit a touch deeper than many other teams, be difficult to break down defensively, and then hit teams on the counterattack. Even if his training sessions lacked consistency and cohesiveness, according to some players, Nelsen raised the bar with the kind of intensive approach he'd grown accustomed to in England. "There was no hiding from him in sessions," said one former player.

Nelsen took a particular shine to young players, working to provide them with guidance about the realities of being a professional abroad.

Doneil Henry, who had been a player of perpetual potential through his time developing in the academy and under different first-team coaches, remembers Nelsen pulling him aside during a training session. He posed a unique, but altogether practical question to Henry: "What do you want from football?"

Henry had never been asked this once throughout his promising career. When he replied that he wanted to play in Europe, Nelsen told him that now was the time. He got him to start taking risks in his career and dreaming of a life beyond his own backyard. The 20-year-old Henry left the conversation with a completely different perspective and began shifting his goals toward a career abroad. Eventually, after a brief stint in Cyprus, Henry landed with Premier League side West Ham United after a recommendation from Nelsen to then West Ham manager Sam Allardyce.

Henry's time in West Ham would prove fruitless, but the confidence Nelsen instilled in him was something that was sometimes lacking during his time at TFC.

"That's when everything started to change for me," reflects Henry, of his conversation with Nelsen.

Not everyone was impressed by Nelsen's first training camp.

Kevin Payne looked at the current crop in camp and didn't believe they were MLS-calibre players. "We [meaning his players] were kind of joking — being paid to go to the gym, now how hard is that?" Payne said in February 2013. "Most people have to spend money to go to the gym and shoe-horn it into their schedule. There's just no excuse for it. In D.C., we didn't accept it and there was an enormous level of peer pressure brought to bear on guys that showed up unfit, and we need to get to that point here. That's not the case right now. I didn't see any evidence of that within the locker room."

Payne came to his final conclusion: many of the players had taken their foot off the gas after they had been eliminated from the playoffs the previous season. "And that, to me, suggested an issue with the culture of the club," he said.

One of the first conversations Payne had with a member of the squad was with DP Eric Hassli, who he believed to be 40 pounds overweight at the start of training camp. Hassli's short stint in Toronto the previous season had not gone according to plan, and immediately Hassli broke down in tears in front of Payne, telling him that his wife would not return to Toronto for another season. "That was my second day on the job," said Payne. "I looked around and said, 'How did this happen? How did his contract get renewed?'"

Instead of building the club in the vision he wanted, focusing on the use of dynamic players largely from South America, Payne recalls trying to get out of contracts that would hamper TFC moving forward. "We had the worst salary cap situation in the history of the league when I arrived there," said Payne. "We had three Designated Players, and not one of them at the time was capable of stepping on the field."

Payne used the one buyout he was allowed on Frings, who would retire in February. The GM then did himself no favours from the outside by flipping Joao Plata, arguably the most promising player in the club's roster, to Real Salt Lake for a second-round pick in the 2015 MLS SuperDraft. Plata had an option in his contract that dictated if he scored 10 goals in the 2013 season, TFC would have to dole out over $1 million, money they didn't have in their current salary cap situation. Plata would go on to score four goals in MLS in 2013 and 13 the following season.

"He had potential to be a great player but not one of the players we wanted to be one of our three Designated Players," said Payne. His goal was simply to become cap compliant and earn some extra allocation money.

Payne considered trading Hassli and his $790,000 guaranteed compensation to FC Dallas for a second-round SuperDraft pick one of his finer moves. "We were completely upside down on that deal," said Payne.

That Payne's early time with the club was largely spent dismantling and rebuilding the roster had limited his ability to exercise the vision he had for the club. "We spent as much time talking about what we were going to have available to us in 2014 as we did talking about trying to win a few more games in 2013," he said.

The continued turnover without anything tangible in return cast a dark cloud over the club before the season had even started. And Nelsen's hands were tied, given that he had to return to play for Queen's Park Rangers intermittently through training camp. That drew the ire of veteran players like Darren O'Dea. "It was a strange one and I wasn't happy with it. I was used to big clubs with big, rich histories and I'm used to professional things being done," he said. Like many, O'Dea was able to get over the fact that Nelsen had never coached before, given his pedigree and quality as a player. But the fact that he was not available throughout training, coupled with the frustration at assistant coach Fran O'Leary's inability to deliver messages to the team properly, got the team off on the wrong foot. Coaching and management had failed to consider many of the details necessary in running the club, most notably a comprehensive plan for training.

Concerns from the players fell on deaf ears. "For me, there was no focal point to communicate with," said O'Dea.

The lack of a comprehensive training camp showed in the team's early season results. They won just two of their first 20 games, effectively eliminating themselves from MLS playoff contention by midsummer. They had failed to score in nine of those games and would eventually finish with the third-worst goal differential in MLS and fourth-worst in franchise history, which was a feat in itself.

To Nelsen, their place in the standings was reflective of the hand he'd been dealt: "Ultimately, I was surprised we even got one point."

He looked around at other MLS squads at that point and felt TFC was "nowhere near where an MLS club should be." He had arrived in Toronto wanting to conquer the mountain many had failed on previously and to change the culture of the club. "But ultimately, you're going to war with a toy gun," he said.

Nelsen realized during the summer that the club would not make the playoffs. Instead of opening up to local media about what he wanted to do with TFC moving forward, he kept his plans to himself. Bruised by his treatment from the unforgiving media in England, he refused to engage with those who wanted answers. His approach was symptomatic of a larger problem that engulfed the club throughout 2013: if there was a plan for the club's direction, it was never communicated. Many club employees felt they were walking aimlessly through the season. Many employees at the time called it a toxic workplace, full of personnel considering nothing beyond their own personal career options.

Gone was the hustle and ambition that a start-up franchise usually has. The novelty had disappeared. With Winter's plan for a franchise built on young Canadian talent diminishing in the rear-view mirror, it had become difficult for fans to connect with the current lineup. And without household names for the franchise to hang their hat on, the long constant that TFC could always bank on — a strong and vibrant home crowd — had also dissipated. The club's 2013 average attendance fell to 18,131, the lowest in franchise history.

All the happiness had been sucked out. "It's draining, keeping everyone positive," said Nelsen.

Even the sure wins for the club were no more. Having won the previous four Canadian Championships, TFC entered the 2013 tournament with expectations of another strong finish. And a 2–0 win at BMO Field in the first leg of the semifinals over the Montreal Impact provided some promise.

One week later, TFC travelled to Montreal for the second leg. Disappointed with how his usual starting 11 had been performing, Nelsen gave many unexpected players a shot in his starting lineup, including recent academy grad and local product Jonathan Osorio and newcomers Danny Califf and Ryan Richter. Nelsen had to see what kind of cards he was now holding.

If 2009 had provided a Miracle in Montreal, 2013 was more akin to a massacre: one goal after another, the Impact picked apart TFC and their hopes for a return to the CONCACAF Champions League. By the time the beatdown was over, TFC had lost 6–0 to their archrivals.

No loss had so comprehensively summarized every failure of the club's entire existence: the club could not score. They could not deliver when it mattered most. "Under pressure, under stress, some of them melted," said Nelsen. And, perhaps most ominously, no one would accept the blame.

"You learn a lot of things," said Nelsen of the loss. As a former player, he was struck by how many "screamers and yellers" there were on the field making a stink, but only for themselves. When they had the ball at their feet, Nelsen found his loudest players didn't back up their words with action. In the dressing room after the game, Nelsen saw more of the same: veteran players who had given up on the pitch were the quickest to start pointing the finger.

Throughout the past few seasons, TFC fans and those within the club had balanced the club's poor results in MLS with the reassurance that there would be another tournament, in which single victories held more weight and the promise of upsetting bigger clubs on their own turf was something of a life raft. Now, robbed of that prospect, many within the club saw that loss as the lowest moment in the club's existence to that point. Danny Koevermans may have said TFC were setting a record as the worst team in the world the previous May. A year later, his prediction had come true.

Nelsen boarded the bus out of the Stade Saputo concerned less with the short-term loss and more about what type of characters he wanted to bring to the team after. That putrid way of thinking that had become a constant in 2013 at the KIA Training Ground had been just as evident on the pitch. "That whole season was a lesson in who could be at TFC for the next five years," said Nelsen.

Tim Leiweke arrived in late April 2013, and he will never forget the look on Jaime McMillan's face. Leiweke was already in the middle of cleaning house at Toronto FC when McMillan, the director of team operations, walked into his office with a face as long as the club's list of losses. "We're embarrassed to tell people where we work," Leiweke remembers her saying.

As the newly hired president and CEO of MLSE, Leiweke had been brought in to deliver stability and success to franchises that sorely lacked it. Having served as the president and CEO of Anschutz Entertainment Group, which maintains ownership either totally or in part of three sports franchises that had won 10 championships under his 17-year watch, Leiweke had the results to back up his boastful, aggressive demeanour. He had made a career of getting what he wanted and delivering results, doing so with a seemingly endless supply of charm delivered through an almost enchanting Midwestern accent. ("Was he charming?" I put to a TFC employee. "He pisses [charm]," they replied.)

Leiweke believed successful franchises had to have four key elements: a great fan base, a vibrant market, resources and an ownership willing to spend, and finally, a talented leadership team of people who are like-minded and ambitious.

It was that final component that, in Leiweke's eyes, was lacking at TFC. So Leiweke, the self-described "glutton for punishment who likes to turn things around," got to work.

"We're going to be just fine," he assured McMillan. "We're going to get this right."

Leiweke spent his first months observing how the club operated. What he saw was a club that had become isolationist, beaten down by years of losses on the pitch and reluctant to open the doors to yet another salesman passing through with a plan tucked in his briefcase. So much so that Leiweke saw a club not utilizing the resources they already had that could set them apart in MLS. "They wanted to be separated from Maple Leaf Sports and Entertainment and many within Maple Leaf Sports and Entertainment wanted nothing to do with TFC because they saw it as a very strong negative," said Leiweke.

To Leiweke, as important as Payne's experience in MLS had been, he saw an executive whose "heart wasn't really into it" and as to direction, the club was in an ocean with no direction and, to Leiweke, "no real purpose."

Payne had previously worked under Leiweke at AEG, as managing director of AEG soccer, originally tasked with six different MLS clubs as part of the league's fledging ownership approach. Payne was well aware of Leiweke's ambition, and tried to quell that ambition in one of their first meetings in Toronto. "One of the great things about Toronto was that we didn't necessarily need to spend crazy sums of money on big name players to be successful," Payne remembers telling Leiweke. He believed the club's audience was sophisticated enough to appreciate good soccer for what it was, and if the team had success, they would support it whether that included household names or not. "And that's not the way Tim wanted to do things."

While Payne wanted to build slowly and methodically with the hopes of long-term success, he saw Leiweke as an executive driven by immediate success and splashes in the market. "If you think of the club like the Charlie Brown Christmas tree, we want to be careful that we don't hang a big, shiny ornament on the tree just to see it droop down to the ground," said Payne.

And that tempered approach from the top of the food chain eventually bled into TFC's identity as a club and what they could become. Leiweke believed Payne's approach had undermined the work put in every day by all the employees clamouring for direction. "And I think that scared everyone away except for me," he said. "I loved it. I saw it as an opportunity to get it right."

Leiweke began by trying to get his employees to rediscover that hustle of a start-up that had defined the club early in its existence. "The culture was defined by the people that had always been there," he said. "We kind of got back to the culture that had been there in the early years, but with an infrastructure and a leadership on the team side that allowed us ultimately to succeed."

Next, Leiweke wanted to ensure that the club's fans, the first element of his four-part plan for a successful franchise, weren't going anywhere. In one-on-one meetings with fans, Leiweke found that they wanted what every fan ultimately wants: a team that was fun to watch, competitive, worth the time, energy, and money they were spending. The temperature of the fans was, after all, at an all-time low.

Leiweke tried then to remind fans that MLSE was taking TFC and everything they encompassed seriously. The resounding sentiment was that the club had been mishandled for years by Anselmi. Though Leiweke readily stuck up for Anselmi, believing his heart was in the right place, he understood why he was "taking a shellacking." Soccer, in Leiweke's view, was "not his area of expertise."

"He didn't know what to do, and that's how it became kind of a stand-alone," said Leiweke. "It was a different business organization. There was a feeling that [TFC] wanted independence. There was no pride of author-ship. The fans were very angry and felt like the problem was MLSE."

He consistently reinforced his belief that the club's greatest asset was MLSE's money and resources at their beck and call and that the fans now had a person in charge with experience with a successful soccer club.

To convince fans that ownership was serious about the club's success, he began leaning on MLSE to begin heavily investing in the club. At first, his requests came as a surprise to those who had hired him. "I think the ownership group was focused on what you'd expect the ownership group to be focused on at the time, which was the Leafs, first and foremost," said Leiweke. The Leafs had just qualified for the playoffs for the first time since 2004, and he saw newfound energy and hope in the team, even if it was, in his mind, slightly misguided. But still, Leiweke knew what he was up against: "It's hockey in Canada. Two of the three partners were distribution partners."

The Leafs' success, unsustainable as it was, was actually a blessing in disguise for Leiweke. It allowed him to keep his hands off of the Leafs for a year to let them continue on their path untouched and meet their own destiny, and Larry Tanenbaum and the MLSE board were easily convinced to let Leiweke turn his focus and attention toward TFC and the Raptors. "I don't want to say they [TFC] were being ignored," said Leiweke, "but they were not the priority."

Leiweke changed that. He wanted the club to make a splash and to utilize MLSE's financial resources in a way they never had previously. "[Larry Tanenbaum] was very good, he believed in the vision," said Leiweke. "He knew [TFC] were trying to set the tone for the rest of the organization."

After all, Leiweke had already laid the groundwork for big spending on big players during his original meetings with MLSE before he was hired. "If I come knocking on your door for a DP, will you spend the money?" he had asked Rogers CEO Nadir Mohamed and George Cope of Bell. When they affirmed in the positive, he followed up. "Okay, well, here's the real question. If I come asking for two DP's, will you spend the money?"

Though the board originally shuffled in their seats, Leiweke insisted that's "how you prove you can win at all costs."

MLSE agreed and gave Leiweke licence to operate the way he always has: without borders of any sort.

Whereas Payne wanted to operate quietly and not bring any extra attention to a club that had been maligned for years, Leiweke wanted to do just the opposite. He wanted everyone within and around the club to use their original ambition as a spark to think bigger than they ever had. "I like taking things and getting beaten because that's what you want to do: rejuvenate franchises that are on the down," he said.

Toronto FC were preparing to depart for a cross-continent journey to Portland ahead of a 4–0 loss to the Timbers when Leiweke fired Payne after less than a year on the job. His vision never matched Leiweke's ambition after he determined that Payne "wasn't there full-time."

"I could kind of feel it coming," said Payne. "I'm not going to pretend that I wasn't angry, disappointed, and bitter. I understood that Tim wanted to do things differently. I disagree with the way he wanted to do them, but he was the one that was given the position at the top of MLSE."

David Miller was still a season-seat holder and sent an open letter to MLSE, decrying the firing of Payne as yet another sign of ineptitude from ownership. He noted in his letter that "There once was magic at BMO Field. The latest reshuffle has made the possibility of that magic returning almost certainly disappear."

He also returned the last of his season tickets for 2013 in an envelope.

"For me, that was the last straw," said Miller. "MLSE had demonstrated a lack of competence and a tin ear to the supporters. We wanted hope. We wanted someone like Kevin Payne, who had a vision and said how we were going to have hope. He provided the building blocks."

And his fellow fans agreed. "Until very recently," said Miller, "almost every day, I would get stopped by someone to say 'Thank you for sending that letter. I was thinking the exact same thing but nobody would listen to me.'"

Miller believed that TFC differed from its MLSE peers in that "soccer clubs came out of communities." And because of this, it was imperative that MLSE get back to the business of understanding what the club's suffering fans were going through. "It's like [TFC fans] own the club, even though we technically don't own it," said Miller. "People felt so strongly about the club but they didn't have a forum to speak out about it. The club needs to respond to us, because it's our club."

By mid-September, Leiweke had gutted the club while simultaneously believing they could grow exponentially in a short amount of time. "If you want to be great, you have to make tough decisions and build a culture with people who understand what you want to do," he said.

At 29, Tim Bezbatchenko began working as the MLS senior director of player relations and competition almost immediately after graduating from law school. And just as quickly, he was familiarized with one of the league's least successful clubs. Working with two other colleagues, his group had to divvy up the teams they'd be responsible for directly working with. Given that Bezbatchenko was the rookie on the team, there was some backroom collusion at play and the young lawyer was dealt a rough hand: three clubs that collectively were not the most successful at that point and also not the easiest to work with, including Toronto FC.

Bezbatchenko knew there would be challenges in his new role, but approached it with wide-eyed optimism. Still, during his first season, 2010, when one of Mo Johnston's proposed trades could not be pushed through because of a technicality that probably should have been vetted on the team's end, he gained a better understanding on the state of the club and their desire for continuous turnover. "There was a culture of change at Toronto FC," he said.

Years later, Bezbatchenko sat on his couch in his Long Island home and watched TFC advance to the CONCACAF Champions League semi-final. Instead of being overjoyed at an MLS club that had very little success otherwise go deep in an international competition, Bezbatchenko was frustrated. He had gotten to where he was by not being afraid to go against the grain and think outside of popular opinion. To Bezbatchenko, the club's Champions League run only perpetuated the course that TFC had been on and held them off from a full-scale audit of the club's goals. "It put lipstick on a pig," he said, tugging at his fashionable glasses and quickly scratching his thin beard. "It didn't force TFC to look into a mirror."

Bezbatchenko freely admits his assessment of the club was made from the "ivory tower of the league office," but he was still enamoured by TFC's potential. He knew the support was there, as evidenced by the routinely high attendance figures. He knew the city, one of the most diverse in the region, was ready for a winning team. And, while he might not have realized it, sitting in New York, hundreds of miles away from BMO Field, he was already formulating a plan for TFC to follow.

"Their success (in the Champions League) was at the cost of the success of the club in MLS," which Bezbatchenko felt needed to be the backbone of the club.

Less than a year later, Bezbatchenko's rise through the MLS ranks was impossible to ignore. He'd gained expertise with the league's complicated salary caps, including negotiating and drafting player contracts and arranging transfers for players coming to and going from MLS. He knew the ins and outs of the entire MLS player pool and each team's salary cap status.

In his time with the league, he'd furthered his belief that homegrown players are the future of the league and had brought forth a number of initiatives to ramp up the signing of homegrown players.

And, perhaps not coincidentally, these were areas of concern for Payne and TFC, so it only made sense that in the spring of 2013 Payne casually gauged Bezbatchenko's interest in becoming the club's assistant general manager. The two had become familiar through the league's competition department, but Bezbatchenko assumed it was nothing more than a friendly offer and didn't give it a second thought.

But on Labour Day, the interest from TFC was confirmed: Bezbatchenko received a call from Todd Durbin, the league's executive vice-president of competition and player relations. Durbin was a mentor of Bezbatchenko's and informed him that he was on the short list of candidates for the TFC's GM job.

Leiweke believed the person tasked with building the current incarnation of TFC needed to be a "capologist," have an analytical mind on player evaluation and, above all, be a person who was not afraid to have huge aspirations to acquire huge players to achieve the goals.

"Tim was all of the above," said Leiweke, affectionately calling him a "cap geek." "He's as smart as there is in the league on managing money, resources, and all of the aspects of the job."

Don Garber had also watched Bezbatchenko grow as an executive, just as the league itself had. "Soccer is a difficult sport to understand," he said. "The idiosyncrasies of a global player pool and the unique structure of MLS make it different from the NHL and the NBA."

Because MLS was still such a young league, it was impossible for the early hires to have grown with the league. But by now Bezbatchenko had, and he had seen the league come into its own.

"People have experience in player personnel and other aspects that allow you to be better and faster than when TFC first started," said Garber, of Bezbatchenko.

Durbin and Bezbatchenko discussed the costs and risks of joining TFC, focusing on all the coaches and GMs the club had gone through. Still, Durbin mentioned how important it would be that, if Bezbatchenko would make the jump out of the league office, he would be going to a club with tremendous resources.

During Leiweke and Bezbatchenko's first meeting, at e11even restaurant near the Air Canada Centre, Bezbatchenko got a sense not just of

TFC's resources, but how tremendous life at the club could be. "We have the potential to be great," Leiweke told him. He pointed to his time at AEG and how he was not afraid to take risks, and after seeing the failures of other leagues, believed that this league would be driven by teams at the top and clubs like TFC had a responsibility to continue pushing the league forward. Leiweke was adamant that he had approval from the MLSE board to go after players the likes of which MLS had never seen before. That approval was part of the reason Leiweke had originally come to MLSE, as the board's vision matched his own. Bigger was better, and Leiweke was daring the normally pragmatic Bezbatchenko to think big as well.

Leiweke told Bezbatchenko that while they would work together on acquiring marketable Designated Players, he would task Bezbatchenko with being the best in the league at drafting, player development, trading, and scouting. At the time, scouting usually fell to a club's assistant coaches. But understanding Bezbatchenko's propensity to think outside the box, Leiweke wanted to utilize that approach in the scouting department.

Yet it was with their Designated Player acquisitions that Leiweke wanted to make the biggest splash. He was so engrossed in signing big name players, he wanted to dive in immediately. During the initial phone conversations, Leiweke instructed Bezbatchenko to prepare a report on possible DP's to acquire.

Leiweke himself didn't have a list, but he had asked Nelsen to submit a list of targeted names, which included Italian strikers Rolando Bianchi, Alberto Gilardino, and then Chelsea legend Frank Lampard. Leiweke wanted two players, either two forwards or a forward and a midfielder, and was largely concerned with how the two players would work together.

Before arriving in Toronto, Leiweke had asked Bezbatchenko to prepare a report on what direction he would take TFC. Bezbatchenko spent 48 hours, missing his son's first birthday party in the process, creating the report.

It was, fitting to Bezbatchenko's personality, an analytically-driven and process-oriented plan. That approach resonated with MLSE Chairman Larry Tanenbaum, and Leiweke was also struck by his vision, save for one element: his Designated Player recommendation.

Now, Bezbatchenko was well aware that Leiweke had been pivotal in bringing David Beckham to MLS, which had shifted the landscape of the entire league. So, he also reached for the stars and suggested the dynamic Swedish forward Zlatan Ibrahimovic, who was then plying his trade at Paris Saint-Germain and would go on to be ranked third in the *Guardian*'s influential Best Footballers of the Year list at the end of 2013.

Given TFC's place at the bottom of the league standings, their lack of success in the past, and Ibrahimovic's flair for the dramatic, it was perhaps even a more drastic pitch than the Beckham play years earlier.

But Leiweke's response? "I don't love your answer."

From a marketing standpoint, as well as how he could impact TFC on the pitch, Bezbatchenko believed Ibrahimovic was a perfect fit. He wondered if he had either overshot the mark or hadn't sold the player well enough, and he secretly wondered if Leiweke was familiar with Ibrahimovic.

Turns out, it was neither. As much as David Beckham taught Leiweke about star players, Robbie Keane taught him even more. Leiweke believes Keane doesn't get enough respect and attention for what he did to boost MLS's profile. "Robbie Keane was the guy that turned L.A. into the greatest team ever," said Leiweke. "He was the juice. He created that culture. There was an energy, excitement, and enthusiasm and confidence with Robbie Keane that was so refreshing. I knew we had to find guys like that: guys who wanted to be part of the organization and … didn't want to ultimately be in retirement mode."

At the time, Leiweke believed Ibrahimovic might have treated MLS as more of a victory lap and less of a place to invest his time in a project. "You don't build around guys like that," said Leiweke of Ibrahimovic, who would eventually sign with the Galaxy in 2018 at 36 after a string of injuries and not gaining any playing time with Manchester United.

"You've got to find people committed to the vision and what you're trying to build," said Leiweke. "You have to find people who have fangs and ultimately a chip on their shoulders. And they relish, and I mean relish, the chance to go to do something special."

Leiweke would assure Bezbatchenko that finding franchise-altering DPs was possible, but he needed to shift his thinking. Leiweke sent him off to write another report to deliver in 72 hours.

This was not how the normally logical Bezbatchenko operated, but Leiweke's own charisma and faith in the project compelled him. On the morning of September 20, the Bezbatchenkos' wedding anniversary, he flew to Toronto to announce that he was becoming TFC's next GM.

He knew that most executives now say they need a few months to evaluate their new companies, but he already knew what he wanted to accomplish, and that allowed him a little levity and presence. Bezbatchenko felt confident in Leiweke's vision and that he had the support of ownership via Leiweke.

Ahead of his first-ever press conference, he received a brief five minutes of media training from TFC's head of media relations, Mike Masaro. It was fast, fun, and exactly what life under Leiweke is like.

Just seconds before Bezbatchenko walked onstage to introduce the umpteenth vision for TFC, Leiweke turned to him. He had gone out on a limb for Bezbatchenko, the unproven "soccer wonk," and Leiweke wanted to make sure Bezbatchenko would be able to prove to one of the biggest markets in the league that he was making the right move. With a slight grin, Leiweke offered him a brief piece of advice: "Don't fuck me."

"If I'm going to exist under Tim Leiweke, I'm going to have to adapt my behaviours to exist in a Tim Leiweke world," said Bezbatchenko. He wanted to be mentored by one of the most successful executives in MLS history and someone who pushes people to their professional limits. As uncomfortable as it would make Bezbatchenko, he was now fully on board and ready to "live on the edge."

Easier said than done.

One of his earliest moves was meant to shore up the player-development side of the club, a task that Leiweke had charged Bezbatchenko with but also one that he held near and dear. In came Greg Vanney as the assistant general manager and academy director. During his time as academy director at Real Salt Lake, Vanney had helped establish the first-ever MLS residential academy in the country and pushed Real Salt Lake toward the forefront of player development in MLS. Vanney, like Bezbatchenko, was a former player, having logged 13 years across MLS and in France while also spending time on the American national team.

"Greg was a smart, young player who was always curious about the game," said former teammate and future assistant coach Robin Fraser. Vanney had been quiet in the L.A. Galaxy locker room and by doing little besides going about his business and doing it well, he had quickly ingratiated himself with the club's veterans.

Still largely reserved now, but not afraid to show off his intellectual approach to the game, Vanney, like Bezbatchenko, wanted to find players who could make a habit of playing the game "between their ears" and considered every tactical nuance on the pitch and every opportunity to develop mentally off of it.

While there was pressure to win immediately on the first team, Vanney did not have those immediate pressures. But he did have Bezbatchenko's ear when it came to mapping out the first team's plan for success. "My role was looking at the academy, looking at the path for the future, trying to add things within academy structure, assessing players, and also at the first team, figuring out where it's all going," said Vanney.

The two men would have conversations about how TFC should be viewed, and they both agreed: the club should attack the ball and play a style of soccer that would keep fans coming back year after year. "It's about longevity," Vanney recalled of his early pitches to Bezbatchenko.

This was not the first time a newcomer at TFC had pitched a plan that would take time. As much as Vanney believed player development through the academy model could create sustainable success, Bezbatchenko knew he was working for a man who preferred banging results out of the table with his fist. "There's a good chance I won't make it a year," he remembers thinking.

Bezbatchenko, Leiweke, and Vanney were on the clock.

So, to both keep a fan base that was turning on the club and to buy Vanney some time, Bezbatchenko swung again, and together with Leiweke, they landed on a player who would alter the course of TFC history.

9

Energy, Vision, and the Bloody Big Bust

TIM LEIWEKE WALKED INTO THE downtown Toronto offices of Budweiser Canada, unsure of what to expect. Since arriving as the president and CEO of Maple Leafs Sports and Entertainment in April 2013, he'd gone against the grain and arranged meetings with the partners and sponsors of all four MLSE sports franchises. He wanted to hear what they believed the organization was doing right, and where it was misstepping, despite many around him telling him that inviting such comment wasn't worth the risk.

Budweiser, a global brand in their own right, was not partnered with MLSE's bigger properties, only with TFC. To say they were a valuable partner would be an understatement.

"All right, let me have it," said Leiweke, his loud Midwestern accent bouncing off the office walls. Given his charm that can stretch around a block, many find it tough not to cozy up to him immediately. "How are we doing?"

The Budweiser executives had no trouble whatsoever telling him how they felt: terrible. They believed the TFC sponsorship deal, incredibly important to the club, was one of the worst deals they'd ever made. Nothing had turned out the way the beer conglomerate thought it would.

They continued to pile on: all the expectations they had, and the commitment MLSE had made, had fallen through. In short, Budweiser believed nothing was working. They gave Leiweke, MLSE COO Dave Hopkinson, and vice-president of corporate partnerships Jeff Deline an earful for half an hour.

"They were right," said Leiweke. Budweiser weren't selling beer because of TFC and they were associated with a product they weren't proud of.

Leiweke, a self-described glutton for punishment who likes to "turn things around," did just that. Once Budweiser had finished reading them something close to the riot act, Leiweke outlined his grand plan for how things would be different under Leiweke, and soon enough, TFC would be great. He had begun his tenure by challenging everyone, not just at TFC, but at MLSE, to ask themselves why, quite simply, they couldn't be great.

Leiweke told them that if by the end of the year they didn't feel better about their partnership, he would let them out of their sponsorship deal. Hopkinson squirmed, reminding Leiweke that the beneficial sponsorship still had another two years left on the contract. "It's the right thing to do," said Leiweke.

He ended with a promise dripping with braggadocio. "We'll never have to have this type of meeting again," he said. "I swear to you." He walked out of the meeting onto Queen's Quay with Hopkinson and Deline and, still dripping with self-confidence, looked each of them in the eye, and promised that they'd never again have to sit quietly while another sponsor unleashed frustration on them the way Budweiser did about TFC. "Bet the house on it," said Leiweke. "We're in this together. Whatever it takes, whatever we have to do, we're going to turn it around."

It was hard for those around him not to buy in to Leiweke's belief that greatness could exist in a space that it never had previously. It would have been even harder to imagine just how different the club would look once Leiweke was finished with it.

By October, Leiweke, Bezbatchenko, and Nelsen had settled on a small list of DP targets that ticked all their boxes. The majority of them were in Europe, so the three men travelled across the Atlantic to London and Italy to sell their vision of the future of the club.

Early on, it became clear that Bezbatchenko and Nelsen did not see eye to eye on where the club was headed from a philosophical standpoint. They were different personalities: Bezbatchenko, the pragmatic, analytically inclined thinker, and Nelsen, the roll-up-your-sleeves-and-dig-in fixer. "There was no chemistry between those two," said Leiweke.

The relationship was complicated by a lack of experience on both ends: Nelsen still had next to no experience as a coach, and while Bezbatchenko was well-versed in how the league operated, he was still lacking practical experience in how to run a club. As both shared their visions, neither had the luxury of simply being able to start an argument with "Well, what I've done in the past with success was …!"

Leiweke sat back and watched. He was not surprised, and he was fine with them not being the best of friends for now. There were, after all, much more pressing priorities; namely, wooing one of the most prolific goal-scorers of one of the biggest clubs in England.

The three men had arrived at Jermain Defoe as the man who could lead TFC to greener pastures. He'd scored 141 goals in all competitions for Tottenham Hotspur since 2003 and, despite a brief two-year stop at Portsmouth, had become the legendary London club's fifth all-time leading goal-scorer. Defoe had international experience, as well, scoring the lone goal in a 1–0 win over Slovenia in a 2010 World Cup group-stage game. That win would send England through to the knockout round.

So, indeed, why wouldn't the club want Defoe?

With his world-class finishing skills, he could be just the man to help rescue TFC from their abysmal goal-scoring record in 2013, when they had tied for second-last on goals-for in MLS.

Convincing him to leave England at just 31 with more seasons likely ahead of him in the most well-regarded league in the world was a different story. The club believed they could sell him on Toronto as London light, a place where Defoe could enjoy everything that a world-class city has to offer with just a fraction of the scrutiny that players in London generally receive.

They wanted to make Defoe the centrepiece of a club that had fans just begging for a championship. He was to be sold on becoming a modern deity in a city known largely for hockey gods.

And there was the small, but impossible to overlook, issue of timing. With the 2014 World Cup approaching and Defoe being thought of as a player on the bubble with Hotspur, TFC could offer him regular minutes and the opportunity to likely score goals at will and showcase that goal-scoring prowess to England manager Roy Hodgson in the hopes of being chosen to travel with England to Brazil.

Finally, the club had an in, which wasn't easy to come by considering the relative stature of TFC and MLS at the time. Nelsen had spent close to four months playing alongside Defoe at Spurs early in 2012. Through Nelsen, the club leaned hard on that familiarity and asked Spurs chairman Daniel Levy for permission to speak with Defoe.

Initially, Nelsen wasn't confident anything would come of the meeting. "I didn't think he'd do it," said Nelsen. "I didn't think it could get done."

But the first meeting saw the full effect of the three-headed monster that was TFC's recruiting squad: Nelsen established trust with Defoe and Bezbatchenko explained the rules, practicalities, and possible salary structure of the move.

The comprehensive approach established a level of comfort for Defoe. But it was when Leiweke began explaining what the club and MLSE could become that Defoe began to envision himself leaving the Premier League. "As soon as I sat down with Tim, I was like, 'Wow.' His energy and his vision that he had; it was almost like I'd made my decision straight away," said Defoe. He was already thinking about his legacy. Even once he'd retired, he felt assured, he would have been part of something bigger.

The trio left believing they'd made an impact, but early returns from his agent led Leiweke to believe they had an outside chance at best. And that didn't sit well with Leiweke, so he reached out to Keane and Beckham to lean on Defoe and sell him on their experience at the Galaxy and how beneficial playing for a Leiweke-led franchise would be. Leiweke further understood that the relationship between Defoe and his mother, Sandra St. Helen, was an important one and required some massaging. So, once she was flown out to Toronto to be wined and dined, Leiweke had LeBron James visit her courtside at a Raptors game to speak highly of the city.

Then, of course, Leiweke had Drake, fresh off being named ambassador of the Toronto Raptors, make a call on TFC's behalf to extend his personal invitation to the city of Toronto. Leiweke was driven to get Defoe to put pen to paper. He wasn't looking two or three years down the road with this signing: Leiweke knew Defoe could make an impact immediately, and that immediacy only strengthened his drive.

All of the lengths Leiweke and TFC went to played into Defoe's interest in coming to a place where he would be the centre of attention. Defoe cuts a shy figure at times, but there was the inherent implication in the TFC sales pitch that Defoe's talents would be thrust to the forefront not only within the team, but within a league that was continuing to grow. And the increased attention could only serve to benefit Defoe's desire to get Hodgson to notice.

Defoe soon had dinner with his agent. Believing that Tottenham wouldn't want to sell him to another English club, he thought the opportunity TFC was presenting was too lucrative to pass up. He informed his agent that he wanted to give Toronto a shot.

The three-man team had a cordial meeting with Chelsea midfielder Frank Lampard, but nothing came of it. It was Defoe they wanted, and though the club had to make a compromise with Jermain's availability and immediately loan him back to Tottenham until the end of February, which cut into his time with the Toronto club in pre-season and training camp, it was Defoe they got. For a hefty transfer fee estimated to be €7.3 million, the club was immediately injected with one of the most talented goal-scorers ever to join the league.

But, a striker sometimes only being as good as the service he receives, Bezbatchenko knew the club needed a midfielder to complement Defoe.

Around Thanksgiving, established agent Ron Waxman visited the TFC training ground on his own to discuss negotiations regarding various players, not including one Michael Bradley. But it was that stalwart American midfielder, then of Serie A side AS Roma, who Bezbatchenko had his eye on. He knew Waxman well from his time working for the league, and had often kicked tires about Michael's interest in one day returning to MLS. Bradley had started his professional career with the New York MetroStars in 2005 before moving to the top Dutch, German, English, and Italian leagues.

Bradley had arrived in Italy in 2011 with Chievo, where he quickly garnered the nickname "The General" for his relentless organization of the club's midfield, a moniker that would stick. A year later, Bradley made the move to the biggest club of his career, and that first season at Roma, with 35 total appearances, met expectations. Bradley had been a favourite of Roma coach Zdeněk Zeman, had established himself within the club, and felt good about the four-year contract he'd signed.

But his fate, as it often is for players, was tied to that of his manager, and when Zeman was relieved of his duties in 2013 after mid-season struggles, Bradley began to wonder if he'd ever be first choice with the club's new management. So he stayed on to see if he could force his way into the good graces of new managers Aurelio Andreazzoli and Rudi Garcia. Bradley's exhaustive work in the midfield on both sides of the ball led him to believe that he deserved more playing time, even if his coaches disagreed.

Halfway through the 2013–14 season in Roma the 26-year-old Bradley, still very much in the prime of his career, began looking for other options. "The reality for me is I love to play and I love to compete too much to sit and watch every week," he said. "It's not in my makeup."

Bradley speaks slowly yet forcefully, carefully considering the impact of every single word before uttering it. His message is a pragmatic, if at times guarded one, hardened by years in an industry that dissects and easily re-interprets every rare quote from a player.

By early December, Bradley had a few leads that looked promising, including interest from one of the top clubs in the Bundesliga. When he shared his concern with Roma's sporting director, Walter Sabatini, he received a different message: Sabatini valued Bradley's contributions, even if the coaches didn't. "Unless I get real big money for you," Bradley was told, "you're not going anywhere."

Bradley was now in a bind, with the coach not seeing him as part of Roma's plans, but the sporting director not planning on letting him leave on loan, either.

So Bradley circled back with Waxman, trying to see if Bezbatchenko's tongue-in-cheek interest at MLS could eventually produce the big money Sabatini was after. He'd visited Toronto previously, most recently spending a week in the city with Roma ahead of a pre-season game against TFC in the summer of 2013. Roma had worked out at TFC's training grounds and Bradley was poking his head around the facilities when Ted Tieu, coordinator of team operations, offered to give him a tour. Bradley liked what he saw, and the brief tour only solidified what he already believed about TFC: that it was in a thriving sports city and relevant with both the city and the media.

Over the Christmas break, Bezbatchenko learned that TFC had a legitimate chance of landing Bradley. He quickly called Leiweke, informing him that Bradley was interested, but that even more money was required. Leiweke had to now go to the MLSE board and ask for the money to get that second DP he'd told them he would want. And Leiweke believed in Bradley, which meant anyone in his path would eventually believe in Bradley, as well. "We found our Robbie Keane in Michael Bradley," said Leiweke.

Leiweke saw immediately how Bradley could be not only a future captain of the franchise, but an indispensable part of what TFC was trying to accomplish. He told Bezbatchenko to go and get the deal done.

In a matter of days, the conversation turned from simply gauging interest to talking real numbers. The actual contract negotiations took no more than a few hours. If Defoe had been a goal-scoring product of the three men at the top of the TFC food chain trying to come together for the greater good, bringing a player like Bradley, who could have a dramatic impact on all areas of the pitch, was Bezbatchenko trying to put his first stamp on the club's direction.

And it was the pace of the negotiations that stood out to Bradley. "That was one of the things I remember as being so impressive and was such a draw to me," he said, "this idea that you had this club and Tim [Bezbatchenko] and Tim [Leiweke] did not mess around."

If Bradley's time in Europe had taught him one thing, it was that discussions very rarely come to anything, and using up time always takes precedence over decision-making. But there was very little waiting with TFC's $10 million transfer of Bradley early in January. "I was sitting in Rome with my eyes wide open, going, 'What's going on here?'" said Bradley.

This was only the beginning of Leiweke's efforts — to borrow an overused but apt cliché — to go big or go home. Brazilian striker Gilberto was added as the club's third DP for a reported transfer fee of over $3 million.

TFC also landed young Designated Player Matias Laba, but with established stars Defoe, Bradley, and Gilberto now on the team, they were over MLS's three-DP limit. They would eventually have to move Laba to the Vancouver Whitecaps for nothing more than future considerations.

And there were now bigger, bloody bigger, fish to fry.

There's no exact figure on how much coffee, tea, and other various beverages were spit out during the shooting of the Bloody Big Deal commercial campaigns. It's not even worth calculating, however, because it is the enormity of The Deal that the commercials were intended to communicate.

The message of the commercials, broadcast across national television, was simple: showcase typical British figures, from police to pub-goers to well-to-do businessmen, who appear to fit the image many North Americans have of normally reserved and stoic Brits, breaking character and spitting out their drinks in horror: Toronto FC have snagged one of their most beloved players. Early versions of the commercials were short and made no mention of Defoe, only increasing the intrigue that much more.

Though the entire campaign had been conceived quite quickly by Canadian-based creative agency Sid Lee, its effects were massive: 60,000 people viewed the ad on YouTube in its first day. "We wanted to energize our fans, we wanted to put TFC back on the map, and we had to take some risks," Shannon Hosford, VP of marketing and communications, said of the 2014 campaign.

The narrative of the club was shifting away from currying the exuberant fans who had been by the club's side since the beginning. Though Defoe would be the obvious centrepiece of TFC's signings, the addition of Bradley and Gilberto, which Leiweke playfully called "financial suicide" during the unveiling press conference, aggressively pitched the club as a major player in the city and the league. "We didn't accomplish anything today," Leiweke reminded those in attendance during the public press conference. "We created a very good opportunity, but the hard work is in front of us."

Still, optimism was the theme of the day.

Every TFC fan in attendance could forgive Leiweke for misattributing his most poignant quote of the day to the Kennedys, when it was, in fact, Bernard Shaw that he was likely paraphrasing when he looked out into the audience and said, "Some people see things as they are and say 'Why?' Others dream of what can be and they say 'Why not?' Today is 'Why not?'"

And with that, Leiweke pushed his thumb and his index finger together with purpose and cocked his head up toward the adoring fans and stopped to emphasize every single word: "Why can't we be great?"

The water bottles by Leiweke shook as he delivered the credo that was becoming his guiding principle with the club. Leiweke played his cards well when he gave full credit to the club's loyal fans, calling the signings "payback" for their patience.

It was the cap on the only rollout campaign in MLS to have rivalled the unveiling of David Beckham years earlier. "The ambition meter had gone up," ESPN national soccer columnist Jeff Carlisle remembers thinking. "This is really upping the ante."

Leiweke had to carry the involved parties on his back. Gilberto, for one, was not in attendance. And Michael Bradley, the man who would be king, appeared the most uneasy, with his opening remarks clocking in at less than two minutes.

While Bradley's conversations with TFC had helped him understand that part of coming to TFC would be the bold marketing, branding, and advertising of his move, it took some getting used to. "Anybody who knows me knows that's not necessarily who I am, naturally," he said. "But I knew that was part of the deal. You can't say, 'I'm not doing this, I'm not doing that.' When you come to the league as a big player, a Designated Player, you have responsibilities in a lot of different areas."

What struck Bradley, and perhaps anyone else tuning in to the live stream, was how the club that had essentially ushered in MLS 2.0 was breaking new ground yet again. "It was incredible, because that wasn't the league I left," said Bradley. "In so many ways it was a new challenge and a situation unlike anything I'd ever seen."

The Bloody Big Deal achieved success on two fronts, one tangible and one less so, but, perhaps even more imperatively, it re-energized the fan base. MLSE recouped obvious financial benefits when approximately 4,000 more season tickets were sold after the announcement. A legitimate case could be made that Defoe carried more clout as an international athlete than any other to have played in Toronto.

Beyond the litres of spit out-tea, however, the signing of Defoe, Bradley, and Gilberto signalled a transition toward a more aware and engaged management than the club had ever had. The real big deal was that Bezbatchenko and Leiweke understood that for DPs to have a long-standing impact on the club, the players needed to be in the prime of their careers. The game, like so many other sports, was trending younger, and while Frings and Koevermans, the club's previous DPs, had been touted for their experience, the Bloody Big Deal solidified the notion that by being ruthless in pursuing them, TFC could attain valuable experience in a player without having to wait until he was past the peak of his career.

At last, TFC was leading the way, not simply reacting to things done by other clubs. "I don't know if anyone else would have had the guts to do it," said MLS commissioner Don Garber, of Leiweke's plan.

Leiweke's insatiable desire for a winning lineup was evident when he went a step further, signing the Brazilian goalkeeper who would eventually be between the sticks for the 2014 World Cup — Júlio César, on loan from Queen's Park Rangers. And he would also bring back Dwayne De Rosario for his final year in MLS.

So surprised was De Rosario that when he originally received the call from Leiweke, he replied, "Get the fuck out of here?"

"This is your hometown," replied Leiweke. "We need you back here. What do I have to do to get you back here?"

The 35-year-old De Rosario was signed to a $173,000 contract, the fifth-highest of any non-DP on the club, after having his option declined by D.C. United and being selected by TFC in the 2013 MLS Re-Entry Draft.

Though their lavish spending would inevitably be criticized as putting the cart before the horse, TFC were again front-page news.

"I don't know a Major League Soccer franchise that wouldn't love that," Leiweke said of the attention. "I know a lot of NHL teams that would love that."

By their nature, goalkeepers are an observant bunch. They are the players who watch scripts unfold on the pitch and often see things that other positional players might miss. But even to TFC goalkeeper Joe Bendik, there was no missing the changes to the club from the start of training camp. "From the minute [Bradley] walked into the training facility, you knew the whole culture of Toronto FC was going to change," he said.

Bradley also had a vision for what TFC could become. He was going to be an extension of Leiweke's ambition, but personified on the pitch. Bradley had never had the opportunity to become the face of a club, not in terms of how the club is represented to fans, but now his work ethic would provide the framework for how his teammates would perform. Bradley had always had an incomparable work ethic, but because he never had a propensity for scoring goals or even for attacking all that often on the pitch, he did not garner headlines. His very position, a "holding," or "defensive," midfielder, doesn't exactly inspire the casual fan.

But on the pitch, as a deep-lying midfielder, any good team's build-up toward a goal begins with a player like Bradley. His work to win balls back from the opposition through tackles or interceptions might be forgotten after a dynamic run from a Number 10 or a highlight-reel finish from a Number 9, but the attack starts with Bradley. He was just months away from covering more distance per 90 minutes (12.6 kilometres) than any other player at the 2014 World Cup, playing for his native United States, and he wanted the rest of the club to follow his lead.

So it was understood: the club's thrust and heft would begin with Bradley. Teammates were struck by his dedication and professionalism from the start of training camp. Bradley would work with the club's front office and coaches to mould it into a winning club. He liked the city, how fanatical it was about its sports teams, so he recognized the opportunity.

As onerous as it sounds, Bradley set out to change the culture in the locker room. He led by example, challenging players to arrive earlier at the training grounds and to stay later after. The hope was to build more of a sense of camaraderie among the squad. "You'd get there at 7:30 a.m.," said Bendik. "And if you got home at four, that would be a pretty average day."

If Bradley was going to put that kind of work in, he expected the same from his teammates. Some bought in, while others were eventually weeded out.

"He raised the intensity level, more than anything," said Creavalle. "He's going to be that guy that will hold players accountable and will make sure that no player is slacking. That's one of the best qualities he brings to a team."

Defoe found himself settling in easily enough early on, finding that the KIA Training Ground was comparable to many of the training grounds in England. By all accounts, Defoe put on no airs and did not play the egotistical superstar inside the dressing room. With a razor-sharp sense of humour, he soon became appreciated. "Even through my first month here, I felt like I'd been there for a year already," he said.

But still, Bradley wasn't convinced. His pragmatism told him that the roster that won just six games the season previous was still largely in place, but now expectations had been raised. "What I realized was how much improvement the team needed; there [were] not enough real guys, not enough talent, we needed more guys with personality, we needed more guys who really understood what it meant to train and work and go for it during moments of pressure," said Bradley.

Throughout pre-season and training camp, many in the squad were under the assumption that when Defoe showed up a week before the season started, he would magically solve the team's problems.

And so it would have appeared, during the club's first game of the season in Seattle.

By the 17th minute, Defoe had yet to get a touch on the ball. But Osorio's deft turn on the ball allowed him enough time to look up and see Defoe having carved a place within the Sounders back line. Defoe played the through ball to perfection, staying onside and turning to fire the shot past Sounders goalkeeper Stefan Frei for the opening goal on his very first shot.

It would be difficult to imagine a better debut in any league than scoring on your very first touch.

Seven minutes later, Bradley pressed Sounders midfielder Clint Dempsey into a regrettable back pass straight to Defoe, who, with more than enough space, needed just two touches this time to bag the brace in the 2–1 win.

One week later, in TFC's home opener, Defoe scored the lone goal in a 1–0 win over D.C. United.

With the dramatic early returns, it seemed TFC had finally turned a corner and were ready for their first-ever playoff berth. Bradley remembers feeling that expectations after those first two games were "twice as high," but still couldn't help thinking, "We still have a long way to go."

TFC would win four games in their first eight, which was as fast as they'd ever gotten to that total in franchise history. But Bradley wasn't convinced. "I know what good teams are," said Bradley. "I know what they feel like."

It was Bradley's belief that although Defoe was scoring at a decent clip, the club could not win on the strength of their DPs alone. He was shouldering too much of the load, both on the pitch and with the off-pitch direction for the team. "When I first got here, the team wasn't as good," Bradley said in 2017. "Not even close. As a result, there was less structure, there was less organization, and for us to have any real chance to win or be successful, it meant I had to play a role where I went for it in terms of attacking, defending, trying to be aggressive, trying to make plays that made a difference in both attack and defence. And obviously there were days where that, within the context of the team, worked well and it allowed us to win some games. And there were other times when that [was] not enough."

What was missing? From the top down, not everyone had bought into Bradley's raised level of intensity and all-encompassing approach. "There weren't enough guys who really *got* it," said Bradley.

There wasn't as much help coming from the coaching staff, either. Nelsen's training sessions relied largely on playing and competing, but he was openly criticized by some players for not having a detailed schedule of how training would evolve every day. Some players wanted more of a description of the process they were undergoing and the discussion over whether Nelsen even wanted to undertake the task of rebuilding TFC as a coach, was growing louder.

"I'm not sure Ryan had his heart set on coaching," said Bradley, convinced that Nelsen's ambition got the best of him when he accepted the coaching position.

And Nelsen, in trying to build a more cohesive squad, was trying to get Bradley to loosen his grip on the team's midfield. "In my opinion, it hurt the team a bit," Nelsen said of Bradley's approach. "That was one of the hardest things for me was to try and tell him: you don't have to do everything."

With the World Cup fast approaching, the news that one of their players would be staying with the club ironically hit them hard: Jermain Defoe was left out of Hodgson's England World Cup squad. Hodgson told Defoe that he was left off because putting him on wouldn't be fair to other players plying their trade in the top European leagues.

It did little to disabuse the notion that Defoe had damaged his career trajectory in signing for TFC. "I always felt like I should have gone to the World Cup anyway," said Defoe. "Maybe if I'd have gone to the World Cup, it would have been different," he adds in retrospect.

Defoe answered with eight goals in the nine games directly after the announcement. England crashed spectacularly out of the World Cup, finishing last in their group and scoring just two goals over one draw and two losses.

With the summer came a sense of exhaustion and frustration: Bradley had just run himself into the ground at the World Cup and was again expected to be the sole driver of the midfield. Gilberto had scored just two goals in 14 appearances. And by August, Defoe had developed a nagging groin injury, causing him to miss the MLS All-Star game in Portland.

Defoe hadn't been happy about having to make the trip across the continent anyway, so it was perhaps just as well. The extensive travel that comes with playing in MLS had yet to sink in to the forward, so used to making short bus trips across England for league games.

Bradley remembers sitting down next to Jermain on their flight to Seattle for the season opener, and having Defoe turn to him to ask how long the flight was. When Bradley informed him that it could be between five and five and a half hours, Defoe looked at him in stunned silence. At first, Defoe thought Bradley was joking. "He thought the flight was two, three hours," recalls Bradley. "It hadn't really dawned on him how big North America is."

Combining the travel with the heat that comes with playing through the summer in North America, and his rapidly developing homesickness, the rumblings over his interest in TFC moving forward persisted. By August, Defoe's appearances in the lineup were becoming less and less frequent, and with his injury worsening, he began returning to England to seek treatment instead of staying in Toronto under the team doctors.

With little information forthcoming in Toronto and plenty of room for speculation, the questions over Defoe's future persisted. Leiweke admits there was friction within MLSE over Defoe, a valued asset. A substantial offer was made, reportedly from Queen's Park Rangers, to transfer Defoe back to England during the summer window. It was, according to Leiweke, a done deal until Tanenbaum stepped in. "He came back and said, 'I don't want to give up on this yet. I know it's a really good deal. I'm hoping that we can still salvage this,'" remembers Leiweke. "To the owner's credit, the amount of money that was on the table, that was huge. It wasn't about the money to our owners. It was about success."

But success was looking less and less probable. Rumours about the influence of Defoe's mother, Sandra St. Helen, were rampant. MLSE had shelled out to woo her, even providing her with a lavish house near to her son in Toronto. But as she grew frustrated with the city, she was rumoured to be laying the groundwork behind MLSE's collective back for a possible transfer deal.

With one of Bradley's fellow Designated Players not available on the pitch, TFC went 2–3–1 in the six games Defoe missed in August and September. It was quickly becoming clear to Bradley that the Defoe experiment just wasn't going to work. "To get Jermain, you need to convince Jermain's mother," Bradley said.

A contingent of the local media began to turn on Defoe, consistently questioning his absences and whether he was still committed to the club. This only furthered his frustration, and he couldn't understand why the local media would be making assumptions about his condition. "It was probably the first time they had to deal with a situation like that," said Defoe.

Defoe insists the experts on the injury he had sustained were in London, and the team doctors in Toronto were unsure, so going to London was the only course of action. He claims that the injury got so bad that his muscle actually became separated from the bone, and that the specialist in London couldn't imagine how he had been able to run even in the months leading up to that point. "If I can't run," said Defoe, "I can't express myself."

In England, Defoe was getting calls from Premier League teams wanting to put pen to paper on a transfer deal. Initially, he refused. "In my mind, I thought I was going back to Toronto after I got fit," he said.

But the longer he stayed in England receiving treatment, the more those around the club assumed he was giving in to obvious homesickness and that he might not return. It was an about-face for a player who TFC had done everything to court.

"When MLSE puts their best foot forward, they do a damn good job and it's tough to say no," said Bradley. "But when Jermain shows up, he hasn't been a part of all of this. He doesn't really know what he's getting into."

Bradley remembers Defoe soaking up the early attention in press conferences and parties after the Bloody Big Deal was unveiled. But teammates saw the grind of an MLS season eventually wear on Defoe. "When all of that dies down, as it inevitably does, and when he doesn't make the England team for the World Cup, and now it's just coming in to train every day and getting ready to play on the weekend, in Toronto, in MLS, he realized he didn't like it. He missed England. He missed what he knew," said Bradley.

"Even with everything that he was given there, he was the show, he was the man, he didn't quite look like he really, really wanted that," added Bendik.

For all the extravagant lengths Leiweke, Bezbatchenko, and MLSE went to to lure Defoe from England, they had perhaps not painted a clear picture of what his day-to-day life would look like in MLS and North America. They had forgone the simple for the exhilarating, and now all Defoe wanted was that seemingly simple life he'd enjoyed in the U.K. "Maybe I missed home a bit, because I've got a big family," said Defoe.

Though the summer transfer window eventually closed and Defoe did return to Toronto, it was all but assumed that in the next transfer window he would be gone. There was little fixing the frayed relationship. Signs littering BMO Field with the words "Bloody Big Bust" summarized the feelings of a large sentiment of the fan base.

"If your heart's not into it," said Leiweke, "your heart's not into it."

In a city where sports figures ripe with an intangible quality like "heart" are often the most revered, it was all Defoe could do to rail against popular opinion and insist he was still happy about coming to TFC in the first place.

"As long as I know why I went, and I believe in my heart that I know why I went," said Defoe, "that's all that matters."

By late August, the distractions surrounding the club had become too much for Tim Bezbatchenko to stand. The club sat third in the Eastern Conference and had two months left to secure their first-ever playoff berth. And with the talent still present in the roster, the GM saw no reason why that shouldn't happen. Tim Leiweke had just announced that he was going to be moving on from MLSE to pursue other challenges. TFC was now firmly Bezbatchenko's club to run, and he didn't like the look of what he saw.

Frustration had seeped into Nelsen's relationship with Bezbatchenko: Nelsen perceived Bezbatchenko to be inexperienced, communicating a message that looked good on paper but that might not work in reality. He wasn't receptive to Bezbatchenko's analytically-driven approach, but knew that the young GM needed to put his own fingerprint on the team. "I think Tim needed to go through that process himself," said Nelsen.

With rumours swirling that Defoe would not stay with the club if Leiweke left, Bezbatchenko and Leiweke had a conversation about how to motivate the squad: they mulled over going into the team's locker room, or perhaps speaking directly to Nelsen, but finally decided the best way to motivate the team was to go public. So, Bezbatchenko held his club to the fire, taking them to task for winning just three of their previous 12 games. "With 11 games remaining, I think what we've been saying is that it's going to take some time to gel. I think that time of gelling is over. We've assembled an extremely talented squad and together it's time for all of that experience to show and take it up a notch," an uncharacteristically aggressive Bezbatchenko told reporters the day before a pivotal home match against the New England Revolution.

Bezbatchenko would continue to press the issue, making thinly veiled criticisms of Nelsen and his team. "Talk is cheap." — "We mean business now. We can be better." —"The last 12 or so games haven't been good enough, at least for making a run in MLS."

Nelsen heard Bezbatchenko's message, loud and clear. "It hurt me. They saw me change. That broke me in a way," said Nelsen. He went to Leiweke to plead for a bit of rationality in what was clearly a troubled time, but Nelsen ultimately knew the season was lost: "You saw the writing on the wall."

With Defoe still out of the lineup with the injury, Nelsen went to a 4-2-3-1 formation in hopes of sparking his team. Almost as if on cue, however, TFC saw the final domino of their season collapse while most of their fans were still in line for beer. Revolution midfielder Lee Nguyen intercepted an errant TFC pass and fired a shot from outside the box past

Bendik in just the second minute. The Revolution drove the nail deeper into the coffin with two more goals.

After the match, knowing he'd be fired soon after, Nelsen shot back at Bezbatchenko, saying that the GM had brought attention to a match that was unnecessarily perceived to be a high-pressure one. "I've won this league, played in it for four years, been in the [English] Premier League for 10 years, played in a World Cup, Olympics. I've played in some pretty hot pressure games. One thing that I do know is this was not one of them," said Nelsen after the match.

Nelsen was clear: Bezbatchenko's message had affected his team and he wished that the GM's frustration had been kept in-house. It would be Nelsen's final press conference.

He told Leiweke that he could still get TFC into playoffs and then step aside, but the philosophical differences were too large to overlook. Bezbatchenko wanted his own choice at the helm and Nelsen had to admit that Bezbatchenko was likely to be with the club long after he was gone. "The working relationship wasn't great," he said.

It was still a bitter pill to swallow. Nelsen had TFC on the verge of a 10-win season for just the second time in franchise history, with 10 games still remaining. He had the necessary ambition to find a place at TFC, but the stress of turning around a franchise while at odds with his boss caused his only head coaching job to come to a close less than two seasons in.

"I had nice black hair before [starting at TFC]," said Nelsen, "but afterward, I was grey as hell."

Following TFC's 3–0 loss, Greg Vanney was asked to sit down with Bezbatchenko and Leiweke. He knew about the situation that had engulfed the club, but his introverted sensibilities didn't allow him to get ahead of himself.

In an office at BMO Field, Vanney was asked two simple questions.

First, "Are you ready to take on this team?"

This was the question Nelsen had been asked, and Vanney's answer was just as affirmative. It was the next question that rang louder, and it was one that perhaps had not been asked clearly enough of Nelsen and even of Defoe. "Do you *want* to take on this team?"

Vanney had not seen the invitation coming. He was happy where he was as academy director. He had even turned down an offer to be an assistant coach in MLS. The head coaching job wasn't on his radar.

Bezbatchenko knew Vanney would eventually become a head coach at some point, but it had never been part of the immediate plan. So it was this question that took a little longer to ponder.

"In the world of soccer and head coaching, you never know when you're going to get a chance," said Vanney, afterward.

Vanney knew what kind of team he wanted: one that could play a fast, attacking style of soccer, could be entertaining as much as it was successful, and finally, could attract fans. Vanney was well-versed in the club's fans, but had seen over the years how difficult it becomes for fans to support a product that doesn't give back. He knew that TFC had put interesting departments in place, including sports science and a brand-new one on cognitive development. With Michael Rabasca at the helm, TFC was developing their players in a way that had never been seen in North American soccer up to that point. And, personally, Vanney wanted to advance his own belief that the best players should have the ability to "play the game in their minds before anything else."

When he realized he had all the tools in place, his decision was made. He wanted to be TFC's coach.

He was announced as the club's ninth coach the next day, and set about trying not just to salvage the season, but to right the wrongs of a tumultuous year and determine whom he could build his team around. Vanney began moving casual relationships with some of the players he knew into personal ones. "He got to work," remembers Bradley. "He wasn't fazed by anything. He wasn't worried about anything going on, on the outside. He was motivated by the challenge and opportunity. He set out right away to build real relationships with myself and some of the other guys who he felt were going to be important going forward."

Director of scouting operations Jack Dodd was brought in to look for available, intelligent, attacking players that fit what Vanney wanted.

Vanney's biggest hurdle was with the players themselves, who he understood might not be keen on hearing yet another new voice. Many had been fond of Nelsen, the gregarious, quintessential player's coach. While he could likely never match Nelsen's natural charm, Vanney still knew he had to come out of his shell and overtly communicate his plans and approach to the game to assuage those who felt Nelsen's time lacked a clear message.

"You have to quickly give the impression that 'this is where we want to go with this,'" said Vanney. He wanted humility in his players, those who were more willing to collaborate and those who essentially "don't even see it as work."

"Every day is a day to try and learn, share your ideas, and get better," said Vanney. "Everybody has to buy in and feel like they're part of it. They have to feel like they're part of driving things forward."

Vanney added his old partner on the Galaxy back line, the sociable Dan Calichman, as assistant coach to help deliver his message with a little more enthusiasm. But the pair's own TFC turnover story came fast and hard. TFC lost the first two games after the coaching switch and would win only two of the remaining final ten.

What had looked like a sure thing midway through the season was now anything but. TFC would miss the playoffs yet again and Defoe would be transferred to Sunderland in the off-season. But, finally, there was synergy at the top: ownership had the GM they wanted and the GM had the coach he wanted.

"We needed [Vanney] to set a high standard on the field just like Tim and I were setting a high standard for what was happening off the field," said Bezbatchenko.

Bradley would take a more vocal approach at the end of the season in what he calls "real, honest, candid" discussions about where TFC was headed. "If I'm going to be a part of something," said Bradley, "you're getting everything from me."

Bradley was named captain ahead of the 2015 season, taking the armband from Steven Caldwell. It was an effort from Bezbatchenko to recognize what they needed to get right, above all: find players who *wanted* to be at the club and were ready to make a difference.

"The players are, especially in soccer, they are the reason they win and lose," said Bezbatchenko. "When they have the balls, there's no plays written. They control the tempo for the club. If you forget that, that's the first step in becoming unsuccessful."

Leiweke and TFC had bet large on their Designated Players, and the tremors from the crashing fall of that approach were felt long after.

Ambition had got the club only as far as the starting block. And as well-placed as it was, what 2014 taught the club is that many hands are required to actually push off that block.

10

Jeans and a Blazer, a Panic Attack, and the Best Player in League History

LIKE MANY OTHERS THAT MORNING, Tim Bezbatchenko stood bleary-eyed in the darkened lobby of the Sheraton Milan on New Year's Day. He had arrived early after a red-eye flight from Toronto. As the hung-over crowd sauntered past him, Bezbatchenko kept his eyes on the lobby doors, waiting for his guest.

It could very well have been a simple day for Bezbatchenko. Have introductory meetings with two players of interest. Sample some fine Italian food. Return with a bit more insight into the direction his club would take.

But everything changed when player agent Andrea D'Amico walked in, like a blaze of light to brighten the drab lobby.

Bezbatchenko was looking at the very picture of a classic Italian gentleman: long, flowing hair, a salt-and-pepper beard, a long overcoat trailing from his shoulders, and a tailored designer suit complete with a pocket square expertly arranged and folded.

After exchanging pleasantries, the two men entered D'Amico's Maserati for the 150-kilometre drive from Milan to Turin. The drive is supposed to take just over two and a half hours, but D'Amico got them to Turin, the home of Juventus, in 90 minutes, driving his Masterati "as fast as the car should go," according to Bezbatchenko.

As Bezbatchenko sailed through the Italian countryside at top speed, the former lawyer from the relatively unsophisticated northern Ohio city of Columbus had to pinch himself. "What world do I live in?" he asked himself. "This is a completely different world than MLS."

The two men were headed to Lentini's Ristorante in Turin to meet a player D'Amico represented. When he met Sebastian Giovinco, the diminutive and insanely talented creative forward, Bezbatchenko's whole approach to his day in Northern Italy began to shift. If he could deflect Giovinco from this old-world environment and sell Giovinco on his vision, and Giovinco himself could find a similar vision for his own path, Bezbatchenko could be changing the course of the entire league. His boss, MLSE president Tim Leiweke, was on his way out of the company and had tasked Bezbatchenko and Bezbatchenko alone with bringing home the club's next DP.

I have to nail this, he said to himself.

Bezbatchenko had gone after TFC's biggest acquisition, Jermain Defoe, alongside Leiweke. But this time, he was going it on his own. The pressure was obvious, and when Giovinco met him outside the restaurant, Bezbatchenko briefly thought he'd blown it.

Giovinco, himself well-groomed and smartly put together, flashed a disarming smile, pointed at Bezbatchenko's blazer and jeans, laughed, and made a comment in Italian to D'Amico. "He expected a suit and an old man," said D'Amico, translating for Giovinco. Bezbatchenko briefly held his breath. "You're wearing jeans and a blazer," continued D'Amico. "He likes the way you're dressed."

Sensing that Giovinco was not like every other player they'd courted to lead the charge at the club, Bezbatchenko smiled back. "I think we're going to get along," he said, as they entered the restaurant, still largely unaware of how a conversation that morning over pizza would help change the perception of an entire league around the world.

Throughout Toronto FC's history, player acquisitions had been mostly one-sided affairs. Agents would approach the club and pitch their players, as with probably 80 percent of the world's soccer clubs.

When Bezbatchenko began at TFC, one of his first missions was to create a scouting department that could scour the planet for talent and essentially flip that model on its head. He understood that TFC was different from many other clubs in that they were trying to create a consistently strong, model franchise, but one that had very little success to build on and to sell to potential players. But with the kind of financial resources that few other clubs in his competing leagues could boast, and with a very clear methodology they wanted to manifest on the pitch through Vanney's vision, Bezbatchenko wanted the club to be able to identify players of interest, and to approach them, rather than waiting to be approached. And by himself recruiting players and selling them on the club's new vision, Bezbatchenko was seeking to retain complete control over player identification and the building of a winning roster.

Throughout 2014, Jack Dodd, the club's director of scouting operations, and Corey Wray, director of team operations, had been identifying players who might steer TFC in the right direction: players who could play the aggressive, attacking brand of soccer that Vanney had begun to establish. They worked to find players of the highest quality who were also attainable, and who could provide value within salary cap restraints.

But they also worked in the rarefied world of Designated Players. In that the club was free to find players of even better quality, and was allowed to pay higher salaries and transfer fees.

One player they'd identified through extensive scouting was Victor Vazquez, the passer extraordinaire and former Barcelona midfielder who was tearing up the Belgian Pro League with Club Brugge. In the middle of a season that would end up seeing Vazquez win the Belgian Professional Footballer of the Year, TFC had made a transfer offer for Vazquez before the meeting with Giovinco, but Club Brugge had turned it down.

Bezbatchenko implored Dodd and Wray to think bigger: to find a player who could potentially have even more of an influence on the club and the league than Defoe had. Someone who could not only lead the team both off the pitch and on it by scoring goals, but someone who could be a difference-maker in the league as a whole. "There's a direct correlation between talent and success," he said of his vision.

Not everyone agreed. Many around MLS, including league executives and other GMs, as well as some within TFC itself, were telling Bezbatchenko to aim a bit lower with his player acquisitions. Partly because of Defoe's premature-exit debacle, but also because he had set such high expectations while the club was still muddling "in the shit," he was repeatedly given the same advice throughout the end of 2014: "Why are you shooting to be great when you just need to be good?"

But Bezbatchenko remained undeterred; he had learned from Leiweke, a man who was always dead set on thinking bigger than his rivals. Bezbatchenko and Leiweke had gone to the MLSE board after it was clear Defoe would not return to Toronto and Leiweke himself had told them, "We are not giving up." Bezbatchenko, too, had given the board explanations for the Defoe exit, and presented research that suggested another high-profile acquisition was necessary for the club's continued ascent. In short, Bezbatchenko had had to explain why, in his words, "this time, it's going to be different."

The board was convinced, and, buoyed by the financial investment MLSE was prepared to make, Bezbatchenko continued his search. Had he listened to the naysayers, given up, and returned to the MLSE board to say that he now didn't want the large-scale financial investment he'd asked for, and that another venture like the one that had almost derailed the club with Defoe would bring too much pressure, he was sure that Leiweke would've fired him. Leiweke and MLSE wanted him to be bold. The once prag-matic lawyer had had to shift his way of thinking to embrace the boldness required for the job. "If you give me a Ferrari I'm not just going to be driv-ing it around the neighbourhood at 25 miles an hour," said Bezbatchenko. "Our board was saying, 'Go. Be great.'"

Dodd and Wray had seen Giovinco play for Juventus. He fit the pro-file in terms of the type of player the club needed, as well as his age and global appeal. Though the Turin-born forward was once looked upon as the heir apparent to Alessandro Del Piero after coming up through the club's academy ranks, after two loan spells at Empoli and Parma, Giovinco was frustrated with the lack of faith in him and playing time he was getting, after spending more than half his life with the club. His obvious qual-ity, vision with the ball, and attacking flair had featured for Italy in the 2012 Euros. In the 2012–13 season, his last season of regular minutes with Juventus, he finished fourth in the club in goals across all competitions. But his lack of playing time through the 2013–14 season may have caused him to miss out on being selected to play for Italy in the 2014 World Cup.

Some commentators in Italy looked at Giovinco as a case of unfulfilled potential, but Bezbatchenko and TFC saw a player whose potential had yet to be properly tapped. "With the resources we had, it would have been silly not to shoot for a player like Giovinco," said Bezbatchenko.

But would a player of Giovinco's quality and age, still in his prime and playing for one of the biggest clubs on the planet, have any interest in MLS?

Corey Wray got the answer when he was originally approached by D'Amico at the Wyscout Forum in 2014. D'Amico had no idea that TFC had been scouting Giovinco previously, but said simply, "I have a player that might be of interest to you."

Wray and D'Amico exchanged ideas and very preliminary financial details that led to a common synergy. Wray immediately phoned Bezbatchenko and told him about the fortuitous meeting.

On Christmas Eve 2014, as Bezbatchenko was driving home to Columbus with his family, he spoke with D'Amico on the phone. "If you're serious, I'll fly over on New Year's Day to see if it's real," Bezbatchenko told him.

When he finally sat down with Giovinco, his brother and father, as well as D'Amico, Bezbatchenko learned of the then 27-year-old's urge to change "everything" in his life.

Bezbatchenko outlined the possibilities for him. "This is going to be hard. But if you come out glorious, you could go down in history as a legend for the club," Bezbatchenko said.

That type of mindset intrigued Giovinco. He didn't just want to dabble in a new league and then retire. The only problem? TFC had been the first club to present a transfer option to Giovinco for that winter transfer window, and even if Giovinco liked their bold approach, he had never heard of the club previously and had never visited Toronto.

Bezbatchenko tried his best to relay information about the club, the city, and its thriving Italian population. But it was only when he pulled out an iPad loaded with videos of the city and fans in Giovinco jerseys, that Giovinco was sold. Giovinco said he believed he could be a pioneer in the game in North America.

Bezbatchenko had a few brief words of reminder. "This isn't an adventure," he said. "Jermain viewed this is as an adventure. You have to view this as a crusade."

Giovinco smiled. He was up to the task, and wanted in.

D'Amico drove Bezbatchenko back to his hotel and they began talking financial terms even during the ride. Bezbatchenko phoned Leiweke to inform him of his successful meeting with a prospective DP. And yet, as good as Bezbatchenko must have felt in luring Giovinco to Toronto, he was still only halfway there. That was just one DP: he wanted two.

Jozy Altidore's flight had just touched down in Toronto, and he didn't move out of his seat. His massive frame stayed put. He looked out the cabin window onto a cold, snowy tarmac and felt a shudder before a wave of anxiety rushed over him.

The then 25-year-old forward was sure of one thing: he didn't believe he should be where he was, returning to MLS after six and a half seasons across five different leagues in Europe. Though he had just come off a dismal season and a half with Sunderland in the Premier League, scoring just one goal in 42 league appearances, there was nothing that could convince him that Toronto, and Major League Soccer, was the answer to his scoring problems.

Altidore had started every game for his native USA in the 2010 World Cup, but in 2014, in Brazil, he had logged just 23 minutes in the World Cup after a hamstring injury forced him to be carried off the pitch on a stretcher. He was a once-prodigious striker, but a severe dip in production had led to personal turmoil off the pitch and Altidore had become much more reserved and protective ahead of being swapped for Jermain Defoe as part of a transfer and a return to MLS.

At the arrivals gate of Toronto's Pearson airport, Altidore's agent, a camera crew, and hordes of fans were waiting to welcome the club's newest DP for a fresh start in his career.

But that sinking feeling in the pit of his stomach wouldn't go away. *This isn't it*, he thought to himself. *I should be in Europe.*

Altidore was one of the last people off the plane, but upon first stepping inside the airport, he still couldn't shake the feeling that he'd made a mistake. Overwhelmed, he took a seat in a gated area on his own to contemplate what had brought him there, into a snowy city he'd only visited briefly previously, and to a club that had never made the playoffs. And he continued to sit. For two hours.

The hulking Altidore isn't the type to panic, but there was simply too much uncertainty for him. "As soon as I get out of here," he remembers thinking, "it's real."

He fielded calls from his agent, who implored him to come out and see the gathered fans. But he wouldn't move. Nearly every member of his family called him and still he wouldn't budge.

Finally, when his sister Sadia called, Altidore calmed down. Her voice soothed him as she instructed the self-confessed family man not to over-think what he was about to do. He'd dealt with personal adversity before. That was the difference, though; for years, it had been people on the outside doubting Altidore.

"It looks as if it's finally time to abandon the notion of Jozy Altidore as the game-changing striker many thought he would become," wrote the *Guardian's* Tom Gottlieb in October 2014.

That sort of doubt over his abilities from the pundits had never much bothered Altidore. Only now, he was doubting himself.

There was still the lingering feeling among many in the soccer world that MLS was less of a league and more of a retirement plan, a destination for players who were comfortable with the notion that they could not compete at a high level elsewhere in the world.

After finally exiting the airport and beginning the drive to the club's training grounds, he couldn't shake that notion. The snow on the ground around him was foreign. He was expected to start fresh, once again, in a place that wasn't immediately warm and welcoming. "It was a cold drive," said Altidore. "A lot of things were going through my mind."

The fears over whether he could adapt back to a new league in a new continent after spending the majority of his professional career in Europe lingered. He was, admittedly, afraid to leave Europe and the style of life that a professional footballer enjoys on that side of the ocean. Teams spare no expense to ensure players are comfortable and ready to perform. He wondered how far away the MLS he left years earlier was from the standard set in Europe.

The transfer of a player who was openly still set on playing in Europe was a dangerous proposition for TFC, given the conditions that had led to Defoe's departure. Bezbatchenko made clear his belief that this wouldn't be an issue with Altidore, even from his opening statements regarding the transfer: "Our top priority is building a winning club with players that are committed to the TFC vision. Jozy is a special player, and checks all of the boxes that we look for in a player."

To convince Altidore that coming to TFC would be the right move for him, the club leaned on Bradley, whom Altidore had known since they were teenagers coming up through the ranks of the U.S. national team program.

Bradley was aware of how tumultuous Altidore's time in England had been and how he had been demoted to being a second-rate striker. He knew Altidore wanted more.

"This can be a good way for you to start fresh," Bradley told him. "This is a club that we can make into the biggest and best in North America."

Altidore trusted Bradley, and was eventually convinced that the club, and their interest in him, wasn't just a passing fancy. He was struck by how serious Bradley was about his dedication to the club.

"That's a big thing, for another player to ask you to come to a franchise and make it relevant, along with Seba," said Altidore, using the familiar nickname for Sebastian Giovinco. Further, he had to admit that in the turbulent world of international soccer, you'd be hard-pressed to find any other such opportunity to help turn around a franchise with someone you've known since you were teenagers.

When Altidore finally arrived at the training grounds, a quick tour was all he needed. Every member of the staff welcomed him with a smile. Every person around him *wanted* him to be where he was. After years of bouncing around Europe, Altidore felt like he had been welcomed into a family. He was ready to call Toronto home.

Giovinco and Altidore quickly hit it off. They ran into each other in a lobby after they were signed within a week of each other and quickly set up shop at a nearby bar to snack on fries and get to know each other.

"He was a bubbly guy, excited," Altidore said of their initial meeting, smiling.

Vanney received word of both of their signings while on the floor of the 2015 MLS SuperDraft. A photo arrived on Vanney's phone with Giovinco holding an Air Canada pen, signing his contract, just before Vanney also got word from Bezbatchenko that the transfer agreement was finalized and Altidore was coming to Toronto. TFC, and perhaps all of MLS, had never had an attacking duo up front with the kind of finish of these two. Vanney's vision of an aggressive brand of soccer was now definitely coming into focus. TFC now had two players who could attack opposition back lines from different angles and become a constant presence on the score sheet.

And the fact that they got along famously so early on in their relationship? That was icing on the cake for TFC. "I've never really played with a player where you become synonymous with that player," said Altidore.

The impact of the acquisitions was immediate. Altidore scored twice in the club's season opener to seal a 3–1 win over the Whitecaps. TFC would then lose their next four matches, but Giovinco scored three of their five goals during that stretch. Altidore then bagged a brace in a 2–0 win over Orlando before Giovinco scored the lone goal in a 1–0 win, with a stunning free kick from distance that would eventually become the norm for the Italian.

In what came as a pleasant surprise to some around the club, Giovinco and Altidore acclimatized to MLS very quickly. No complaining, no questioning of methods. After the drama that accompanied Defoe during his time in Toronto, there was an expectation that Giovinco would bring the same. Players with that kind of quality often carry with them equally noticeable personalities, but Giovinco proved the opposite. "[Giovinco] you would think would have been more of an issue, but he was very humble, very good," said Fraser.

The addition of the star duo meant Bradley had two more allies in his quest to turn TFC into a top-flight club. Having trained in and around Europe's best, Altidore and Giovinco understood the demands that the sport's elite place on themselves and were ready to bring that level of quality and expectations of others to TFC.

Vanney and the coaching staff were pleasantly surprised by the level of professionalism TFC had adopted, though a familiar concern about the team's style of play didn't just linger, it had gotten worse. In 2014, TFC managed to keep six clean sheets. This was far from respectable, but at least it was something to build on defensively. In 2015, that number lowered to five, with one of those being a 0–0 draw against D.C. United. TFC was easily one of the worst teams in the league defensively, highlighted by a five-game stretch through July and August when they allowed three or more goals in four of those matches. It was these defensive woes that were not only keeping Vanney awake at night, but also preventing TFC from becoming a truly championship-calibre club.

"It was hard to get a foundation of confidence if you're also leaking goals," said Vanney.

All told, TFC would win a franchise-high 15 matches that season. And the forward duo scored in all but one of those games, including seven one-goal wins, creating an almost immeasurable impact on the standings. While it's naturally impossible to imagine how the club would have fared without them, or had TFC pursued other attacking options, those numbers alone place responsibility for the turnaround the franchise experienced in 2015 squarely on one pair of very broad, and another pair of much smaller, shoulders.

Those small shoulders were quickly changing the expectations many outsiders had of players within MLS. Giovinco's 22 goals would tie for the league lead and equalled the total scored by all the other players on TFC, if you leave out Altidore. But it was the way Giovinco attacked defences and moved the ball with the kind of creative and dramatic flair one would expect only in La Liga or Serie A that made him a two-foot putt for MLS MVP in 2015.

The finesse and power with which he scored made the scrappy goals of Danny Dichio look like hieroglyphics: from another era, and almost impossible to compare with what was happening before fans' eyes now. For years, North American soccer had struggled to find its footing from a tactical standpoint: Canada and the United States were melting pots of international cultures, and as a result, their citizens brought wave after wave of soccer ideologies. And each belief in how to play the game was intertwined with a brutally physical approach deriving from the classic American belief that, on any field, brawn beats beauty.

Giovinco would seemingly effortlessly erase any preconceived notions of what soccer is, or what it could be, in Toronto and North America with a quick, graceful turn with the ball around hapless defenders or a perfectly placed free kick, of which Giovinco still refuses to share the secret.

He was a superstar in a city that felt robbed of one a year earlier. But he was a superstar who moved almost whimsically, clearly blessed with talent in a city that loves its heroes hard-nosed and big-hearted. Local papers such as the *Globe and Mail* were already calling him the best player in North America and stopping inches short of calling him the best in MLS history midway through his first season.

In Bezbatchenko's and TFC management's dreams, managing a player of Giovinco's otherworldly talent would be the daily routine. But in 2015, it was a new, fresh challenge. Asking him simply to show up for training five days a week and then score at a league-leading clip would not be enough. As good as Giovinco, and Altidore, for that matter, were, their presence ensured that the coaching staff raised the bar in a club that had once simply relied on small-sided games to fill a training session.

"You make sure that everything you do makes sense," said assistant coach Robin Fraser, of the coaching staff's approach in 2015 with that top-end talent included. When the training sessions appear randomly planned and don't provide a clear means to an end, players such as Giovinco and Altidore lose interest. Their output on the pitch suffers. "Because the big players, I think in my experience, when the things you do make sense, when you ask, when what you demand, when it has a purpose, then everyone's on board."

Giovinco came to Toronto to escape the shackles of a club that did not appreciate him. The result was evident on the pitch. "For a player like me, playing in America is fun," said Giovinco. "Especially for the first year, nobody knew me. So when I played, I played like I was free, like I was liberated."

Altidore and Giovinco fell hard for Toronto in their first season. Altidore loved the glamour, if in modest proportions, that came with the city. He could mingle with the city's athletic glitterati, but not be bound by the same expectations.

And Giovinco, too, didn't mind being recognized at the odd Raptors game, but still appreciated being able to walk the high-end streets of Yorkville without being mobbed by the fanatics that came with the territory in Turin.

By the end of the summer, Altidore had shed any fears of what a return to North America could bring.

The two had been isolated in their respective careers for too long. Here, many hands were making for light, and inspiring, work.

"I've never played with a guy," said Altidore, "where the plan was just to build."

Toward the end of the 2015 season, TFC ventured farther into uncharted waters as they went on their first-ever four-game winning streak. Throughout this stretch, Vanney saw progress not only on the pitch, but off it, as well. With new faces providing a level of quality that had never existed previously in Toronto, the squad was finally solid. For the first time, Vanney glimpsed a team that truly believed they could "be a champion in this league."

The streak was capped with a win over the eventual Supporters' Shield winners, the New York Red Bulls. On the other side of the Gardiner Expressway that evening, the Blue Jays were making history with a climactic Game 5 win over the Texas Rangers, highlighted by José Bautista's now infamous bat flip, in the American League Division Series.

But south of the Gardiner, Giovinco wrote his own chapter in the TFC history books. He had played in the Italian national team for a Euro 2016 qualifier the previous day, and entered the game in Toronto as a substitute in the 62nd minute. There had been serious doubts about whether Giovinco would return in time for the pivotal game against the Red Bulls, at all. Some in Toronto saw an ominous parallel with Vince Carter, the best in Toronto Raptors basketball history, and his decision to fly to North Carolina for his college graduation ceremony the morning of Game 7 of the Eastern Conference Semifinal. Carter had scored 20 points in a loss to the Philadelphia 76ers, one many Raptors fans have etched in their memory.

But Giovinco was determined, as he always had been in Toronto, to be different. He texted Vanney after Italy's 2–1 win over Norway, then as he boarded a flight and again when he landed in Toronto three hours before the BMO Field kickoff, every time affirming that he would play against the Red Bulls.

And while few would have faulted Giovinco too much had he missed the game — as TFC still had two more opportunities to clinch their first-ever playoff spot — that he was so determined to play speaks to just how much Giovinco truly wanted to shift the perception both of his abilities and of MLS. Here was a goal-scorer, at the height of his powers, who had just been called into one of the most established national sides on the planet, who was determined to play for an MLS side after flying across an ocean.

Forget Danny Dichio. And that one incident alone made the Jermain Defoe saga fade almost into oblivion.

And Giovinco didn't just clock in and clock out for duty. In approximately eight seconds, Giovinco forced naysayers to accept that MLS was not a league for international has-beens, but one where some of the world's most dynamic players can thrive.

"He was the proof of concept," said ESPN soccer columnist Jeff Carlisle, noting how Giovinco's arrival didn't bring the wide-scale attention that perhaps David Beckham's did. But his arrival signified that soccer in North America could thrive. "He changed the league in a different way."

With the ball near the touchline halfway between the Red Bulls box and his own half, Giovinco quickly dummied two Red Bulls players with deft movement on the ball as he attacked the opponents' back line.

"There's an air of expectation ..." Nigel Reed said in the broadcast, himself almost holding his breath in anticipation.

Still with the ball, Giovinco embarrassed centre-back Ronald Zubar by crossing over to his left, leaving Zubar fighting for table scraps. Now with a clear look at the net, Giovinco launched a shot, with his wrong foot, past experienced goalkeeper Luis Robles.

Colour commentator Jason deVos quickly called it the goal of the season on the broadcast, but in retrospect, with the obvious context of Giovinco having played international soccer the day before, it might very well have been the best goal in MLS history.

Ask most sports fans in Toronto to recall October 14, 2015, and many will fondly recount where they were and who they were with when José Bautista hit a three-run home run, flipped his bat, set off a bench-clearing brawl, and ultimately sank the Texas Rangers. It was a moment of epic proportions in Toronto sports history that can bring together a city.

But ask Toronto FC fans where they were on that same day and they'll recount their own story, of when Giovinco undressed an entire back line and propelled TFC to the MLS playoffs for the first time in franchise history.

It's horribly ironic that the most important goal in Toronto FC history came as another moment a couple of thousand metres away would overshadow it. And while Bautista's home run provided a spark for a fan base and perhaps a city, it did not represent a turning point in the history of the sport in Canada. It was an addition to the top-10 lists of one franchise.

Giovinco's goal changed the course of Toronto FC and showed what North America could be: a place where great players in the world's biggest sport could thrive. Giovinco repaid the faith that Bezbatchenko showed in him ahead of the season by bringing the club to the playoffs for the first time. As Giovinco ran to the sidelines to celebrate, he did so by twirling his right hand as he would if he were mixing in a bowl. It was a similar celebration to what the Jays had used all season. He had bought into the city and the sports infrastructure that supported it.

Giovinco, like Altidore, was happy in Toronto. Giovinco wanted to create a new sporting culture in the city. And as fans close to him, and the mob of his teammates that surrounded him, after the goal bowed down repeatedly in sheer adoration, it was hard not to think that he had begun to do so. The first of the club's objectives in turning the franchise around had been accomplished: they were no longer "that club that hasn't made the playoffs."

Elite-level soccer can very often feel distant in North America. The world's best appear Saturday mornings on TV screens, competing in places many children have to look up on a map. When the name brands of the sport do visit North America, it's on victory laps in their careers or during cookie-cutter tournaments that have no real consequences. Giovinco's investment was a long-term one, one that would be felt in the generations of children growing up in Toronto who understood, that after his goal, it was possible not just to be one of the sport's most impactful players, but also to call Toronto "home."

Once the celebration of making the playoffs ended, there were still questions about where TFC would finish in the standings and who they would face. A first-round bye wasn't out of the question with two games remaining. And as well as TFC had played during their four-game streak, Vanney knew that the teams that perform well in the playoffs are those who enter the post-season with momentum.

Their final two opponents were both in the tightly contested Eastern Conference, and a win against either the Columbus Crew or the Montreal Impact would go a long way to leapfrogging other clubs in the standings.

But by this point the secret of this revamped TFC outfit was out: they could score in bunches. They had been scoring all season, with 58, tied for second in the league. But their leaky defending still hadn't been fixed, and their 58 goals against were tied for the worst in the league. Any team that could shut down Altidore and Giovinco, as monumental a task as that would be, might well earn themselves a victory.

And that's what happened in the final two games of the regular season, as the Crew helped themselves secure the first-round bye with a 2–0 win over TFC. Then, on Decision Day, TFC travelled to Montreal, where the Impact were sitting in fourth place with the all-important home-field advantage.

A textbook cross from Giovinco and finish by Altidore made it look like TFC would head into the playoffs on a high note, until the Impact's established foreign man struck: Didier Drogba's world-class deft touch around a hapless Ahmed Kantari levelled before he struck again to take the lead with a TFC back line sitting on their hands. The 2–1 result would stand.

Very quickly, TFC found themselves in sixth place in the Eastern Conference with no momentum to speak of. The loss in Montreal meant they'd have to make the trip back east again to the Stade Saputo just four days later for their first-ever playoff game. Whereas TFC were now slightly out of form heading into the playoffs, the Impact had found their stride, winning their last three regular-season games.

Besides a few staffers, there was virtually no connection now between the club entering the pressure cooker of a first playoff game in 2015, and the 2009 side that had bottled it with their season on the line. Still, the same question that haunted TFC throughout their franchise existence emerged: *Would TFC disappoint, as they always had?*

The short layoff forced Vanney not to stray far from the lineup that lost in Montreal days earlier. Lining up in a flat 4-4-2 that had hardly been customary, Vanney threw Jackson in at right back, despite the fact that he'd been used in different positions throughout the season.

As much as TFC wanted to rise to the occasion, Vanney acknowledges that his squad "weren't quite ready" to enter that aforementioned pressure cooker. From opening kickoff, the Impact were relentless off the ball, pressuring TFC into multiple turnovers.

Seventeen minutes in, three Impact players worked their way through six TFC defenders to expose a hole on Jackson's side of the pitch. Ignacio Piatti's low shot was stopped by TFC's goalkeeper Chris Konopka, but it had become clear early on that TFC were going to be chasing the match.

One minute later, the Impact broke up a TFC attack and caught Jackson flat-footed and far too high up the pitch. With Jackson unable to break up an outlet pass, Piatti was able to dribble through the heart of the TFC midfield untouched. A quick through ball to Patrice Bernier allowed the veteran Canadian to open the scoring with a single touch. TFC's defending was as shambolic as it had been all season.

"What had been our Achilles heel all year was our Achilles heel in the first 20 minutes," said Vanney.

Fifteen minutes later, things went from bad to worse when Ahmed Kantari chose to move the ball into a dangerous area in the middle of the pitch just outside of TFC's box with Piatti and Drogba pressing, instead of keeping the ball wide. Josh Williams slipped when trying to receive the pass and Piatti made no mistake, doubling the lead with another low shot.

"On the night, so much of what could go wrong, did go wrong," said Bradley.

The rout was officially on when, six minutes later, TFC threw eight outfield players into the box to break up a Bernier chip across to Drogba. That idea, like so much of the rest of TFC's approach that evening, didn't work. Drogba tapped the cross into an open net and sunk any lingering hopes of TFC advancing. A few of those eight heads looked to the sky, while others lowered to look at the ground. Jackson unleashed a verbal tirade on Robbie Findley, who had run into the box to mark Drogba, then slowed up.

TFC were being shown up by Drogba, an aging star finishing his career in MLS, while one of the most dynamic players ever in the league was being limited. While that first half didn't quite stoop to the depths that TFC had explored in the past, that the Reds laid an egg during their first-ever playoff game spoke to how far they still had to go.

"In 90 minutes, it feels as if you undo all the progress you've made all season," said Bradley, shaking his head.

The last thing Vanney wanted to do, against his club's great rivals no less, was go down by several goals and lose the little confidence that had been built up all season. After years of losing seasons, Vanney now had his own special TFC horror story to share with past players and coaches. He couldn't help fearing, too, that this loss might have his elite players reconsidering their decision to join the Reds. "There's such a stress to win with this club, they all want to prove that their decision to come to this league is beneficial," he said.

He wanted to think long-term and think of the loss as a "massive building block," so his message to his squad after the game was simple: take what you can from this loss to help you when you return to this stage.

TFC left Montreal humbled, but with a valuable lesson about sustainable success in MLS: sheer talent alone doesn't always equate to results.

Though fans might have felt that the era of learning and gleaning lessons from losses was past, inside the dressing room, TFC thought differently. "I don't think we recognized the moment. There's no way you can tell me that Montreal team was more talented than us, even with Drogba," said Altidore. And while he might have felt at home in his first season, he wasn't convinced everyone else beside him felt the same way.

"We weren't ready to take that next step, for each other."

11

Finding the Last Piece of the Puzzle, Getting Goosebumps, and Feeling Numb

BILL MANNING DOES NOT LIKE to be embarrassed. Throughout his 24-year career in sports management, including stops with the Philadelphia Eagles and the Houston Rockets, he never had been.

He didn't think he would be embarrassed when, barely two weeks after being named president of TFC, he sat down with Larry Tanenbaum and Don Garber at the Stade Saputo to witness his new club's first-ever playoff game on that chilly evening in late October. But that's exactly what had happened: as TFC continued to leak goals en route to a 3–0 drubbing at the hands of their rivals, Manning was flat-out ashamed in front of the man who essentially signed his paycheque and another man who had been pumping the tires of his new club for years despite constant losing records.

The Impact brought the different level of intensity that MLS playoffs demand. They were ready for the occasion, and TFC were not.

Manning believed TFC had the pieces to contend, but early on in his tenure at the club, there was now very little separating him from the perpetual embarrassment that had dogged the franchise.

So, when Manning left the stadium that evening, he summoned his inner Tim Leiweke and made a simple vow: he would figure out how to stop the bleeding and would not allow TFC to be embarrassed again.

From his desk at the BMO Training Grounds, Manning can look out of wide windows onto every training pitch. He likes being able to have a grasp on everything that's happening within the club. When he walks into a room, it's hard not to be drawn to his imposing figure. His is a handshake that nearly crumbles you before you're brought back to life by his Grand Canyon–sized smile.

Manning has never shied away from a challenge. Which is why, midway through 2015, when he heard TFC were looking for a president, he reached out to Larry Tanenbaum through a mutual friend to express his interest. He was still under contract with Real Salt Lake and couldn't speak formally about a contract, but TFC had always intrigued Manning from afar.

His track record at Real Salt Lake spoke for itself. Under his watch as club president, RSL won an MLS Cup and were MLS Cup and CONCACAF Champions League runners-up. He was awarded MLS's Doug Hamilton Executive of the Year award in 2012 and 2014.

RSL's growth was also exponential, from the opening of Rio Tinto Stadium, to the increase in ticket sales, and partnerships.

Once Manning was officially out of contract on August 15, he began fielding calls from various MLS clubs. He visited four different teams in two weeks, but still didn't receive a call from MLSE. Quietly, he held out hope that TFC would enter into the bidding. "I actually felt Toronto would be the best turnaround," he said, of the chance to remake the franchise.

After just landing from a flight to visit another MLS team, Manning finally got the call he was hoping for. "Before you do anything, I want you to come to Toronto," said Tanenbaum.

Two days later, Manning was in Toronto to meet briefly with Tanenbaum, before another trip to meet with Tanenbaum, George Cope, and Guy Laurence. Sensing that they were close to an agreement, Laurence suggested Manning return once more, his third trip in 10 days, this time with his wife. With the wounds of Defoe's leaving Toronto still fresh, MLSE wanted to be sure: if Manning was going to take the job, ownership had to be sure his family would embrace Toronto.

When Manning and his wife arrived at their hotel, they were surrounded by TFC gear in their sons' sizes. They were treated to Raptors games, dinner at Buca, and lunch at Harbour Sixty Steakhouse. After just a few days, Manning and his family did indeed feel like they were home.

"The one thing I learned quickly is MLSE is professional," said Manning. His only concern was that TFC would not be held in the same regard as

MLSE's other sports properties. He was assured the opposite was true: MLSE wanted TFC's status within the city and across MLS to be elevated. There was an admitted lack of soccer expertise at 50 Bay Street, but Manning found an astonishing depth of understanding of the game at the club's training grounds. He wanted the resources to better serve those at the training ground, and Tanenbaum wanted someone who he could trust with the club who wouldn't have to be micromanaged. They'd done the same with the hiring of Masai Ujiri for the Raptors, and Brendan Shanahan for the Leafs, to immediate success. MLSE, in short, wanted someone who could focus on winning.

"That was music to my ears," said Manning. "I believe winning supports the business."

To develop a winning franchise, Manning sold MLSE on a refreshing concept: long-term stability instead of quick fixes. "The last thing you guys need, and I will represent change, but we need to keep a foundation here," Manning told MLSE. He wanted to keep the club's staff in place and believed that if the entire club was aligned, "good things can happen."

As for the squad itself, Manning shared part of his recipe for success at Real Salt Lake with MLSE, what he called the "Rule of 14."

Essentially, Manning believed that in order to develop a stable, successful roster of a club's top 14 players in terms of minutes played, at least 10 should return for the following season. With that, players would not be constantly looking over their shoulders and worrying about their positions being taken. Manning's plan would liberate players mentally and allow them to perform to their full capacity on the pitch.

TFC, he told MLSE, was jarringly different from RSL. In 2009, just seven of TFC's top 14 minutes-earners had returned. Then that number fell every season to a low of just three players of 14 returning for 2012.

Only in 2015 did that number begin to rise, this time to six. Manning wanted to build on that number and create stability in the roster, telling MLSE that, ideally, he would like to see 10 to 12 of the club's top minute-earners return every season. (It's worth noting that in 2017, for the first time in club history, 10 of the club's top minute-earners were returning players. Manning beams with pride when he points this out.)

Two weeks after his final exploratory meeting with MLSE, a deal was agreed on, and October 12, 2015, Manning was announced as club president.

The hire was an aggressive move, but one that further showcased the change in attitude throughout the organization. TFC were aiming to throw off the shackles of embarrassment that had long hindered them. By utilizing the full scale of resources afforded to them through ownership in every possible facet of the club, from the pitch to the boardroom and everywhere in between, TFC wanted to frame themselves as a club that would strive for excellence at all costs, not unlike the Maple Leafs and the Raptors. And by swinging for the fences with every transaction, TFC believed they could lap some of their counterparts in MLS, who treated every season as an opportunity to simply put one more small piece into the jigsaw puzzle. TFC didn't just believe they could be measured alongside some of the most prominent sports organizations in North America; they acted with that same swagger as well. The club had learned that they needed to add big on the pitch and carefully consider every element needed for success off of it. They had become the club that was thrown back in the faces of MLS haters when it was suggested that the league was small-time.

Manning's first order of off-season business was ensuring that what had happened in Montreal wouldn't happen again. Some fires needed to be put out.

First, was addressing "#VanneyOut," the growing calls for the young coach's dismissal. That Vanney couldn't deliver during the club's first-ever playoff game was enough for many to believe a coach with more experience would be better suited to lead what had become a talented core of players.

Manning saw potential in Vanney, but was still unsure if he could grow into the coach TFC needed. Nevertheless, having been in MLS throughout the past decade, Manning knew that turnover was TFC's unfortunate hallmark. In his mind, the last thing the club needed at that moment was a coaching change.

In their first post-season meeting, Manning made his intentions clear: the team's defending needed to be improved. Almost immediately, Vanney opened up his notebook full of plans and pointed to the top entry in his off-season "To do" list: "Improve TFC's back line."

Both Manning and Vanney wanted defenders with practical MLS experience, so they turned to the league's first-ever crop of free agents. Near the top of the list was defensive stalwart Drew Moor, who had previously won an MLS Cup in 2010 with the Colorado Rapids.

A vocal commander in a back line, Moor was also the calming influence that had been missing in TFC's previous playoff run. His voice could often be heard even from the stands, directing traffic and keeping the lines of communication wide open.

For Manning's first proper acquisition, he had to pay forward the good will that MLSE had shown to him on his initial trips to Toronto. Moor and his wife, Shelby, were expecting their first child and wanted to sign with a club that would take care of their family.

So Manning suggested Shelby visit Toronto. When she arrived, the club introduced her to some of the support they provided spouses: a family room during games with babysitters, and a club-organized "Girls night" once a month, where a sense of community can be built. "It's an organization that tries to do everything right," said Moor.

And any fears Moor had about the TFC of old creeping up were assuaged through the conversations he had with club staff: "One thing that I like about the people I spoke to, the people that have been with TFC the longest embraced their past, regardless of what people thought of it. They learned from it what they want to do better."

And in the short-term, that included getting better defensively.

Moor insists he didn't feel the weight of expectations being brought in as a centre-back to a club that was porous defensively. "Bringing me in wasn't going to solve all the problems," he said.

What his addition would do was make TFC louder on the pitch. Moor remembers going up against TFC outfits in the past and noticing that as a unit, they were "too quiet." Moor urged his teammates, especially the younger ones, to express themselves vocally on the pitch. "Even if you're not saying the right thing, you're saying something."

His presence was augmented days later with the additions of defender and former Supporters' Shield winner Steven Beitashour, Canadian defensive midfielder Will Johnson, and, the following month, goalkeeper and former teammate of Moor's, Clint Irwin.

There were now pieces in place that could help TFC on the pitch, and characters that could contribute to a healthier environment off of it.

Moor may very well have been the final piece of the puzzle that Michael Bradley was helping to construct. From the moment Bradley arrived in Toronto, he had recognized that the majority of players he was surrounded by were not players who were playing for the common goal of winning the MLS Cup. He needed to be surrounded by more "real men." And, by the start of the 2016 season, he saw the team get rid of the "dead weight, the bad guys, the guys who are going to let you down in the biggest moments, guys only there for themselves."

From the early days of training camp, Bradley noticed a difference from the 2015 squad. "When you replace bad personalities and bad players with amazing personalities and amazing players, it starts to feel like it should. Like a real team. Like a group of guys who are committed to going after things in the right way," said Bradley.

The change wasn't lost on assistant coach Robin Fraser, either. The first training camp sessions revealed Moor to be a confident, capable defender who stepped into the squad rather easily by giving information "in the tone in which it needs to be given."

Immediately, Moor won respect in the TFC locker room by delivering a balance of tough love to fellow defenders when need be, but also providing an ear for younger players. While there was no reason to doubt Moor's ability on the pitch, Fraser was integral in helping TFC identify players whose personal attributes sometimes overshadowed their on-field contributions. "We want characters," he said. "We want good characters to help create the culture we have now. Guys who are unselfish, respectful. Those things are huge. If you look at our team, we have guys in leadership roles but there's a respect for everyone. That speaks to the type of people we have."

Throughout pre-season and the team's training camp in Orlando, Vanney began leaning heavily on Moor because the theme of those early months was tightening up defensively. One defensive drill begat another defensive drill and Moor laughs now when recalling how frustrated the team's attacking players must have gotten.

In Orlando, everyone gathered to determine their goals for the season and those characters made themselves known immediately. TFC didn't just plan on getting back to the playoffs and finally winning their first post-season game. They put, in writing, a lofty goal: win the MLS Cup in 2016.

To those who thought that might be too ambitious, Moor reminded the group of his time with the 2010 Colorado Rapids. Moor's old team snuck into the playoffs tied (with 46 points) for the final playoff position. After a win on penalties in the conference semifinal, Moor's Rapids continued to gut out wins that propelled them to the MLS Cup.

If those Rapids could grind out wins to an MLS Cup, so, too, could this TFC team loaded with talent. "Every team should set the goal to win MLS Cup," said Moor, shrugging his shoulders. "It's different from Supporters' Shield obviously. It's the ultimate prize."

Fans had to wait to get a good look at the new makeup of this defensively-sound squad. BMO Field had undergone major renovations and additional seating had been added, particularly in the east stands. The capacity for BMO Field would be 30,000 for the 2016 season and the stadium would welcome the CFL's Toronto Argonauts as cohabiters, even at the disdain of many TFC supporters who would wear "No Argos at BMO" shirts.

The ongoing renovations meant TFC would play their first eight games of the MLS regular season on the road, in seven different U.S. states and one Canadian province. Given how gruelling road games can be in the league, few were complaining when they finally returned home with a record of 3–3–2. And even fewer could complain about the play of Sebastian Giovinco, who showed no signs of letting up after his MVP campaign. With six goals in eight games, Giovinco was the difference early on, winning games almost singlehandedly.

He was determined to show that the 2015 season was not a fluke and that his impact would be felt beyond BMO Field. "I came here to win for sure," said Giovinco of his start in 2016, "to change soccer in Canada and in North America. And to win in North America was important …"

Giovinco's dream of making an impact on the sport away from his native Italy was dealt a serious blow early on in the season when, despite his ludicrous goal-scoring prowess, he was left off Antonio Conte's 2016 Italian European Championship roster.

Conte didn't hold back when addressing why Giovinco and fellow countryman Andrea Pirlo of New York City FC, both of whom had previously logged plenty of time for the Azzuri, were left off the team. Conte attributed it to their choice to play in North America."It's clear that if you make such choices in football then at the end you might pay the consequences," Conte told reporters.

Giovinco remained tactful in addressing Conte's comments. "At the end of the day, you need to see what the coach says, and how he interprets things when he chooses his team. It can be right, it can be wrong, but it's really not my place to say. He knows what's best and I think it's a good decision if that's what he thinks," said Giovinco.

When the club returned for their home opener on May 7, Giovinco broke out for a 10-shot, one-assist performance in a 1–1 draw. The rest of the club picked up the slack when Giovinco went goalless in eight games, including local product Jordan Hamilton, who had three goals in a four-game stretch through the summer.

And a last-minute goal from Will Johnson to win the Canadian Championship, their first since 2012, on away goals, gave the team belief that championships were again possible.

It was during that summer stretch that the defensive work done through training camp began to foster results. Between July 2 and September 10, a 13-game stretch, TFC allowed more than one goal in a game just once and would only lose twice. Their playoff spot was looking like more and more of a given with a 7–2–3 record during that span.

It was during this stretch that Vanney's master plan was finally coming into focus. He wanted a team that would not get bogged down by a single loss as TFC teams had in the past. The losses would build up throughout the early seasons in TFC's history because, in short, some players didn't know any different. As the losses piled up, and as the losing seasons also piled up, a winning "culture" became more and more difficult to attain. If losing is expected, then a club very often just meets expectations.

The shift in 2016 occurred with Vanney's ability to convince the team to, as overwrought a sports cliché as it is, take the season just one game at a time. And Vanney's 2016 team refused to fall victim to the losing mentality that festered in past squads. Coupled with the veteran experience that Moor and Beitashour brought, the entire team's master plan was finally evident.

COME ON YOU REDS

For a team that lost back-to-back games on four separate occasions in 2015, the turnaround was compelling. After dropping two 1–0 results in a row on the road very early in the season, TFC would not lose twice in a row again all year, finishing with a goal differential of +12. They'd end up third in the Eastern Conference and fifth in MLS with 53 points, a club record.

Toward the end of the season, that shift in mentality was the most marked difference from the squad of a year earlier. "If you lose a game, how quickly can you get back to the other side?" Vanney would continually ask his team.

While they lost just once in the final six games of the regular season, the fact that they allowed two or more goals in four different games and could muster just one win (on the final day of the season) meant TFC were headed back to the playoffs again not on a high, but with questions. The obvious one rang out: would the same defensively unstable team show up in the post-season this year, or would TFC finally get a playoff win?

For Vanney, Fraser, and the rest of the TFC coaching staff, what had been lost over that late-season stretch, and that they needed to reclaim, was the ability to control games.

Having finished third in the Eastern Conference, TFC, for the first time ever, hosted a playoff game, a one-game knockout-round match against the Philadelphia Union. With a cold wind blowing off Lake Ontario making temperatures feel close to freezing in late October, Vanney stressed the need to control the game from the start.

And they did that, with two bona fide chances, both just missing wide, from Giovinco and Armando Cooper, within the first 10 minutes. The Union had little answer and chased the game early on, most notably when four separate Union defenders kept their eyes focused squarely on Altidore as he corralled a loose ball and knocked it over his head to a man that, historically speaking, shouldn't be left unwatched in the box. Giovinco volleyed Altidore's ball into a wide-open net and TFC had their first playoff goal. Giovinco smacked the corner post in a mix of elation and relief. Later in the first half, Giovinco missed a gorgeous free kick just wide. TFC were on their way, and didn't let up early in the second half when Giovinco played a corner kick in that landed on the foot of Osorio, who doubled their lead from short the distance.

And though nine separate TFC outfielders within the box could not control a corner kick that bounced off three separate Union players before being knocked in for a goal, Vanney still knew what everyone else could see: TFC had dominated, and would not take their foot off the gas.

Eight minutes later, Altidore pounced on some shambolic defending and, on his own, pushed a dagger into the Union's chances with an 85th minute goal.

It was a wholly individual effort, but it changed the perception of an entire franchise. With success on the line, TFC had finally embraced the idea that they deserved to think big. Not only had they learned from their excruciating loss in Montreal the previous year, they were using it as fuel. "You have to win the first playoff game in order to have the freedom to move on," said Vanney. "You have to get that monkey off your back. I don't know that it was our best performance, but it was a freeing performance. We knew that if we could win a one-off game and we get into a two-game series with anyone, we can win this."

The wait for their first-ever two-game MLS playoff series was short. Four days after the win against Philadelphia, MLS MVP and 2010 World Cup winner David Villa and New York City FC arrived in Toronto. Though NYCFC finished with just one more point in the regular season than TFC, it was hard not to favour those in the light and dark blue kits, especially considering they would be welcoming the Reds back to Yankee Stadium for the pivotal second leg.

Vanney went with the same formation and lineup as he had against Philadelphia, with the focus the same it had been all season: keep a clean sheet and avoid allowing the pivotal away goal.

For 80 minutes, a tightly-contested, if at times overtly technical, 0–0 draw, which would have certainly benefited TFC, looked like the obvious result. That is until — much as against Philadelphia — TFC pounced on a back line that was unable to clear a loose ball in the 84th minute. Altidore found the back of an empty net and Tosaint Ricketts scored an insurance marker in extra time to send TFC back to New York with a two-goal cushion.

All the planning heading out on the road was focused on Patrick Vieira's tactical approach. Vanney saw Vieira and NYCFC as a very ideological team, one that would play the same way through any game, through thick and thin. For Vanney, his preparation was clear-cut, because it was his belief that "it's not like they're going to do anything different."

Buoyed by a two-goal lead in the series, Vanney wanted to attack NYCFC aggressively early on. TFC employed a high press in specific areas of the pitch. Almost every minute of training ahead of the second leg was dedicated to working tirelessly on how TFC would pressure New York and win balls back in good spots in NYCFC's end. The coaching staff believed that if they could win balls back in specific areas, they'd be rewarded with promising scoring chances.

"Credit to the players," said Fraser, "they were so up for it and they didn't give New York a second to breathe."

For the fourth game in a row, Vanney's lineup was unchanged. On a strange-looking pitch, in the middle of an iconic baseball stadium, his faith and nuanced planning were rewarded. Six minutes in, TFC defender Justin Morrow allowed NYCFC defender Frederic Brilliant limited time and space. His slow pass found Jack Harrison who was quickly pounced on by Osorio. Harrison's errant first touch meant Altidore could easily play a through ball to Giovinco. Inside the box, one quick turn was all that was needed to give him a clear look at net and the pivotal away goal.

Fourteen minutes later, Brilliant could not handle Giovinco's run through the box and conceded a blatant foul. Giovinco converted from the spot and the rout was on. Ten minutes later, TFC defender Eriq Zavaleta's perfectly placed long ball meant Altidore could box out his defender and volley the third goal in just under the crossbar. Altidore, with his third goal in as many playoff games, ran to the sidelines, held his hands to his ears, and saw beer cups rain down upon him.

More pressing meant more questionable passes and a Jonathan Osorio goal before Giovinco added his third with a dipping strike in added time.

It was a performance few outside of the TFC dressing room could have predicted. With the Impact having eliminated the top-ranked New York Red Bulls in the other conference semifinal, an all-Canadian conference final was set. It was hard not to now consider TFC the favourites, an offensive train impossible to slow down.

That, coincidentally or not, was exactly what happened when TFC travelled to Montreal for the first leg, to be played at Olympic Stadium, with its 60,000+ seats, where the game was moved to just for the occasion.

With the stadium rarely used for soccer, packed with the then second-largest MLS playoff crowd, for an 8:00 p.m. kickoff, match officials noticed an egregious error: the 18-yard penalty box markings were too small. The faulty lines were painted green and a rudimentary machine painted white lines in their proper spaces.

As if that wasn't comical enough, a machine not unlike a leaf-blower was then produced to help dry the paint.

For 40 minutes, fans were tortured by actually having to live the phrase: they watched paint dry.

And in the dressing room, TFC waited.

Moor couldn't help letting the blunder affect him. "It throws your rhythm off," he said. "For your entire life, you prepare, you get to the stadium, you put your warm-up gear on, you warm up, you put on your gear, you play. Now you have a 30-minute gap in there."

There was a lot of laughter, simply out of surprise, but after the game, Bradley would raise his concerns that perhaps the Impact had orchestrated the blunder themselves. "Probably not totally out of the realm of possibilities that they did it on purpose, maybe. Add to the drama of it all. I don't know," said Bradley, smiling.

Once the match did kick off, there was little reason to smile. Two quick passes sliced through the midfield and a missed assignment saw former TFC forward Dominic Oduro clear through with the game's opening goal for the Impact, just 10 minutes in.

Two minutes later, the horrors of the previous year's playoffs began to stir, as Matteo Mancosu wasn't properly marked by TFC defender Nick Hagglund and doubled up on the lead.

At halftime, again facing a seemingly insurmountable lead as they had a year earlier in Montreal, Bradley went to speak to the club. Instead of seeing bowed heads, the change he saw in attitude was palpable:

> It'd be so easy at that point to go, "Are you fucking kidding me? Is this happening again?" And instead, it was just

different. You came inside, you look around; obviously there's frustration. Really quickly what you say is "Forget that. That's over with. Now, for the next 45 minutes, it's just about one goal at a time. How many away goals can we leave here with?"

A year earlier, when Bradley delivered a similar speech, he found that he was talking to a wall in many regards. This time around, players were buying in.

Though Ambroise Oyongo added to the lead in the 53rd minute, Altidore continued his playoff scoring streak minutes later with a header in close. He mauled Impact defender Laurent Ciman for the ball after scooping it from the back of the net to run it to the half line and get play started again.

Bradley added the crucial second away goal with a clean, well-placed shot into the corner of the net from just inside the box.

Though TFC would leave the game down 3–2, Bradley and TFC still felt like they'd escaped death in some manner. When they pulled out of the Olympic Stadium in the team bus, they shared a common belief: if, at the beginning of the season, they had been offered 90 minutes at home to win and go to the final, to a man they would've signed that proposal.

Eight days later, TFC were afforded that chance in what would stand as one of the wildest games in MLS history.

Twenty-four minutes in, Hagglund's missed coverage again allowed Oduro to walk through the box and send a low shot past Irwin. Not only were TFC down 4–2 on aggregate, the Impact had an away goal they could build on. Oduro ran to the south end and raised his index finger to his mouth to try and silence the crowd.

And for a minute, Bradley thought TFC might have lost their all-important home crowd. He briefly recalled similar situations in his past, when going down early at home would lead to booing from the hometown fans. "There was the obvious silence when [Oduro] first scored," Bradley recalls.

But when we got the ball back, the place was louder. It was like everybody inside the stadium said to each other,

"We're going to be here for the next 60 minutes. We can either be quiet or we can, together with the guys on the field, make this a special night." They got louder and we put more into it.

A leaping header from Nick Hagglund off a corner kick nearly tied the game before Cooper scored his first MLS goal on the rebound.

Rain started to fall even harder right before halftime as Giovinco went to take a corner kick. Seconds before, Altidore had jogged to the corner, bent over, and Giovinco had whispered into his ear, *Go to the near post and be ready.*

"Maybe it's better to go to the first post because I know how to kick there," Giovinco said later, shrugging and smiling.

Giovinco's soft kick in was redirected with an even softer touch of the head by Altidore into a slim space between the near post and Impact goalkeeper Evan Bush.

"Jozy Altidore cannot stop scoring right now," exclaimed play-by-play man Luke Wileman, as Altidore ran along the sidelines with his now trademark scream. He continued his celebratory run clear along a quarter of the pitch to his teammates on the bench. Five straight goals in five straight playoff games.

Looking back, Altidore found it impossible not to elevate his own game when the stakes were higher. "The games are different, they're not boring, they're tense, they're like a chess match," he said. "For me, it's just recognizing the opportunity to do what I want to do and win that trophy."

After halftime, Hagglund again got beat by his man, this time Ignacio Piatti as he willed his way through the TFC box before scoring a slow, rolling goal. Not only did Montreal have their own second away goal, they also had a 5–4 lead on aggregate.

The skies were now wide open, the rain pouring down, and match reports were being crafted, questioning Hagglund's role in what was supposed to be a championship-ready back line.

The rain seemed to only call more out of the BMO Field crowd during their Viking clap in the 68th minute. As it built to a climax, Morrow chipped a cross into the box. Hagglund ran back from his place near the penalty spot before turning around at the edge of the box and sprinting back in toward the chaos in front of Bush. Hagglund launched himself up, far higher than any defender, and forcibly headed the chip into the net. Atrocious defending capitalized upon.

It was now 5–5 on aggregate.

"What a night at BMO Field!" proclaimed Wileman.

Extra time was inevitable. The sense of drama was only heightened when Giovinco was subbed off with a calf cramp in the 97th minute, replaced by French veteran Benoit Cheyrou.

"You can go from winning to losing like that," said Fraser, snapping his fingers.

"I was frustrated because they had nothing," Vanney recalls of the 5–5 aggregate score. But his message, along with the rest of the coaching staff, was the same during the break. Keep doing what you're doing. Maintain an aggressive mindset. You will be rewarded.

In the 98th minute Bradley stood with the ball midway between half and the edge of the box with his head up, surveying his options. On the right flank, Beitashour raised his hand as he made his run. Bradley flipped the ball forward to Altidore, who slipped the ball deftly over to Beitashour. After a quick touch, Beitashour felt like something of a quarterback, not trying to aim for either Ricketts or Cheyrou, but instead for a "danger spot" he sensed. As his marker tried to force him more to the edge of the pitch, Beitashour stopped, moved the ball to his left, and swung the cross in with his left foot.

The cross sailed over Ricketts's leaping head, but eventually found a diving Benoit Cheyrou. He pushed off Osorio and ran to the south stands to celebrate the biggest goal in TFC history, having just come off the bench.

A minute later, a Herculian individual effort from Altidore to move the ball down the flank caught the Impact on their heels, and unable to lock down on Ricketts. He jumped in toward Bush to deflect Altidore's cross into the net.

Nine previous years of misery led to the most cathartic of roars from BMO Field.

"It still," said Moor, raising his arms as evidence, "brings goosebumps."

The 5–2 win and 7–5 aggregate were far from the prettiest or even most convincing of results. But it was emblematic of who TFC had become. In the pouring rain, on a night that could have turned out miserably and been met with equally miserable fans, the club instead scraped and clawed its way into history. "One of the most exciting sports events," said Fraser, "I've ever seen."

Nothing had ever come easy for the squad, or its fans. Years of disappointment on the pitch had led to the pervasive belief that if something could go wrong for TFC, it would. But both the squad and the fans played their parts in propelling the club to a situation that, perhaps up until a week or two earlier, seemed like a laughable proposal: hosting the MLS Cup final. The opportunity to erase years of misery hung in the balance.

Michael Bradley awoke early in the Ritz-Carlton on the morning of the final. With two young children, Bradley is accustomed to waking early. He took Will Johnson and Nick Hagglund out for a coffee. The three teammates quickly made a startling realization: temperatures were already well below freezing, and at BMO Field, close to the lake, they'd be in for one of the coldest games of their lives.

Returning to the hotel, they found an anxious group. Some chose to watch Bradley's father, Bob, coach English side Swansea against Sunderland and their former teammate Jermain Defoe. "You're really just trying to kill the day off," said Bradley, "and make time go as quickly as possible."

As the hours wore on toward kickoff, Bradley kept his nerves at bay. There was little that could surprise him. After agreeing as a group close to 11 months earlier that their goal for the season would be to win the MLS Cup, and after the steam built up through an improbable playoff run, Bradley was not about to be pragmatic about the final: "I had only prepared for one possible outcome — that we were going to win. We felt that when we were at our best, we were invincible."

While some will stop short of calling it "destiny," the narrative was definitely working in TFC's favour. From the embarrassments of years past, to the recent embarrassment from a year previous, TFC had arrived. The final would not be their coming-out party, but instead a fitting end to a transformative season.

But even after the final whistle in the TV game and the auspicious 3–0 win that Swansea and Bradley's father delivered, there was still eight hours to go before the MLS Cup final, and the wait was getting to Altidore. "I was anxious," he said. "I'd be lying if I said I wasn't."

In many ways, the weight of TFC's fortunes rested on Altidore's shoulders. His playoff performance up to that point had changed the course of the club's history, and if anyone was going to break through a stingy Seattle Sounders outfit that had allowed just three goals in five playoff games, it was going to be Altidore.

And that much was known about the Sounders. They were not a relentlessly aggressive, offensive team like TFC. As impressive as their three goals conceded in the playoffs were, they'd only scored eight goals of their own in that span. The Sounders ranked in the bottom half of MLS with just 44 goals scored through 34 regular season games. Without a top-rate goal-scorer in Seattle's fold, a tentative final was expected.

But from the opening kickoff, tentative as a descriptor for the final became an understatement. Moor watched the ball played all the way to Seattle's back line before a long ball was played in the air deep into TFC's end, but to no one in particular. TFC immediately gained possession on the ensuing throw-in. "They must have messed it up," Moor recalls thinking.

They hadn't. Even the most casual observer would have noticed the Sounders parking the bus and waiting for, in Moor's words, one "half chance."

Altidore understood the need for a visiting club to be diligent, but after an early chance of his just drifted past the far post, the minutes continued to tick away. He noticed the way the Sounders communicated, moving their arms to instruct every supporting player to play safe.

And when he used his Spanish to pick up on Osvaldo Alonso telling the Sounders to "stay deep, keep it deep, stay compact," he knew TFC would be dealing with a very defensive posture all night. Parking the bus allowed Seattle to keep the tempo of the game slow, which was aided by the weather and the fact that the ball moves that much slower on a cold pitch.

After 90 minutes, TFC had not produced any noteworthy chances. But the Sounders? They had yet to register a single shot on goal.

Bradley grew frustrated that TFC could not "get that final play right," through 90 minutes. The goal, he and the rest of BMO Field, thought, would certainly come in extra time as the Sounders defensive approach would surely relent to TFC's aggressive approach.

Bradley's belief wasn't encouraged when, in extra time, Sebastian Giovinco informed Vanney that he was having trouble moving well and needed to be substituted off.

On the sidelines, Vanney and Fraser were in constant communication. "How much do you want to potentially expose yourself, to try and create a little bit more on the other side, or do you have enough to get the one goal?" they would ask each other. "Is one goal enough to make a tactical switch? Do we make a broad technical change, to take our guys out of the five back to a four back to add more pressure up the field?"

The pressure mounted to a boiling point when Ricketts sent a shot inches wide of the post and then, 75 seconds later, when Altidore had the chance he'd been waiting for all game.

Ricketts evaded a Roman Torres challenge and, summing up his inner Justin Morrow, sent a chip into the box. Unmarked, Altidore put his head on the ball to send it sailing toward the top right corner of the net. The ball hung long enough in the air, a full second, for Altidore to begin his run toward the sidelines to celebrate. He thought he had the winner, and TFC fans probably thought they had a suitable candidate for the next mayoral race as well.

Stefan Frei had other ideas. He leapt into the air, and with the top of his left hand, reached across the goal line and deep into the hearts of TFC fans.

Fuck, Altidore said to himself. *How are we going to crack this?*

They wouldn't; 120 minutes brought no goals, and still not a shot on net from the Sounders. Any action on the pitch was as frozen as the fingers and toes of the thousands of fans in the stadium. If relief, and redemption, were to come, fans would have to wait a little longer: penalties would decide the MLS Cup for the fourth time in its history.

Drew Moor began to look around and consider who the penalty-takers might be: Altidore, Bradley, Cheyrou, Johnson ... And then he realized ... "I might be the fifth guy."

When Vanney first asked Moor, he told him to kick tires with the rest of the team. But Vanney wanted veteran presence, and circled back to Moor to take the first shot.

"It's a bit of an out-of-body experience," said Moor, who put his penalty into the bottom left corner. Cheyrou, Johnson, and Altidore would all score their penalties.

Bradley took a long run up to his penalty. After the year of expectations that had weighed on him, and a game in which he once again ran himself ragged, he was drained and had nothing more to give. His shot lacked enough power and was stopped by Frei. "I didn't have anything left to shoot with in that moment," he said.

After five rounds, the two clubs were still deadlocked. Justin Morrow was called up to take the all-important sixth penalty in what had become a sudden-death round.

He hit the ball firmly, and would have beaten Frei, but saw it bounce squarely off the crossbar.

It was up to Roman Torres to finish TFC.

With a clean shot to the right of Irwin, who guessed and went to the other side of the net, Torres did just that. The image of Torres's braided, spiked hair bouncing as he ran toward the middle to find his Sounders teammates quickly took its place in the pantheon of disappointing memories in the life of a TFC fan.

Bradley walked off the pitch with a player and a fan base of thousands never having felt more connected. "I was numb," he said.

The Sounders were a club that had never taken their sights off the MLS Cup and, while they were at one point in the season in last place in the Western Conference, they truly believed it was their trophy to win.

And as bad as the loss in Montreal had been in 2015, the current crop of TFC players was still largely separated from the anguish that had plagued the club early on. The reckoning with the loss was a quiet one. Altidore first saw Corey Wray, and the two embraced for minutes on end. The TFC dressing room, with the smell of alcohol from the visitors' dressing room wafting through, was painfully silent. Some buried their heads in their hands and others stared blankly into their own encroaching feelings of regret and longing. Not a single player said a word.

While Vanney fulfilled his duties in the post-game press conference, the silence continued for close to 20 minutes. Even Bradley couldn't summon up an encouraging word or two. "There's nothing really you can say," said Moor.

After his press conference, during which he told the media that he, like Bradley, was still numb, Vanney returned to the dressing room. Having lost three MLS Cup finals as a player, Vanney remembers how he and his teammates internalized their frustration, so he made a point of directing his energy toward specific individuals, especially Justin Morrow, instead of giving an all-encompassing team talk. When he did address the group before the media entered the dressing room, he found it difficult to logically explain the loss.

> When we came into this game, we said we wanted to be the aggressors and leave nothing out there. We did that. We were the better team. We played to win the game. But that's soccer.

Moor then took time to console Osorio, who, as one of the local products on the team, was wearing the loss especially hard. Days earlier, it had been Osorio who had clutched the Eastern Conference trophy for long stretches at a time, and now his head was buried in his hands.

"I know it hurts," said Moor.

Altidore sensed the need to eventually address the group.

"Bottle this up," he told the group. "Remember this feeling. Before you know it, we're going to be back here. When it's time to let it out, let it out."

Days later, in the team's final media availability, frustration was still evident. Giovinco not-so-subtly blamed the Argonauts for tearing up the BMO Field pitch, which he believed led to his cramping. Altidore lamented the team's lack of a "creative" midfielder who could have better linked up with him and Giovinco and all but insisted TFC find that type of player in the off-season.

Few had answers for the loss, then. And even far separated from the loss, with many of that group having eventually become parts of what would be known as the greatest MLS side of all time, it's one that most still cannot come to terms with.

"I feel," said Moor, much later, his palms stretched open wide, "like I should have one more championship than I do."

12

One Game at a Time, One Trophy at a Time, and More Than One Drink at a Time

FROM THE MOMENT TORONTO FC returned to training camp from a brief 43-day respite after losing the MLS Cup on home soil, one thing became painfully obvious: this was not going to be a very fun team to be around.

There was a noticeable absence of photos from the team's off-season vacations on their various social media channels; a rarity. considering the lavish lifestyles many of the team's stars enjoyed. Quietly, many who had covered the team wondered if the sting of the finals loss would carry over to 2017. If their window had closed, would there be any interest from the players in opening themselves up throughout the season?

Having fun, of course, isn't a contributor of any sort to success on the pitch and so there was no need for TFC to entertain the ever-growing crowd of reporters who would attend training sessions and matches. Players treated those who were near the club every day with all the affection that one might show an employee of another company taking the same elevator in the morning. There was work to be done, and pleasantries were kept to a bare minimum. To look into the world of the 2017 squad was to see just one objective: return to the MLS Cup.

For Torontonians who had been swept up in TFC fever months earlier and gotten on board as part of a new fan after years of dismal losses, there was a sense of bewilderment that the club's off-season could be so short. How could a return could be welcomed, with a thick layer of snow on the streets and the pitches of the city?

Behind the closed doors of the KIA Training Grounds, there were very few questions about whether the club could rebound from the loss. The club's lack of off-season visibility came from the players' shared belief inside the dressing room: they would rather not have had an off-season at all. "If we could have started pre-season that morning," Michael Bradley said of the day after MLS Cup 2016, "we would have."

The club convened first in Toronto before departing for Irvine, California, to begin training camp. There, they held court in a meeting room at the team hotel and broke off into small groups to discuss their mutual objectives for the 2017 season. Returning to, and winning, the MLS Cup was obvious. But Bradley challenged the club to think even bigger, and Vanney implored the club: there was enough talent and depth to go around that they could "be different" and accomplish things that no other MLS club had before.

So, as a group, it was decided. In 2017, Toronto FC would win the Canadian Championship midway through the season, finish the season by winning their last three games to gain steam heading into the playoffs, win the Supporters' Shield, and also keep the lowest goals-against average in the league. Oh, and win the MLS Cup, becoming the first-ever MLS club to win the much-vaunted treble.

When the club's collective goals were relayed back to the coaching staff, they didn't bat an eye. "Everyone says they want to play attractive, attacking soccer. Everyone has lofty goals. But if there's substance behind it, then there's reason for belief," said Fraser.

It was the club's desire to allow fewer goals than the rest of MLS that stuck out. To Fraser and Vanney that was going to be the real measure of how good this team could actually be.

No one wore their obsession — of not only returning to the MLS Cup but of creating the kind of memorable season that would define a career — more than Bradley. Just over four months earlier, Bradley was driving a club to get over the hump that for so long had haunted them: to win their first-ever playoff game. Now, he was part of a leadership group pushing the club to do something that had never been done in league history.

His relentless drive would certainly rub some newcomers the wrong way. Soccer was work for Bradley, and he would hold players to the highest of standards that he would hold for himself in 2017. Days off would come because they were mandated, not because they were wanted. "I don't think I've ever seen him sleep," said Drew Moor of Bradley. "I think he just plugs in."

When Moor hears Bradley speak, he's not surprised, having been in the league long enough and knowing what's necessary to win the MLS Cup. But the veteran defender appreciates how Bradley's approach might surprise a first-year player.

For his part, Bradley had heard the rumblings of what some thought of as his tireless approach and work ethic, and proudly shares them: "Michael's crazy. Michael's too hard on me. Michael pushes us too strong. He wants too much."

Yet there was a difference, heading into his fourth season at TFC: now, not only did Bradley continue to want "too much," everyone else alongside him did, as well. If his no-nonsense demeanour grated on some players, they would be in the minority.

"He's the captain that all captains wish they could be like," Moor said, of Bradley's leadership efforts.

For all the club's lofty ambitions ahead of the season, they still stumbled out of the gate, winning just one of their first six matches. Part of the reason for their struggles? Two of their most notable off-season acquisitions, creative midfielder Victor Vazquez and defender Chris Mavinga, were struggling to adapt to the rigours of a new league.

Vazquez was signed to be the playmaking midfielder Altidore had all but asked for in the club's season-end media availability. Raised in Barcelona's famed *La Masia* academy, the Spanish midfielder was best known for having been a teammate of Lionel Messi, despite having been named Belgian Footballer of the Year in 2014–15 as part of a successful four-year stint at Club Brugge.

At 30 years of age when he signed with TFC, Vazquez was happy to escape the shackles of his last season with Mexican side Cruz Azul. Injuries, the lack of privacy afforded to a soccer player in Mexico, and the constant congestion within Mexico City had caused him to fear for his safety and that of his wife and young son, Leo.

"I know that it's a hard world," said Vazquez, "but it's not safe in Mexico City."

When TFC came calling again as they had in 2014, Vazquez told his wife that this was too good an opportunity to pass up. "Maybe it might not come again," he said.

As he entered the locker room on his first day after arriving late in February, Bradley was the first player who approached him. Bradley gave him his phone number, with the promise to be ready to help the new player with anything he needed to ease his transition.

"Now I feel [at] home," Vazquez remembers thinking. Immediately, Bradley reminded him of the legendary defensive midfielder and one of Belgian's most accomplished leaders, Timmy Simons, who treated newcomers the same way at Club Brugge. "That's a captain," Vazquez said, nodding his head. "It doesn't matter if you're a big name or not."

Immediately, Vazquez noticed how much more physical a league MLS was compared to Liga MX. Even though he scored in his third game, he was still the victim of heavy fouling and at times seemed to drift slowly in and out of the attack.

Vazquez took it upon himself to study the movements of those he had to link up with on the pitch. He'd approach them personally to best determine how they like balls played to them. He'd watch how they ran, and eventually came to understand that Giovinco likes the ball played directly to his feet, Altidore prefers the ball played into space, and Bradley can be left alone to do what Vazquez calls "the dirty jobs."

The Spaniard would be the final piece of the puzzle that would help cement the vision Vanney had for TFC all along: lightning-quick ball movement, based on just one or two touches of the ball to break teams down with precision passing.

The results began to show on the score sheet: Vazquez logged five assists in three games in April en route to 16 assists on the season, second in MLS. "When you know each other, you can be more relaxed," Vazquez said, smiling.

And it was that relaxed mentality that presented a healthy balance to many in the squad throughout the season. Vazquez approached every stranger he came across with a beaming smile, placing his hand on your arm as an expression of the warmth of his convivial Spanish character and his happiness to be in a place where his wife and child can walk the streets with ease.

Chris Mavinga's start to the season was perhaps even rockier. The French Congolese defender had spent time with both Paris Saint-Germain and Liverpool's reserve squads before bouncing around a handful of Belgian, French, and Russian sides. Six years of his career were marred by changes in coaches who would promptly diminish his playing time. He had grown increasingly frustrated before TFC called to offer him a spot patrolling the left flank.

With his international pedigree, Mavinga entered the season unaware of the challenges MLS would bring. Speaking quietly, using his limited English softly and hesitantly, Mavinga openly admitted that he was naïve to the quality within the league.

That much was evident during his first start for TFC. Caught wildly out of position on both Atlanta United goals as his marker scored twice, Mavinga could not escape blame from Vanney after the game. "No matter how fast you are as a human being, if you don't pick up on the plays early enough, you're not going to make up the ground. For me, as of tonight, he wasn't ready for the speed of the action in the transition," said Vanney.

Vanney understood that Mavinga's confidence could have taken a hit because of both his own play and his coach's assessment, but followed up his comments with a promise: "He'll get another shot down the road."

For four straight games, Mavinga was glued to the bench and didn't see a minute of playing time. There were whispers, as soft as Mavinga's own voice, that TFC might have a bust on their hands.

But Vanney would make good on his promise, starting him in the nine MLS games that followed. The man-management that was often nonexistent in TFC coaches of the past had become Vanney's calling card, and he forced Mavinga to gain a better understanding of the league. And, as he did, throughout the summer Vanney saw Mavinga blossom into one of the league's most athletic and durable defenders, able to break up attacks with well-positioned and clean tackles. "If I'm being honest, if one player has been critiqued on one performance more than he has for his performance against Atlanta, I don't know who that player is," Vanney said in July. "That one game keeps coming up over and over and over. It's like that game defined him. So you didn't have a great game. That doesn't mean that's him. People need to stop talking about it because that doesn't define who he is."

Vanney's business-like approach, and his insistence on taking the season one game at a time and not being consumed by the big picture, may have been the height of sporting clichés and worn thin on the pack of reporters following the team, but it was beginning to ring true to his team.

Though Mavinga worried at one point his debut season with TFC was over before it began, once he blocked out all else and simply focused on winning every tackle, he became an indispensable part of TFC's starting 11. "My last year was not good," Mavinga said in July. "I didn't have the confidence from my old coach. But with Greg being confident in me, it's easy for me to be ready for the game. I can do my best for him."

Both Vazquez and Mavinga looked at Toronto as an opportunity to get their careers back on track. It was that motivation that in part brought them to the notice of TFC assistant GM Corey Wray. In looking for new players, Wray, Bezbatchenko, and TFC's recruitment staff were at a point where understanding what motivates a player was near the top of what they were looking for. They could be selective, and target players that fit their mould as a club.

"You don't have to sell the project anymore," said Wray.

Another element of the club's recruitment process that had become more prevalent under Bezbatchenko, and by extension, Wray, was their use of analytics in identifying players for the club. Driven by Devin Pleuler, the club's senior manager of analytics, TFC had established themselves at the forefront of analytics use in the league.

Bezbatchenko and the analytics team developed their own model to break down performance that is "formulated to our own style of play" according to Bezbatchenko, and it is used on the technical and scouting side of the game. "It definitely gives us more insight," said Wray, while also emphasizing that the club does not use analytics as the sole factor in decision-making. But it does still play a significant role. "As much information as you can get about a decision, that's good," said Wray.

Analytics helps TFC whittle down a player pool that is much larger than that of any other sport in the world. The club's analytics model assists them in making a short list of players that would fit in well with the club. They then follow up by closely watching the player in videos and in person. "And we use our analysis to match what we're watching to what it was saying before," said Wray.

For years, Wray and TFC had invested heavily in collecting data on both their own players and those around the world. Early on, they were unsure of how to best utilize the data. But by 2017, their use of analytics to follow players abroad and measure the training loads of their own players had given them enough of an understanding of how and which trends were developing. It might have taken longer than expected, but the trends noticed through use of past data would help the club make a better prediction about a player's future.

It's safe to assume that Wray and TFC are fans of George Santayana — at least, of one of his most quoted beliefs: "Those who cannot remember the past are condemned to repeat it."

"We're interested in learning more about the game," said Wray.

At many other clubs across the league, there is a divide between traditional scouting departments and the analytics department. What Wray and many others within TFC were proud of was their ability to bridge the divide and ensure the two schools of thought are working together for the greater good. He'll often hear a question that many old-school thinkers would likely never utter: "Did my eyes deceive me?"

To start the 2017 season, Expected Goals, a stat that measures the chances of a shot finding the back of the net based on a variety of factors, including location of the shot and the part of the body the shot is hit with, was in vogue and being used on a wide scale as a predictor.

Wray shakes his head. The start of the season saw TFC having improved so many elements. And how they approached analytics was one. "It's not [Greg Vanney's] concern what the Expected Goals are," said Wray. Instead, Wray and Pleuler would analyze the bigger question: How did that chance develop?

The ambition that had seized the club was now just as evident with the way the club treated the accumulation of data. When Vanney and other coaches would visit the analytics department to ask for more information about a single play, the conversation would not run merely to a formula. People like Pleuler would instead stop Vanney and ask *him*, "What do you want to learn?"

With their early season MLS Cup hangover shaken off, TFC could return to being, according to Vanney, "the best version of ourselves."

It was that quote that was repeated ad nauseam in 2017, so much so that reporters would begin taking bets after training sessions on how many times the phrase would be used.

TFC weren't catering to fans' demands or to media pressure, as they had in part in the past. Being the best version of themselves meant shutting out all the chatter around them, including questions about how they would handle a stretch of six games in three weeks after looking unconvincing early on.

But TFC, far from just wanting to get out of those six games alive, regarded them as their coming-out party. With Vazquez now the key cog in the middle of the pitch who could properly execute Vanney's vision of a team that does not rely on possession as much as it does on quick, precise movement of the ball, one game after another actually worked out as they hoped. "To say we fought is one thing," said Fraser of that six-game stretch. "To say we fought intelligently is another."

When the team travelled to Seattle in a MLS Cup rematch, they were met with blazing heat for the first time that season, and had a depleted lineup: Giovinco, Vazquez, and Moor were all unavailable because of injury. Depth players, including Canadians Jay Chapman and Raheem Edwards, made an impact and transitioned seamlessly into the lineup. A 1–0 win on an Altidore penalty over the team that had sunk them five months earlier was of little consolation. Instead, the forward was beginning to recognize what could set this team apart from the team that lost to the Sounders in December. "I saw a group of fighters, for each other," said Altidore.

It was that fourth win in a row, without the help of three of the club's stars, which gave Fraser pause. "You look around and think, 'Alright, this team's got something.'"

Two more wins capped off an impressive six-game win streak, and the realization league-wide was that TFC were once again MLS Cup contenders. To prove their mettle, the first trophy opportunity came not long after that six-game stretch. After advancing to the two-leg Canadian Championship final against the Montreal Impact, TFC would have to play four games in 10 days. A pair of 2–0 wins at home in league play kept the Supporters' Shield within reach, but a 1–1 draw in the first leg of the Canadian Championship final in Montreal meant another win, or at least not allowing Montreal to score a road goal, was needed.

The push toward the Canadian Championship was hampered by a dip in production from Giovinco. He'd suffered a quad strain in May and throughout the first half of the season didn't look close to the player who had taken the league by storm two years earlier, forcing shots from bad positions and unable to break down defenders who were sometimes triple-teaming him in the box.

And Giovinco's passionate approach to the game had begun to drift toward the petulant, with Instagram posts complaining about the team not listening to him despite his health after the quad strain, and then an outburst after being subbed off, during which he smacked a barrier on the side of the pitch. TFC had raised the bar in such a manner that it was surprising Giovinco could not keep up in a consistent manner.

On the night of the second leg at BMO Field, Giovinco had even more eyes on him than normal. The Italian had always fancied himself a big-game player, but had not dominated a game yet in 2017. Giovinco did not speak to the media during this poor stretch, and was never the type to tip his emotional hand either way in his limited English. So, whether the questions about his performance made their way back to him may never be known. The club's circle in 2017 was a tight one. Whatever the explanation, Giovinco saw an opportunity during the second leg of the final and took it, putting up one of the single best performances in Toronto FC history. A fantastic turn after receiving a high cross was enough to give him a sliver of a look at the net past two defenders for his first goal, and with his left foot, no less.

In the 87th minute, with the score deadlocked at one, Giovinco made a tremendous run through the box that forced Kyle Fisher to make a jumping tackle that easily could have been called a penalty. Giovinco emerged from the heap and raised his hands to his head. While Altidore began to implore a penalty call out of the referee, a slight smile emerged on Giovinco's face, almost as if he knew something everyone else on the pitch did not.

Eight minutes later, with the game seemingly destined for extra time, Giovinco stretched back into the midfield to write his own script: a recovery of the ball after a Michael Bradley dispossession, a quick dummy of two defenders, a safe lay off of the ball to his left, a straight run to the goal, and then a redirection of a Raheem Edwards cross for the brace and the Canadian Championship.

And for the climax? Giovinco ran straight to the south end, leapt over the barrier, and into the arms of those who appreciated him the most — his adoring, frenzied fans.

The dénouement came after the match and the Voyageurs Cup trophy presentation when Giovinco, the MVP of the tournament, stood on his own in the middle of the pitch. Fireworks rang off to the north of BMO Field to mark the win and Giovinco stood transfixed. It was a moment dripping with symbolism, much to the delight of nearby photographers: Giovinco reclaiming his spot as a star on the team and TFC accomplishing the first of their goals of the 2017 season.

A variety of alcoholic beverages were waiting for the team in their dressing room. But training the next day was also waiting for TFC. Winning a trophy represents the end of the line for many clubs, but for Giovinco and TFC, it marked only the first leg of their quest to win the treble. As TFC players filtered out of the dressing room, there were more full bottles of beer than empty ones. There was more work to do, starting the very next day.

"It's okay to celebrate success … that night," said Bill Manning.

As in the season previous, it was that first trophy that convinced many of the players that the lofty goals they'd set for themselves were possible. They'd crossed the first one off the list. From a psychological standpoint, many became convinced of their own potential. The idea of winning immediately became contagious and spread like wildfire through the locker room. Midsummer signing and Lichtenstein international Nicolas Hasler arrived in large part to replace the injured Steven Beitashour, and said he had never been a part of a team that had such high expectations for themselves. TFC were moving the ball with the kind of conviction rarely seen in MLS. Success had become a drug, and as the dog days of summer rolled around, the club had lost just three MLS matches all season.

The wins continued to pile up, including comprehensive beatdowns of some of the league's best. Clinical four-goal performances over New York City FC and the Portland Timbers shifted the perception of the club away from just being Supporters' Shield favourites. By that point, their closest competitors were already conceding that trophy.

"It was important to win because I believe it's always good to get close to Toronto," NYCFC coach Patrick Vieira said after an August win of his own, "but I believe Toronto's already the champions."

The confidence inside the club was palpable. During their strong summer stretch, a club employee took a few reporters on a tour of a renovated section of the training grounds that in part would serve as a new press conference room and media centre. The employee stated matter-of-factly that the room would be ready for the MLS Cup.

"*If* you get to MLS Cup," replied one reporter.

The employee turned, did not reply, but instead shot the reporter a straight-faced look that would have been used just as easily if the reporter questioned the necessity of oxygen to his survival.

As August turned to September, and two more 4–0 wins felt more like the club was just meeting expectations, a 19-year-old record was ripe for the taking: the Los Angeles Galaxy's single-season total of 68 points.

A friend sent Vanney a snapshot of the first article written about TFC's chances of toppling the Galaxy's record. Instead of getting giddy at the possibility, Vanney found his resolve steeled. If he, who stayed about as far away from social media as humanly possible, could hear the chatter about TFC breaking the single-season points record, then it was very likely that his players had as well.

At training the next day, Vanney wondered briefly if the mantra he had repeated from the first day of the season — "One game at a time" — should only get louder. Thinking ahead of themselves could sink this team.

Instead, he assured himself, with Fraser and Calichman concurring, that he didn't need to remind his team of the task at hand. All season, every single moment of their preparation focused only on the team closest in the schedule and on no team beyond that.

Being with Fraser and Calichman, people he could trust, allowed Vanney to better deliver his message without fearing any deviation. Fraser is more analytically inclined, and will assess a lot of the bigger-picture questions, as well. While Vanney and Fraser are sterner, more reserved figures, Calichman is the jovial one whose lightheartedness provides a healthy balance. His booming voice somehow echoes throughout a flat pitch, homing in on specific efforts from a player and bellowing out support.

Though they often looked at their daily tasks in different ways, both Calichman and Fraser, colleagues ever since they had shared the back line at the Galaxy, had recognized that Vanney would be a strong coach.

Curiosity about how to improve drove Vanney's instinct about the game. "There's a reason why there are great players that are very instinctive," said Fraser. "They think differently and move differently. It doesn't mean they're exploring their thoughts, they're always just curious. To them, the Xs and the Os matter. Things have to make sense. When things make sense, there's a proper playing environment."

Throughout his early career as a coach, Vanney spent the little down-time he had reading and watching speakers deliver their thoughts on team culture and messaging. Once he arrived at TFC, he had set to work trying to get a better sense of what made his audience tick. He saw an organization that was hungry for success, so he, along with management, began studying other successful organizations, including the San Antonio Spurs, the New England Patriots, and the New Zealand All Blacks. *Legacy*, the James Kerr book that examines what made that rugby team so successful, particularly rang true to him.

The similarities between the teams he studied? "Be consistent, then eventually people will jump onboard," said Vanney. Wavering from the message, regardless of the results, would only hurt the club's performance. By 2017, Vanney could put what he had learned into practice.

Vanney's obsession stretched outward, as he became deeply intrigued by talented people of every ilk. Even sitting in a bar watching a talented guitarist, he couldn't help locking into a state of observation, taking notes on what makes that performance stand out. That obsession even hindered a date night or two with his wife. On a night out at a Lady Gaga concert, Vanney couldn't help recognizing her talent. So, instead of just taking another sip of his beer and sharing his appreciation with his wife, he meticulously analyzed every part of her performance, the charisma she displayed, and how he could utilize some of that Gaga charm on his own audience. "Why?" he asks, recalling the concert. "What does she do to captivate an audience? You have to look at all the little details of what she does."

Vanney's message had moved beyond a cliché and had become a way of life for TFC. Having never strayed from his belief that the club should stay meticulous in its approach, and should try to ignore the expectations surrounding them — and the bigger question of what their team was capable of accomplishing — Vanney had achieved what Toronto-based sports psychologist Brenley Shapiro called a "present and process-oriented focus."

"The more you repeat something, you're training the brain to adapt to and incorporate that method," said Shapiro.

Shapiro marvels at how Vanney was able to keep TFC focused on working in the present tense but also to still be concerned with the progress they were making. Most importantly, she notes, Vanney had to ensure that there were actions to back up his words. "The repetition is a pathway in the forest," she said. "The brain works the same way. Just like a pathway in a forest, it takes many footsteps to do it. The repetition of that method is really working to develop that pathway in the player's mind so it becomes something to live by."

Vanney had buy-in from his entire team, which can be a rarity in modern sports when clubs comprise wildly different personalities from widely different backgrounds.

It started at the top. Bradley believed that by 2017, the "One game at a time" approach was part of an unspoken agreement in the squad. The summer brought more games, but Bradley and TFC had learned to eschew the losing mentality of squads of the past and to welcome the challenge. "If you think that you can look past something, things are going to get shoved down your throat really quickly," said Bradley. "It serves as motivation in every way."

With five games left in the regular season after finishing their second six-game win streak of the season, TFC had their motivation: they needed just seven points from those five games to topple the points record.

Shocking losses to subpar Impact and Revolution sides only briefly put the points record in jeopardy before TFC rebounded with home wins against the Red Bulls and the Impact. TFC would head to Atlanta to face the expansion United FC and their upstart, dynamic attacking lineup in the last game of the regular season, needing a draw — a single point — to secure the points record.

The game would be played in the Atlanta Falcons' Mercedes-Benz Stadium, with a crowd of more than 70,000 — the largest in MLS history — likely to attend.

A hostile crowd was to be expected as the United fans hoped to play spoiler for the giants from north of the border. But that nationalistic element was skewed when, less than two weeks before the match, Altidore and Bradley were part of an American national team squad that simply had to win their final game of World Cup qualifying against last-place Trinidad and Tobago to secure the country's place in Russia. Despite rumblings about discontent in their new coach, Bruce Arena, it was almost impossible to imagine a World Cup without the United States. Still, the American side had continued to drop points in what were believed to be winnable games against inferior opponents.

Bradley, the team's captain, and Altidore, the goal-scoring threat, in particular, were torn apart by many media outlets.

"Michael Bradley, the U.S. does not need you to be zen. The U.S. needs you to play better. Jozy Altidore, is this really as good as it gets? Because it's still not good enough," said Fox soccer analyst and former U.S. national men's team defender Alexi Lalas ahead of the match.

The strange summer of World Cup qualification continued with the U.S. losing a shocking 2–1 match to Trinidad and Tobago to miss out on the World Cup for the first time since 1986. Bradley said after that no one deserved blame but the players themselves.

Altidore was equally critical. "If you don't look at yourself after this individually," he said after the game, "I think you're fucked up in the head."

Altidore himself could only shutter the blinds and not leave his house after returning from Trinidad and Tobago. He battled bouts of depression and was unable to report to training sessions. "You let a lot of people down," he said. "And there's a very small window to get over it."

Eventually, Altidore found redemption in the joy he could provide the fans that had welcomed him to their home years earlier. "Was I going to sulk, or go back to Toronto where there's a group of fans and group of guys that has nothing to do with this?" asked Altidore. "They want, and expect, the best of me."

In Atlanta, however, thousands in attendance were quick to remind Bradley and Altidore of their national team failures. With every touch, the two were booed mercilessly. "There's so many people out there that love to celebrate your failures," said Altidore. "They love to see you not do well."

The boos perhaps rang the loudest after Altidore's deft touch of the ball past American keeper Brad Guzan knotted the score at one.

After the goal, Altidore ran over to a group of hometown fans behind the net and cupped his hand to his ear. When a beer was thrown down toward Altidore, Giovinco, arriving late to the scene, picked it up and promptly downed it.

The fans were then treated to the best of the club in the 84th minute when Altidore's long-time friend, Giovinco, tied the score with perhaps his most impressive free kick to that point, a screamer off the crossbar past Guzan.

Minutes later, the final whistle came and TFC hit 69 points, securing the record for most points in the regular season.

They'd won the Supporters' Shield three weeks earlier with the win over the Red Bulls, but Vanney's message had become so effective that the group had added a list of accomplishments that few, if anyone, had believed possible ahead of the season.

TFC drew Red Bulls in the Eastern Conference semifinals and began the playoffs with a typically resounding performance on the road. The boos didn't just continue toward Bradley and Altidore; some fans took to hurling insults about the former Red Bull's faith as a Jehovah's Witness at him. Giovinco eventually silenced the crowd with another perfect free kick to give TFC two crucial away goals and a 2–1 lead heading home.

Back in Toronto, Vanney was well aware that the Red Bulls' plan was to create a sense of chaos during the match. Their high-pressing system would only be part of the equation, however.

Just before halftime, Altidore and his former teammate on the U.S. national team Sacha Kljestan engaged in a brief altercation. Debating the validity of a foul, Kljestan gave Altidore a slight shove and Altidore hit the pitch immediately. Both players were given yellow cards. Moments later, as they walked through the player's tunnel at the end of the half, the fracas continued as Kljestan and other Red Bulls tried to confront TFC players in an area of the tunnel that the visiting team is not allowed to walk through. A melee ensued under the glow of penetrating red lights, all in plain sight of the BMO Field VIP bar. It was alleged that Kljestan tried to take a swing at Altidore as he headed toward the TFC dressing room. By the time the police arrived to separate the two teams, Altidore and Kljestan were in completely different areas of the tunnel. Bradley, Vanney, Calichman, goalkeeper coach Jon Conway, and Alex Bono stepped in at the front of the pack to try to separate the two teams. Red Bulls coach Jesse Marsch wouldn't let it go, drawing the ire of Bradley, who screamed, "Why are you here?" in an uncharacteristically high-pitched tone.

By the time the two teams took the pitch for the second half and news of the fracas had made its way out, Altidore and Kljestan had both been handed red cards, ruling them ineligible for the next game and reducing both teams to 10 men.

"We got fucked," said Vanney, who found out 90 seconds before the second half that Altidore had been handed a red card. In losing Kljestan, Vanney believed Marsch was not forced to dramatically change his diamond midfield shape and still line up in a positive posture. But TFC were reduced to playing a completely unorthodox 5-3-1, and had a hard time moving the play forward, just as the rain that had been drizzling began to fall that much harder.

That much was evident when Bradley Wright-Phillips accidentally deflected a shot from long distance that rendered Bono helpless. Tied 2–2 on aggregate but still holding the lead on away goals, TFC was forced to hang on for dear life.

Bono's right leg save in the 62nd minute at point-blank range with Wright-Phillips sprung free is perhaps the least discussed season-changing moment for the club. "At that point, it's all reactionary," said Bono. "You're just trying to make yourself big."

Bono was perhaps the unsung hero of the 2017 season, making 29 appearances in TFC's 34 regular season games and playing every minute of the playoffs. In just his second full season with the club, Bono kept 10 clean sheets and was top 10 in the league in save percentage.

"That's just a small contribution that I was able to make," said Bono.

TFC would go on to have two goals called back after the save, including a quickly taken free kick from Victor Vazquez from a near goal-line angle that saw the normally pleasant Spaniard's eyes bulge in anger when it was denied.

They'd get out of BMO Field alive, but those disallowed goals would stick with Vanney. (In an interview to open the 2018 season, Vanney cited the two disallowed goals as a deficiency of the newly-adopted Video Assistant Referee system, which was being used to ensure the correct calls were made on the pitch.)

A little over two weeks later, TFC would head to Columbus to face the Crew in the Eastern Conference Final. The Crew had been under a cloud for their entire season, because it had become apparent that owner Anthony Precourt was hell-bent on relocating the team to Austin. And TFC were without the services of Giovinco and Altidore after yellow-red card accumulation.

Yes, everyone was getting screwed all right.

A cold night in Columbus produced a 0–0 draw with very few chances for TFC and, perhaps to be expected by this point, a heroic singular effort from Bradley amid even more booing from the Crew fans.

The typically descriptive Vanney showed the determined, forceful attitude that had characterized TFC early in the season. "I have no idea," he said after being asked for his reaction to the constant negative attention from fans surrounding Bradley. "I think he is probably focused on just whatever his job is and the task. At this point I think he thinks nothing of it."

Aside from another point-blank save from Bono on a Harrison Afful shot in close in the 85th minute, it was arguably the drabbest and most uninspiring game of TFC's season.

"Ultimately, we're going to take what the game gives us," said TFC defender Eriq Zavaleta before the series began. "We'd like to play beautiful soccer. You will see that at times throughout this series. I don't want to say easier, but more in the style of the way that this series goes, more than last series."

With two goalless playoff games in a row, TFC's play began being labelled as ugly by many in their growing media contingent.

"It's pragmatic," said Fraser of their approach. "And it's hard not to say the proof is in the pudding. People didn't think about how good New York and Columbus [are]. Those are factors that are going to change a game."

Altidore had tried his best to keep calm. He watched the game from a private box with Giovinco, who only made things worse. "Seba's not great at hiding his nerves," said Altidore.

Altidore did his best to share that sense of poise with Bradley, texting him immediately after the players entered the dressing room and Altidore and Giovinco were led up the MAPFRE Stadium stairs: "You get through this game, I'll bring it home."

The Crew would press early in the second leg, including a clear chance for Justin Meram that required Bradley to sprint 30 yards back toward his own goal and provide a leaping slide tackle, eerily reminiscent of Philipp Lahm's game-saving tackle for Germany against Brazil's Marcelo in the 2014 World Cup semifinal, to keep the clean sheet early on.

Victor Vazquez's penalty effort in the 26th minute provided BMO Field with heart palpitations, and the collective heart rate only increased early in the second half when Altidore was accidentally knocked over by Afful close to the Crew goal. When he finally stood up, it was all Altidore could do to hobble to the sidelines. He threw his gloves to the ground in frustration.

There was a brief conversation with Vanney about his status. His ankle was badly swollen and it was all he could do to move at a reduced pace.

Over his time at TFC, Vanney had learned to trust his players. Altidore said he wanted in. Just over 10 minutes later, Vanney was reminded why that trust is important. A lengthy goal kick was played out from Bono. It landed at Giovinco's feet close to the Crew's 18-yard box. Quickly, Giovinco, Altidore, and Vazquez set up a triangle. Giovinco nudged a back-heel pass to Altidore, who played a one-touch to Vazquez and ran into the Crew box.

Vazquez took the pass and waited. And waited. He cocked his right leg back and, holding the faith of BMO Field with that right leg, allowed Altidore to gain a few extra yards in the Crew box. His pass was weighted perfectly and Altidore hit his pass first time past the right hand of Crew goalkeeper Zack Steffen for the game- and series-winning goal.

"My house!" Altidore screamed as he ran to the southwest corner of BMO Field, the communal elation of the crowd providing more of a relief to his injured ankle than the many shots of Toradol he would receive afterward to treat the injury.

Five minutes after the final whistle had blown in the Eastern Conference Final and TFC were through to their second straight MLS Cup, there was no champagne. Only a few cans of beer could be found in the TFC dressing room. Their work was not done. And Greg Vanney could not relax either. In that five-minute span, he made a decision. On the cusp of the biggest match of his career, he would abandon the 3-5-2 formation that TFC had used for nearly their entire historic season. Tactically, TFC was almost unbeatable, but he'd seen enough through the playoffs so far to decide that more possession was needed and that Vazquez, perhaps driven in part by how well he linked up with his forwards during that series-clinching goal, needed to be closer to his two forwards in the final.

The early feedback was not positive.

"I was pretty much the only one in the staff that thought that way," said Vanney. One day after their win over the Crew, the Seattle Sounders advanced out of the Western Conference, setting up a rematch of the 2016 MLS Cup Final.

"I also thought, coming into a final, [the Sounders] would not be prepared for a shift," said Vanney.

The first four days of training, before the national media arrived to cover the final, were spent solely on getting his team ready for the game by working on the diamond 4-4-2 formation.

By the Wednesday of the week of the final, TFC were preparing for a training session that involved a 10-on-10 drill. Fraser had started handing out the coloured shirts to differentiate the two teams and defender Jason Hernandez started questioning aloud whether their secret would be found out. Vanney assured him not to worry.

As soon as the doors to TFC's training pitches opened and reporters entered midway through a training session, Vanney threw a different coloured shirt to his nephew, Eriq Zavaleta, to put on as a signal: Revert back to the 3-5-2 and keep the formation change under your hat. The reporters will be none the wiser.

On that first day, Hernandez walked by Fraser and gave him a low five. Everyone inside the squad was on the same page, and ready for the final.

From the outside, the team's coy approach to the final was making headlines. The *Globe and Mail* called TFC "men of few words" after the official MLS Cup press conference. Vanney and the TFC players had cut a dour figure, while their opponents appeared relaxed. With an MLS Cup in their back pocket, the smiles came fast and easy from the Sounders.

Just as they had been to start the season, Bradley and TFC remained impervious to much of what was being said outside their own dressing room. They, after all, had a secret they couldn't wait to share.

"In the biggest games," said Bradley, "guys have to be fearless."

Victor Vazquez never gets anxious before important matches. The night before his debut with Barcelona in the UEFA Champions League? He slept fine. Throughout a surprise run to the quarterfinals of the Europa League and a Belgian Cup win with Club Brugge? Just another day at a time for the Spaniard.

So when, two nights before MLS Cup final with TFC, Vazquez sat surrounded by his wife, Andrea, and his close friends Carlos and Cookie, who had flown in from Barcelona for the match as they do for many of his big games, Vazquez was calm. They sat at the dinner table in Vazquez's home, drinking red wine and eating *tortillas patatas* with tomatoes, ham, and bread, a favourite of Vazquez's.

Just another day.

But Carlos, Cookie, and Andrea emanated an anxious sense of excitement. They knew Vazquez was on the cusp of winning a title, but they also knew how Vazquez has eschewed the spotlight throughout his entire career. With 16 assists in his first MLS regular season, second in the league, it became clear that he would literally rather pass away glory than have it for himself.

For one day, however, his friends and his wife wanted more. As the wine kept flowing, they came up with a plan that showed eerily accurate foresight. Carlos and Cookie predicted that, toward the end of the MLS Cup game, Vazquez would score.

At first, Vazquez scoffed. "Toward the end of the game is when I feel tired, I am almost dead," he told his friends. But they persisted and felt sure that he would score.

And if he did score, they implored him to make a promise: that he would take off his jersey and turn the back of the jersey, with his name and number 7 on the back, straight to the fans, much like his childhood teammate Lionel Messi had done in the April 2017 El Clasico in front of rival fans in Madrid. They wanted him, for a brief second, to enjoy some personal glory. All season long, after Vazquez's eight goals, he would try to find his wife in the crowd and pull his hands together in the shape of a heart. He felt a debt of gratitude to her for moving away from her family and friends in Barcelona to be with him wherever his career took him.

"It will be just for the history, to do something different," Andrea insisted.

Eventually, as Andrea continued, Vazquez relented. He didn't admit that he didn't believe he'd score, of course, but he couldn't stop the passion from those closest to him. "I wanted them to feel part of the game," he said.

He slept easy that night, as he usually does, confident about the game while also believing that he would probably keep his shirt on his back throughout the match.

One hour before kickoff in the BMO Field press box, the news of the switch to the 4-4-2 drew gasps. "What is Vanney thinking?" became the common refrain.

A few floors below, there was no shortage of confidence, and no concern from the club about the task at hand. There were no rousing pregame speeches out of a Disney film from Vanney and Bradley. Giovinco felt "tranquil." In a season filled with "one game at a time" speeches, there was no need to remind players what they were playing for. They showed up at BMO Field on another cold Saturday in December, ready for work.

Drew Moor quickly thought back to the opening kickoff of the previous year's final, when the Sounders controlled the ball and quickly confused TFC.

Not again.

Not two minutes into the final, Moor sent a header off a Vazquez corner kick just over the bar.

With the lineups for beer still long in the BMO Field concourse, TFC had already established dominance. "And I thought, we're just going to kill 'em tonight," said Moor.

Eight minutes later, a long ball from Michael Bradley found its way to Jonathan Osorio, whose left-footed shot was stopped by a diving Stefan Frei.

Not one minute later, a Sounders turnover caused by Michael Bradley, the last man back for TFC, led to a stunning transition driven by quick ball movement that ended in a Giovinco shot that shaved the outside of the far post.

Moor looked over to see Sounders midfielder Cristian Roldan holding his hands up in exasperation. "They had no answer," said Moor.

In the 23rd minute, another Giovinco shot was stabbed over the net by Frei.

Delgado's sailing shot in the 35th minute was served a similar shot by the Sounders' goalkeeper.

Blink and you would have thought you were watching a replay when in the 41st minute Frei again stretched out to save a low Vazquez shot.

As TFC walked into their dressing room at halftime, Fraser was concerned and wondered to himself: *After TFC dominated the first half, would the momentum flip in the second?*

Fraser looked to Vanney, who kept his message succinct. Don't do anything different. The Sounders will crack.

Three minutes into the second half, Fraser was assured that the momentum would stay in TFC's favour when more effective ball movement led to a Steven Beitashour shot that just sailed over the post.

Two-thirds of the way through the game, the one player who had not been granted a clear chance at goal was the one whom the club had depended on for two seasons now to provide goals when it mattered. Jozy Altidore could not escape the pain of his swollen ankle. Had it been a regular-season game, Altidore readily admitted that he would not have played. For 66 minutes he waited, not at top speed, for his chance.

Now, just because there were no Disney-ready speeches at halftime didn't mean the club couldn't produce on a cinematic level. They had approached the entire season with a methodical mentality. The final was their opportunity to demonstrate on the biggest stage the results of that business-like approach. All season, they'd worked with that quick ball movement to the point of banality.

But when Marky Delgado tracked back to intercept a Sounders through ball in the 67th minute, no one at BMO Field was complaining. What's not often remembered is how quiet the crowd became when Delgado intercepted the pass. They dug in to watch, having seen this kind of ball movement before. Delgado pushed the ball to Moor, who one-touched it to the team's distributor, Bradley.

Bradley turned and one-touched the ball over an approaching Sounder to Morrow, waiting with his hands wide open.

Morrow kept the bouncing ball in the air, one-touching it over to Vazquez, still in the centre of the pitch.

Vazquez allowed the ball to bounce twice. In doing so, three Sounders crowded him and left Giovinco open.

Vazquez one-touched a pass to Giovinco. With its single bounce the crowd picked up again. The ball was over half and Altidore was turning to cut between two Sounders defenders.

Giovinco took one touch to control, turned, and Sounders defender Chad Marshall tried to be a hero, attacking Giovinco. In doing so, he created a wide hole in the middle of the pitch. Giovinco pushed the ball through to Altidore. And, on cue, the crowd erupted. They'd seen this film before. They knew how it ended. It was an ending they would never tire of.

The Sounders had been trained to defend Toronto's wide areas, as is customary when playing TFC's 3-5-2 formation. But in doing so, Sounders defenders Joevin Jones and Roman Torres had left Altidore with entirely too much space. Altidore was onside, and moved like a man who had never suffered an ankle injury in his life.

Altidore couldn't break from tradition either. He took one step with the ball to push it to the right of Frei, and with both Jones and Frei stretching out on him, Altidore chipped the ball over the fray and into the back of the net.

Though it took less than 14 seconds for TFC to move the ball from the interception to the goal, the high-pitched screams of delirium heard after spoke to the 364 days everyone around the club had waited for Altidore's goal. He ran behind the net, a bull let loose, and charged toward the sidelines, where he was mobbed. "Finally," Giovinco remembers saying to himself, his eyes growing wide as he recalls the moment. "This is why we always train because we have the players, the quality to do this."

There were 23 minutes left in the game, and Vanney would lock the game down with three defensive-minded substitutions. The man who could slow the game to a crawl with his dribbling, Armando Cooper; defender Nick Hagglund for Altidore — to give him a hero's send-off; and, in anticipation of his likely upcoming retirement, 36-year-old veteran midfielder Benoit Cheyrou.

A year earlier, TFC fans had sat on their hands, overcome with nerves and hardened by season upon season of disappointment. But after Altidore's goal, the fans got even louder. It was hard not to anticipate the new inevitable: TFC were minutes away from the MLS Cup.

Bright red and white smoke and flares had been set off in the south end in added time when Morrow intercepted a Sounders pass and pushed it along the wing to Vazquez. Along with Giovinco and Cooper, the 3-on-2 break was on. Giovinco collected the ball on top of the Sounders box and sprung Cooper through. A deft fake on Frei meant he had a wide open net.

Vazquez, like the other 30,000 or so people at BMO Field, assumed Cooper would safely find the back of the net. But he kept running forward, unable to control the momentum he'd built up.

When Cooper's shot bounced off the post, Vazquez didn't hammer the rebound home. Instead, overcome by shock, he had no choice but to see the ball bounce awkwardly off his thigh and into the back of the net.

He ran out from the net, pointed quickly to the family and friends section at the other end of the stadium before stopping in front of the south end faithful and, true to Carlos, Cookie, and Andrea, took off his jersey and proudly displayed it to the fans who were falling over themselves to get closer to Vazquez.

Giovinco was the first one to him, leaping onto his back. Vazquez was soon mobbed by his teammates on the pitch and on the bench. Bradley ran toward them but stopped short, his arms wide.

Moor ran to him. "He was the first guy I wanted to find and embrace because I know how much time and energy he's put into winning championships with this club," said Moor. "You remember the guys you do it with."

The TSN camera feed quickly panned to the TFC coaches, all embracing in a five-way hug. A friend of Fraser's captured a screen shot of that moment, and when he brings out his phone to show me the photo, his eyes cloud over with pride. After the four coaches let go of each other, Fraser turned to Vanney. "We fucking did it," he said.

Vanney laughed, but Fraser stopped, looked him dead in the eyes and extended his hand in congratulations. Through the formation and personnel changes, the club's principles had always remained the same. Vanney had prepared the team to be adaptable in a way no other MLS club had. "You didn't really put a foot wrong all year," Fraser told Vanney.

Ninety-seven seconds later, Allen Chapman blew the final whistle.

"Even when I think about it now, I get emotional," said Altidore, bringing his hands up in surprise on reflecting on that final whistle. "To have our moment, to say 'Ha, we came, we saw, we conquered.' It was pass or fail for us."

Minutes later, Bradley calmly walked with the MLS Cup up the stairs to teammates and executives gathered onstage. As many people from the organization as possible had crowded onto the stage, providing a glimpse into the totality of a project that was, at least for the time being, complete.

"It's unique," said Fraser, "to see a group pull in one direction."

Vanney was the first to welcome Bradley, bowing his head, waving him in before patting him on the back. Giovinco wiggled like a cartoon character, looking more animated than he had since he arrived in Toronto. Osorio held back the entire group for Bradley to take centre stage and raise the trophy for a scene that, up until a few years earlier, had seemed impossible.

With the work done (for now), the party finally started. The TFC dressing room exploded in a sea of champagne and beer and the party didn't stop for days.

After answering the assembled media's questions in the 20-minute post-game press conference, Bradley took a moment to himself in the corner of TFC's dressing room. As his teammates drank in celebration, Bradley began coughing furiously. A year's worth of anguish over the MLS Cup loss in 2016 came out. A small handful of reporters watched as Bradley, unexpectedly, let his guard down and continued in what began to feel like an exorcism.

When he finally finished coughing, he turned to face the reporters watching curiously.

"Are you okay?" one reporter asked.

"Never better," Bradley said, grinning widely.

The Maple Leafs had a rare Sunday game the next day and welcomed TFC to a private box. The club sat in Larry Tanenbaum's lounge before the game, when they were told that Manning, Bezbatchenko, Vanney, Vazquez, Moor, Osorio, Giovinco, Altidore, and, of course, Bradley, would be asked to come on the ice for a ceremonial puck drop. The Leafs organization came around with Leafs jerseys. When Bradley was given his, he stopped and felt a brief lump in his throat. Bradley's jersey had a "C" stitched above his heart. The Leafs themselves did not have a captain at the time and Bradley was overcome with emotion. "I know what it means," he said slowly, "to have a C on your jersey for the Maple Leafs."

After Bradley dropped the puck, a spontaneous "TFC!" chant broke out in the Air Canada Centre.

"In that moment, it dawned on me, because along the way, we've gotten real relevance in the city," said Bradley. A club that once stood on the fringes was now centre stage on hallowed ground — or hallowed ice.

Altidore, never much of a hockey fan from the time he arrived in Toronto, had eventually grown to understand the cultural dominance the Leafs had. And the chant left him speechless, as he recorded the entire scene on his phone. "That's when it hit me," he said. "This is big time."

So overcome by the moment, Altidore even forgot to shake the hand of Leaf Leo Komarov during the puck drop. Oh, and also, he was still drunk from the night before. Altidore would apologize via Twitter, but the party would continue the next day when TFC hopped on a double-decker bus for a parade through downtown Toronto.

Standing atop the bus, guzzling champagne like it was water, Altidore thought back to the time when Leiweke was trying to bring him to the city. Leiweke had promised him that if he brought a championship to TFC fans, he would see passion unlike any he'd ever seen in North America. As hundreds of fans lined the streets, in the middle of a workday, no less, Altidore's own journey came into focus. "It was everything everyone said it would be and more," he said, admitting that he didn't sleep for three days straight.

The parade culminated in a rally at Nathan Phillips Square. Mayor John Tory proclaimed December 11, 2017, as "Reds Day." Bradley called Toronto the greatest city in the world.

Vanney took the stage and grew reflective. "We started on a mission here a couple of years ago with our guys. Everybody behind me joined this because we wanted to do something special for this city. And we had a motto and that motto was: 'They'll remember how you make them feel.'"

Vanney stopped, summoning every ounce of enthusiasm out of his normally pragmatic self. "So, I just have one question," he said. "How do you feel?"

As the thousands of fans cheered on the organization, more champagne appeared onstage. Altidore would not leave the stage after the proceedings finished. "My drink of choice was *everything*," Altidore said of the week after winning the MLS Cup. "Because everywhere I went someone bought me a drink."

Altidore grabbed the microphone unprompted and set the crowd and social media alight with a drunken speech that managed to take cheeky shots at the Impact, boast about the club's historic season as the first-ever MLS team to win a domestic treble, and shout out to Drake and his lyrics, but not before proclaiming, albeit soaked in alcohol, a statement that the thousands in attendance felt proud to agree with, once again: "Baby, I'm TFC 'til I die."

"These are moments, as athletes, that you want," reflects Altidore. "You want to be looked at and loved, the way we are."

Nearby, the club's coaching staff stood and smiled, while also shaking their heads.

So, was it tough for Fraser to see his players drunk on a stage, finally swallowing up the adoration of the thousands of fans who had stood by the club for 12 years? "Hell no," he said, shaking his head. "It was like nothing I've seen in soccer in North America."

13

Fans, Family, and BMO Field

I STARTED BY ASKING A SIMPLE question: What does it mean to be a fan of Toronto FC? But, as so often happens, the answer was complex.

After all, it was clear from those very early meetings at the Duke of York that the club's fans, and how they showcased that fandom, would be, well, different. They began as fans of a game that was far down the pecking order in a city that could arguably be described as the capital of another, more dominant sport. And they immediately became fans of a club that had no historical precedent, while two of the oldest franchises in North American sports called Toronto home.

That the club could draw more than 20,000 fans on average during their inaugural season, good for second in the league, suggests that Toronto held more than just a few thousand fans who enjoyed watching soccer as a solitary pursuit. And then to continually rank in the upper echelon of MLS average attendance, even as ticket prices rose and the results on the pitch never improved, suggests that BMO Field wasn't just being filled by fans there for the novelty of a new team.

Maybe, according to some fans, misery just loves company.

"It's a small community," said Kristin Knowles. "But it's a really big small community. Part of the reason we're so passionate about the club is because they sucked for so long."

Knowles, who is part of the The Vocal Minority website and podcast, is one of TFC's most fervent fans both in the south end and online. She has hosted Bill Manning at her dining room table for a podcast recording and presented the Voyageurs Cup after TFC won the Canadian Championship in 2017.

As an ardent soccer fan, she felt disconnected from any local soccer presence. In an attempt to connect her with the burgeoning new club, her father and stepmother gave her season tickets for Christmas 2006. "I stared at [the tickets] in shock and awe, for so long," remembers Knowles.

After the monumental first home game, her father called her for an update on the stadium and the game. He was confused: were the cameras at the stadium not fastened properly? Why were they shaking during the broadcast?

"'The stadium was really shaking because everyone was so hyped and enthusiastic,'" Knowles told her father. "And it started from there. It was such a great thrill to finally have a team to support."

Knowles would at first go to matches alone. Through Twitter, she connected with the people she calls her "tribe" and moved to the south end. She began writing for the TFC blog *Waking the Red*. Born in Canada, Knowles didn't feel a connection to any European or South American clubs as many local soccer fans did. But she saw a collection of fans gathering and an opportunity to be a part of something "in your own backyard."

"We wanted something real," reflects Knowles. "We wanted our own club."

In connecting with other fans online, Knowles didn't just find new fans to sit beside: she found a sense of belonging. "Once I was able to find people, this was what I wanted," she told me. "These were the people I wanted to talk to and share my joy and pain with when it comes to the club."

And there was pain, for a long time. That sort of pain on the pitch usually results in dropping attendance numbers, especially when there are two other major-league franchises to compete with.

Yet because the club sprang from such humble but intense roots, a sense of ownership of the club and ownership of their lack of success grew as the team continued to perform poorly. All around her, Knowles saw fans who had suffered as previous soccer teams in Toronto lost their way and fell off the map entirely. There was little chance of that happening with TFC, however. What began as each fan's love for a sport considered on the fringes of North American popular culture had evolved into a shared sense of belonging and a belief that, while the losing might continue, no fan can fall if there are other fans around to keep you standing.

"They put us through the wringer," Knowles said of TFC's lean years. "And once you've gone through that, it's hard to not have that bond."

It culminated at the end of the miserable 2012 season.

"You were there to keep everyone's spirits lifted," said Knowles. "You weren't there to enjoy the football. You were there to enjoy your soccer family."

And TFC has provided the opportunity for families, those united by blood and not a sport, to further their connection. Keeps your ears open at BMO Field as you mingle amid the deep red seats and you'll hear, not passing strangers trying to make a point to whoever is next to them, but friends who have developed their own habitual way of communicating, without banal pleasantries and full of knowing, impassioned discourse. The comfort of having an argument and then being excited to return the following Saturday to continue that argument.

TFC GM Tim Bezbatchenko puts it succinctly: "We're living in a different world than other MLS markets."

Lauren Wharton and her father would butt heads through her teenage years. He of old (and, in her perception) stuffy British ways, embarrassed the hell out of Lauren. Born in England, Lauren's father, Dave, was a Manchester United fan and skeptical about how Toronto's new soccer team would pan out.

Lauren's parents had divorced early in her life and she never saw her father much. They had little in common and even fewer shared experiences. But they took a chance on this new team, given Lauren's budding interest in the sport just as it was exploding in North America.

They attended home matches to begin the inaugural season. After Danny Dichio's goal in 2007, after which Wharton and her father launched their seat cushions into the air in unison, they were hooked. Finally, they had a memory to share. "It was one of those surreal moments because it wasn't planned," said Wharton. "We talk about it all the time."

Slowly, Wharton saw a pattern developing. Finally, they had something to share and, without the trappings of societal obligations that their relationship usually fell victim to, they began to develop the relationship they never had and to see each other as family first and fans second. "I learned to see him less as an embarrassing dad and embrace him for who he is," said Wharton. "That's the place where he is his most comfortable and that's how I'd prefer to see him."

The relationship they now share is one they don't have with other family members. They've been season seat holders ever since. Whatever has happened in each of their lives, they know they'll be together on match days. That shared passion has become the thing that keeps driving each of them forward. In the summer of 2016, Lauren saw her father become a Canadian citizen. And, naturally, his allegiance shifted.

"He feels so much more connected to TFC than United," said Wharton of her father. "We both consider BMO Field a second home."

Fans of a club don't get to choose the players who wear the crest they love, much as all of us don't get to choose our family. And being part of a family that supports you at your lowest isn't a given, either. That's what TFC fans have found in each other, however. People that once did not have a place to gather were made to suffer a little longer through a fandom they felt had to be part of their DNA.

After some excruciatingly difficult seasons, there is no greater pride among the TFC faithful than being able to call themselves "Day One" fans. Yet those days of pitch invasions, seat cushions falling from the sky, a quaint stadium with a view, and a rotating cast of characters are long gone.

And yet, as the team, and the sport as a whole, continues to grow, it will be the connection that each of those fans have to each other that will last. "Not many sports fans can say they've been there since the beginning of the team," said Wharton. "And I think that's what connects TFC to their fans. We've had the ability to be there from the beginning. Though the team is in its infancy, but to see how far it's come. It's amazing."

EPILOGUE

A Strange New World

THE SUN, AS IT HAD been for days, was relentless in Guadalajara that afternoon. Try as one might, there was little escape from the heat in Mexico's second-largest city. Even sitting on the edges of the second-floor lobby of Toronto FC's hotel meant being subject to the constant, glaring sun with the doors wide open.

Late in the afternoon, Greg Vanney walked up behind me, patted me on the back, and as he slumped into his chair, tried to put forth a positive spin. "Nice day today."

Vanney's stubble was approaching full beard, with more of a coating than a few dashes of salt noticeable in the pepper. The sun caused him not just to squint, but to look at me through the thinnest of openings in his eyes. The creases in his face had become more and more evident, and the then 43-year-old coach looked like a man who had lived through many more years than that.

And, in a way, he had. Vanney had returned to Mexico for the third time in a little over a month, trying to lead his team to an unprecedented CONCACAF Champions League victory and become the first-ever MLS team to do so.

"This tournament was a grind for us," Vanney would say, later.

It seemed like a noble venture when, at TFC's season-opening breakfast in February 2018, club president Bill Manning threw down the gauntlet and said that his team were as well-equipped as any MLS team ever to win the CONCACAF tournament. They had won the treble in 2017, and TFC could easily claim to be the best MLS side of all time. They'd even bolstered their lineup with Gregory van der Wiel, who had legitimate experience at Paris Saint-Germain and Ajax Amsterdam and could immediately lay claim to being one of the best outside backs in MLS. And the addition of Brazilian defender Auro Jr. and Spanish creative midfielder Ager Aketxe had made an impenetrable squad even better. That much was evident when they steamrolled through their first round opponents in the Champions League, the lowly Colorado Rapids, 2–0 on aggregate, barely hitting third gear.

But by early March, the reality of what it would take to become crowned the club champions of North and Central America had set in. TFC had been placed on the unforgiving side of the draw, and would need to get through both Monterrey's Tigres (the recent Liga MX champions) and Mexico City's Club America, the most famous of all Mexican sides, who play in the legendary 87,000-seat Estadio Azteca.

For Vanney and TFC, everything would have to fall into place just right.

Up to that point, an MLS side had beaten a Mexican team in Mexico just twice in CONCACAF Champions League play. Just getting out of their own side of the bracket was going to reveal a lot about this team. Warranted or not, the inclusion in 2018 of Toronto FC, the winningest team in a single season in the entire history of MLS, and two other MLS sides that had experienced domestic success — the Seattle Sounders and the New York Red Bulls — led to the inevitable comparisons between MLS and Liga MX and which league was "better," as subjective a term as that might be.

That debate only increased after the first leg of the quarterfinals, during which the Sounders, Red Bulls, and Toronto FC all defeated their Liga MX opponents. While the Red Bulls joined the ranks of a celebrated few MLS teams by beating Tijuana in Mexico, TFC's win was perhaps the most impressive — a come-from-behind 2–1 win over Tigres, the 2017 Liga MX Apertura champions. No team could boast about their sheer array of individual talent up and down the roster the way Tigres could. Ecuadorian international Enner Valencia, Chilean international Eduardo Vargas, and powerful French forward André Pierre Gignac, who had nearly won Euro 2016 for France just over a year earlier, made up the kind of attacking trio most MLS sides could only dream of. On a chewed-up pitch that clearly had been beaten up by an unusually long and wet Toronto winter, TFC went down in the 52nd minute on a stunning Vargas strike. It was a crucial away goal in the aggregate series, in which away goals would act as the tiebreaker.

"Well, it was nice for TFC to dream," said one member of Toronto FC's media corps, while the visiting Mexican media could not restrain their excitement and hooted and hollered over the goal, clearly unwilling to abide by the unwritten rule of "no cheering in the press box."

TFC had not seen an opponent that could move the ball as fluidly as Tigres did in well over a year. No other MLS team could hold a candle to the kind of talent many of the best Mexican teams were built upon.

In Tigres, and perhaps in other Mexican teams moving forward, TFC had finally met their match.

Yet as the match hit the one-hour mark, almost on cue, Jozy Altidore awoke from his slumber and realized that a hero was needed, just as he had against Columbus and Seattle during the previous MLS Cup playoffs.

Midfielder Marky Delgado stood wide open in the middle of what resembled a cow patch waving his hands in the air. Sebastian Giovinco played a ball across the pitch to Delgado, who then one-touched a pass to Altidore, just beginning his run.

And as much as the BMO Field grounds crew probably took their fair share of heat for the state of the pitch, they may end up being known as accidental saviours as Delgado's through ball hit a bump in the pitch and deflected inches outside of Altidore, enough for him to gain a step on his marker and fire his one-touch shot under diving Tigres goalkeeper Nahuel Guzman.

Dramatic as it may have been, TFC still needed more, and got it from a player who had emerged as one of TFC's best over the previous six months. In the 89th minute, Giovinco received a pass inside the corner of the Tigres box and, since the defenders naturally expected him to shoot, had four Tigres defenders crowd him. That left Toronto's own Jonathan Osorio wide open in front of the net.

Just under a year earlier, Osorio appeared to have lost all of his confidence in his game, sending shots from in close over the bar, losing his spot in the starting 11, apologizing to fans via Twitter for his poor performance, and engaging in dust-ups with reporters when questioned about his play.

But all the promise that had kept Osorio with the club as their all-time appearances leader was finally manifested in what he would agree after the match was the "goal of his career."

Giovinco's short pass came a second earlier than expected and Osorio was forced to corral the ball with his back to the net. In one fluid, and admittedly absurd moment, Osorio rolled the pass off his off foot while turning 360 degrees and put the ball into the back of the net.

The late-game eruption in front of the south end had become commonplace.

"It's a little bit of a Jedi mind trick that I put on him," said Vanney, after the match. "I told him to drop a little deeper, not worry about scoring goals, and now he's in front of the net all the time."

Whatever Vanney had done, it worked. With one flick of the heel, the perception of TFC's chances in the tournament utterly changed. It was the first taste of a best-on-best match between the two leagues in this tournament, and TFC's victory, combined with the success of the other two teams, sent shockwaves through the Mexican soccer landscape. "Insulting and unacceptable" read the front page of Mexican daily sports newspaper *Récord* after the first-leg results.

And, despite being pressed repeatedly by Mexican media about the state of MLS compared to Liga MX, TFC never completely bought into the hype, though they did take pride in their result.

"The opportunity to prove ourselves to a few people who don't think we're as good, or the quality of the league is as good," said TFC captain Michael Bradley, "we take that responsibility very seriously."

Vanney, though never one to pump his own tires, would admit that the tactical precision with which many MLS teams operated, including his own team, was improving. "It wasn't that long ago that MLS was a very improvisational league, and a lot of teams were just off the cuff playing, and you had good players, and they either made plays or they didn't," said Vanney. "Now tactics are more sophisticated in the league, and teams have clearer (tactical) identities, and I think that's helping."

Was a 2–1 result enough, though, given that Gignac was likely to be deployed for a full 90 minutes in Monterrey instead of the 45 minutes he was used for in Toronto?

In Monterrey, through the first half of scoreless soccer, it looked like the result would stand. And of course, once the clock passed the one-hour mark, the skies opened. An own goal in the 64th minute gave TFC a crucial away goal, but Tigres kept things interesting and converted a corner kick off of some questionable defending in the 69th minute. Squeaky-bum time, as Sir Alex Ferguson would have called it.

In the 73rd minute, Giovinco was awarded his second free kick of the match, just over 20 yards from goal. His first effort, from a similar spot, had been saved by Guzman.

Yet this time the Argentinian goalkeeper couldn't quite get to Giovinco's precisely placed shot into the top corner. TSN play-by-play man Luke Wileman's voice cracked as he screamed Giovinco's name in elation. "The man for the big moment," Wileman proclaimed, "does it again!"

TFC's 4–2 lead on aggregate, with two vital away goals, was now insurmountable for Tigres. They would score two late goals, but TFC would still advance on away goals from the 4–4 result.

Belief in TFC's chances in the Champions League were growing.

"It's big for our club and our league to be able to go through the Mexican champions," said Vanney.

TFC would have to return to Mexico for the semifinals against Mexico City's Club America, easily the most recognizable team in Mexican soccer. TFC would first welcome Club America and their dramatic, eccentric coach Miguel Herrera to BMO Field for the first leg. Rain poured down early on as Giovinco was awarded a penalty kick in the 9th minute and calmly sent it straight down the middle and into the back of the net. Andrés Ibargüen levelled in the 21st minute with an incredible solo effort, embarrassing a few of TFC's defenders with impeccable dribbling and a bullet of a shot past Alex Bono.

But just before halftime, Altidore showed up earlier than expected with the go-ahead goal.

The testy affair spilled over into familiar surroundings at halftime, when Osorio and Club America coaches were involved in a fracas in the BMO Field tunnel. The teams' coaches offered different takes on the event, with Herrera proclaiming that a member of the Toronto Police Services hit Club America players, while Vanney said one Club America coach took exception to Giovinco being awarded the penalty kick and confronted him, before Osorio stepped in to defend his teammate. Vanney said that a Club America coach elbowed Osorio in the nose.

"I saw a couple of their staff, I don't know what they were doing to [Giovinco]; it looked like they were harassing him," Osorio said. "It didn't look like it was a friendly conversation. I just stepped in for my teammate and I caught an elbow to the chin from one of their staff and it escalated to a little bit of a thing but nothing happened after that."

Osorio, already riding the aforementioned wave of confidence, said the incident "sparked" him. It may have sparked his Toronto brethren, too, as Ashtone Morgan scored just the second goal in his career with TFC to send the team back to Mexico with a 3–1 lead.

Osorio continued his hot streak at Estadio Azteca, providing the dagger after some one-touch ball movement for his 12th-minute goal. On the sidelines, a normally reserved and pragmatic Vanney could not contain his emotion. The matches and miles of travel were piling up early in the season, as were the doubts if TFC had enough in the tank to get through Mexican teams in mid-season form. He shouted and pumped his fists in elation. Early in the game as it might have been, that goal was likely enough to send TFC through to the Champions League finals, making them just the third MLS team to do so.

And it was. TFC reverted to shutdown soccer for the rest of the match, allowing only an Andres Uribe penalty kick in added time. TFC were heading to the Champions League final.

The cracks were beginning to show for TFC, however. Victor Vazquez was held out of the lineup for his second straight Champions League game with nerve issues in his back, and Altidore had to be subbed off in just the 7th minute of the second leg.

TFC had also stumbled in MLS early on, winning just one of their first three matches of 2018. They grabbed a break when D.C. United allowed their April 7 match, supposed to be held just three days before the second leg against Club America, to be rescheduled. But with their third trip to Mexico looming, changes were needed. The squad had had just six weeks of rest from the end of the previous regular season to the start of training camp, and included in that training camp was a week-long stint in Mexico.

There is nothing to suggest that TFC underestimated what it would take to compete in CONCACAF Champions League. And yet, as so often in the franchise turnaround since 2015, the enormity of the moment was beginning to loom for the club.

In preparation for the two-leg final against Mexican fan favourite Chivas Guadalajara, Vanney and his coaching staff elected to rest the majority of their starters in an away game to the lowly Colorado Rapids three days before the first leg. A squad built largely on TFC II players was beaten by the Rapids, 2–0. TFC asked to have their away match one week later against the Houston Dynamo rescheduled, but lightning didn't strike twice, and those same reserves were again picked apart, suffering a 5–1 loss.

Chivas had experienced poor form in the 2018 Liga MX Clausura, falling into the bottom three of the league through 15 matches. Having dispatched two superior teams in the previous legs, TFC were now considered the favourites. And the first leg of the final against Chivas was there for the taking. With three of their starters ineligible due to suspension, the Mexican-only squad looked vulnerable. But the wear and tear on TFC was impossible to ignore. Injuries were piling up. Vazquez was left out of the squad, and Chris Mavinga, Justin Morrow, and Eriq Zavaleta would be good for only about 45 minutes each.

One of the main forces behind TFC's winning the Supporters' Shield in 2017 had been the drive to play their final post-season game at home. TFC didn't have that advantage in the two-leg final. Chivas came to Toronto for the first leg, at BMO Field.

TFC were arguably too friendly as hosts, as some porous marking allowed a Chivas pass to trickle through TFC's backline before Rodolfo Pizzaro capitalized for an early, crucial away goal. Osorio would equalize 17 minutes later, becoming the tournament's leading scorer with four goals — one against each opponent. Yet Chivas's intense man-marking approach stifled TFC as, without Vazquez, they were unable to break it down.

As snow started to fall, so, too, did TFC's hopes. An Alan Pulido free kick from a near-impossible angle close to the touchline stretched over Bono into the far corner.

"Now we are in the hole going to Mexico," Vanney stated matter-of-factly, after the 2–1 loss.

And that brings the story out of the snow and into the blazing sun.

Instead of smiles at the chance to defeat a Mexican team and enjoy some respite from a never-ending Toronto winter, there was palpable tension in TFC's camp. Vanney, in particular, couldn't help looking back instead of forward, noting the tens of thousands of kilometres his team had travelled in the previous months, the different altitudes they had played and the different surfaces they had played on, from Montreal's turf to Colorado's frozen field. They'd already played 12 matches in less than two months before the second leg, whereas the majority of their MLS counterparts had played half of that. And they'd beaten two of the best Mexican teams in that process.

But they were at the end of their rope.

"To be one hundred percent honest, the group, as a whole, it's very difficult to have guys very physically prepared for that in four weeks," Vanney said. "So what you see is, guys naturally break down."

Defender Drew Moor had suffered an injury in training two days before the second leg of the final that would rule him out of the lineup, while Mavinga, Morrow, and Zavaleta were all unfit to play.

Then, two days before the final, the match took an unprecedented emotional turn: 10 people were killed and 16 were injured after a Toronto man allegedly drove a rented van up onto the sidewalks of Yonge Street. It was a senseless act of extreme violence the likes of which the city had never seen.

Four thousand kilometres away, feelings of helplessness were rampant among TFC.

"I almost wish that we could be there to give support to the city in this dark time," said Bono. "It's a shame that something like this happens in our city…. We're playing with heavy hearts. We have Toronto in our minds and our hearts all the time. Even more so now."

Sports, meaningless as they can be, can also be unifying. Bradley wanted TFC to be a force for the latter. "When we get our chance tomorrow night, we're going to see if we can do something special and make it a night that everybody watching back home can be proud of," he said, the day before the match.

And they did. Amid a wildly raucous crowd of 36,000-plus, TFC held their own. With Moor out, Bradley was forced into an unfamiliar centre-back role. TFC came out swinging, eager for the two away goals needed to at the very least force penalties.

They didn't back down even when Chivas midfielder Orbelín Pineda cut through TFC's backline and sent Chivas up 1–0. Six minutes later, Altidore showed up even earlier than he had against Club America, finishing after some tremendous work from Nicolas Hasler close to the Chivas goal. And, after showing his frustration at a no-call after what he believed to be an egregious foul, Giovinco stormed in on his own toward the Chivas goal and finished his shot short-side to tie the series on aggregate at 3–3 before halftime.

By the start of the second half, via the TV feed, TFC had the eyes of an emotionally drained city on them. Earlier that evening, the Maple Leafs had been eliminated from the playoffs; the Blue Jays had lost to their American League East rivals, the Boston Red Sox; and the Raptors had taken Game 5 of their first-round playoff series against the Washington Wizards. Now the attention was on the Reds.

The sun had set in Toronto, and as the minutes passed in the second half, TFC hung on for dear life. Altidore pulled up with a leg injury late in the match as Chivas kept up intense pressure. Under tournament rules there would be no extra time after a draw, so penalties looked inevitable. Without Altidore and Vazquez, who had been subbed off in the second half, the battered squad tried to extract every chance possible from every final inch of rope.

After the final whistle, Vanney collected his troops to prepare for penalties. He got a firsthand look at the effects of a successful season and the little rest that comes with it. "We had guys who were cramping, who were struggling physically," said Vanney. "What more can you say to them?"

One by one, all four Chivas players buried their kicks from the spot.

Giovinco scored. Osorio's kick hit the crossbar. And Delgado scored (some small act of redemption after missing a clear chance late in regulation).

Bradley was up next, with an opportunity to keep TFC's Champions League hopes alive, just as he had in the 2016 MLS Cup final. Before his kick, he carved in a small hole with his boot near the spot, delicately placed the ball in his preferred location, and took 11 paces back.

His shot had power and location, as Chivas goalkeeper Rodolfo Cota guessed incorrectly. But the shot also had height, and sailed over the net.

Cups of beer sailed down from the cheap seats in Estadio Akron. Bradley collapsed onto the pitch. Vazquez was the first to console him.

After the match, one by one, TFC players, all dressed in black, left Estadio Akron quietly as the celebration of Chivas players and fans could be heard ringing out throughout the bowels of the stadium.

"This is the way the game goes," said Bono, of losing on penalties. "It's unjust sometimes. It feels like your heart's been ripped out of your chest sometimes. But that's just the things you have to deal with in football."

Perhaps had the match gone to extra time, as any soccer match should have, TFC might not have lasted the continued offensive onslaught from Chivas, given how depleted they looked through the final 20 minutes.

It was all irrelevant to Bradley after the match. "In the biggest moments, we fuckin' went for it," said Bradley. "And that's all you can ask for.

"We threw caution to the wind and played with balls and bravery and pride in ourselves, each other, our club and our city," he added. "And unfortunately, at the end, one team has to lose."

Given TFC's success of the previous season, fans and onlookers could be forgiven for forgetting that the last part of Bradley's statement is indeed true. It was impossible not to look back on the rapid ascent of the club: less than three years earlier, TFC had only just snuck into the MLS Cup playoffs for the first time before being battered in their first playoff game.

Now, once again, TFC had a look at the peak of the mountain, but did not scale it.

Memories of TFC falling and standing back up again came flooding back. Of their 2015 playoff loss in Montreal, and then winning the Eastern Conference in 2016. Of falling short on penalties in the 2016 MLS Cup final, and then winning an unprecedented treble in 2017.

In his post-match press conference, Vanney nodded when asked to recall a conversation we had in Irvine, California, months earlier, during TFC's training camp, about the club's stumbles ahead of their successes.

"You lose," Vanney said in January 2018, "to then learn something to win the next time."

Vanney was then asked, could this loss serve as motivation for the future of the club?

The coach inhaled. Looking out into the crowd of reporters, he answered with the same air of defiance that had gotten the club to where they were — in one of the soccer capitals of the world, still fighting for recognition.

"It has to."

Acknowledgements

FOR A FEW YEARS THERE I was getting anxious about what my next book would be and when it would come. Then, like a quick counterattack, this project came up and I hunkered down in my basement, at my kitchen table, in hotel rooms, press boxes, and maybe a bar or two to get this ship off to sea in a short amount of time.

First, I sincerely hope that the Toronto FC fans out there find some value in this book. You're the engine that has kept the club moving along, and for every day spent with your club at the stadium, in pubs, or at home, I hope I've done right by your fandom. If I've missed a moment in the club's history that you identify with, please don't take it as a slight. TFC is simply a club that, in the words of my good friend James Grossi, "has lived many lives."

It's a strange thing, supporting a club. But if you love your club and the game enough, both will eventually love you back. I'm sure of it.

Thank you to the staff at Dundurn Press, including Scott Fraser for inviting me in and believing in my passion for this project from the beginning. Allison Hirst kept this book moving along with her thoughtful edits and encouragement. Kendra Martin, Michelle Melski, Elena Radic, and Sheila Douglas were also incredibly helpful throughout the entire process.

My good friend and brother, Adam Kesek, was there every step of the way, whether it was hearing out ideas over pints at our local or providing vital feedback on every chapter. I'm lucky to have him in my life.

And I'd be remiss if I didn't thank the staff at Shox Billiard Lounge, where so much of this book was written.

My editors at the Athletic, James Mirtle, Sean Fitz-Gerald, Kaitlyn McGrath, and Sunaya Sapurji, were supportive and understanding of the time needed to complete this book. All four of them have worked to make me a better writer, so if this book is any good at all, they deserve the credit.

A number of local soccer journalists were both encouraging and resourceful along the way: James Grossi, Amil Delic, James Sharman, Oliver Platt, and Steve Gennaro. John Molinaro, the great-grandfather of Toronto FC coverage, deserves big-time praise here, and he knows why.

Thank you to everyone who agreed to be interviewed and to give their time and perspectives. Special thanks to Michael Bradley, who was generous with his time and agreed to represent his club with the foreword for this book.

I'm indebted to the MLSE and Toronto FC media relations staffs for not only helping arrange time with important interview subjects, but for being behind this project as well. Thank you to Dave Haggith, Jeff Bradley, Anthony Cozzetto, and in particular Mike Masaro for putting up with countless emails, texts, and phone calls. They'll say they were just doing their jobs, but they went above and beyond to help make this book happen.

Thank you to every other media relations member from MLS and teams throughout the world for helping coordinate interviews. You know who you are, and you are appreciated.

The good people of Südkurve Toronto, including but not limited to Ryan Tune, Jimmy Czikk, Matthew and Sebastian Moreno, Lilli Tang, Jarek Zlamal, and Julia Albus, were uplifting in their support. *Mia san mia!*

Thank you to my colleagues at Seneca College, who were always curious and optimistic about this project.

Al Gregory and David Trumble probably got annoyed with me rambling on about this book, but their friendship has always meant the world to me.

My parents and sister also became fans of Toronto FC in a short amount of time, and their encouragement kept the train moving along.

Finally, to my wife and best friend, Jess: This book would not exist without you. Thank you for every single moment we share. Can't wait for what comes next.

SOURCES

Interviews, 2017–18

Jozy Altidore

Tom Anselmi

David Bailey

Chad Barrett

Armen Bedakian

Paul Beirne

Joe Bendik

Tim Bezbatchenko

Alex Bono

Michael Bradley

Jim Brennan

Jeff Carlisle

John Carver

Tomer Chechinski

Earl Cochrane

Warren Creavalle

Sam Cronin

Chris Cummins

Nick Dasovic

Julian de Guzman

Bob de Klerk

Dwayne De Rosario

Jermain Defoe

Jack DePoe

Danny Dichio

Mike Dubrick

Terry Dunfield

Robin Fraser

Don Garber

Sebastian Giovinco

Jeremy Hall

Doneil Henry

Sean Keay

Eddie Kehoe

Kristin Knowles

Danny Koevermans

Tim Leiweke

Michelle Lissel

Daniel Lovitz

Bill Manning

David Miller

John Molinaro

Drew Moor

Ashtone Morgan

Stuart Neely

Ryan Nelsen

Darren O'Dea

Pat Onstad

Kevin Payne

Richard Peddie

Predrag Radosavljević

Marco Reda

Carl Robinson

Duane Rollins

Ryan Smolkin

Greg Sutton

Greg Vanney

Victor Vazquez

Lauren Wharton

Paul Winsper

Aron Winter

Corey Wray

Marvell Wynne

Websites

bigsoccer.com

bleacherreport.com

canadasoccer.com

cbc.ca

deadspin.com

espn.com

espn.in

facebook.com

mlssoccer.com

nytimes.com

sify.com

socceramerica.com

sportsnet.ca

strategyonline.ca

theathletic.com

theglobeandmail.com

theguardian.com

thescore.com

thestar.com

torontosun.com

usatoday.com

wakingthered.com

youtube.com

INDEX

Hall, Jeremy, 130,
142–44
Henry, Doneil, 139, 151
Homegrown Player
Rule, 120
Houston arrests, 141–43

Johnston, Maurice
"Mo," 45–50, 54–55,
62–71, 91, 95, 102,
107, 111, 115–16

Keay, Sean, 20–21, 34, 37
Kehoe, Eddie, 50, 53,
63–64
Klinsmann, Jurgen, 14,
116–18, 120–21, 140
Knowles, Kristin,
251–53
Koevermans, Danny,
121–22, 234, 124,
132, 134–38, 142,
144, 155

La Barra Brava, 59
Leiweke, Tim, 116, 155–
59, 161–65, 166–69
171–76, 179–83,
186, 190–91, 249
Liberty Village, 27, 130
Lissel, Michelle, 65–66,
73–75, 92
Los Angeles Galaxy, 39,
116, 130, 132, 234

Major League Soccer
(MLS), 9, 16–17, 19,

21–24, 28–33, 44,
50, 53–55, 58–59,
61, 64–66, 69–73,
77–78, 80–82, 92,
94, 96, 98–100,
102–6, 108, 115–16,
118, 120–25,
128–31, 134–35,
137, 139, 143–46,
150–54, 156, 159–
64, 168–72, 174–75,
179, 181–82, 187,
189, 191–94, 197,
199, 203–7, 212–13,
215–17, 220, 225,
227, 233, 236,
250, 255–58, 260,
262–64;
MVP awards, 80,
121, 196, 210, 213
Manning, Bill, 98,
204–8, 233, 249,
251, 255
Maple Leaf Sports
and Entertainment
(MLSE), 19, 21–24,
29–32, 36, 40–41,
46–48, 74, 81,
111–12, 116–18,
120, 129, 139,
145–46, 155–59,
166–67, 172, 174,
179–82, 205–6
Mavinga, Chris, 226,
228–29
message boards, 20–22,
33–35

Miller, David, 25–30,
66, 68, 159; season
tickets returned,
151
Miracle in Montreal, 89,
154
MLS Cup, 9, 16, 80,
98, 130, 146, 149,
205, 208–10, 219,
221, 222, 224–26,
231, 234, 242–43,
247–48, 263–64
Molinaro, John, 64,
66–67, 108, 148–49
Montreal Impact, 16,
30, 85–88, 134, 143,
154, 201–2, 204,
214–18, 231, 236,
250; rivalry, 134
Moor, Drew, 208–11,
215, 218, 220–23,
225–26, 231,
244–47, 249, 262
Morgan, Ashtone, 113–
15, 120, 167–27,
139, 260
Morrow, Justin, 214,
217, 221–23,
246–47, 261–62

Neely, Stuart, 43–44, 119
Nelsen, Ryan, 148–55,
162, 167–69, 178,
182–85
North American Soccer
League (NASL), 15,
42

Book Credits

Acquiring Editor: Scott Fraser
Developmental Editor: Allison Hirst
Project Editor: Elena Radic
Copy Editor: Laurie Miller
Proofreader: Dawn Hunter

Cover Designer: Carmen Giraudy
Interior Designer: Jennifer Gallinger

Publicist: Elham Ali

Dundurn

Publisher: J. Kirk Howard
Vice-President: Carl A. Brand
Editorial Director: Kathryn Lane
Artistic Director: Laura Boyle
Director of Sales and Marketing: Synora Van Drine
Publicity Manager: Michelle Melski

Editorial: Allison Hirst, Dominic Farrell, Jenny McWha, Rachel Spence, Elena Radic
Marketing and Publicity: Kendra Martin, Kathryn Bassett, Elham Ali

dundurn.com   dundurnpress
@dundurnpress   dundurnpress
dundurnpress   info@dundurn.com

FIND US ON NETGALLEY & GOODREADS TOO!

DUNDURN